All At Sea Yarns

Cap'n Fatty Goodlander

Copyright © 2009 Gary "Cap'n Fatty" Goodlander

All rights reserved. The entire contents of this book are copyrighted 1986-2009 by Gary M. Goodlander aka Cap'n Fatty. Except as permitted under the United States Copyright Act of 1976, no part of this material can be reproduced or distributed in any form or by any means, or stored in a data base or retrieval system, without the prior permission of the author.

*Contact: Gary Goodlander at Fatty@fattygoodlander.com
or visit our website: FattyGoodlander.com*

*All our books are available in Kindle and other E-book formats.
Amazon.com
Smashwords.com*

Dedication

To Chris, Nicole, Griffith, and Josephine Kennan for being my wonderful literary support team for so many years.

And to Gary E. Brown for watching my back and aggressively advocating for my benefit—when it was clearly against his own financial self-interest to do so.

Table of Contents

Introduction 6
Preface 7
Sailing Away from the Dream Crushers 19
The Ghosts of September 23
Rigging the Facts on Freudian Sloops 27
Avoiding Work 30
Dastardly Diesel Mechanics 33
Racing to a Halt 36
Inside the Outboard Conspiracy 39
Fuel Docks, Blow Boats, and Other Natural Enemies 42
Insuring Yourself Against Idiocy! 45
Repowering 48
Born-again Stinkpotter 51
Two Grumpy Old Farts Spew 55
The Romance and Reality of Single-handing 59
Gybing into Nirvana 62
Bad Marine Trends: Here, There, and Everywhere 67
Bringing Fire to Curacao 71
Christmas Afloat with Cap'n Scrooge 74
A Lively Tale of Boredom 78
Empty Nesters 81
Perverting the USCG Regulations 84
Customizing Your Boat 87
Yacht Racing Withdrawal 90
Fat Family Reunions 93
On Being Childish and Childless 96
Getting Off On Shoving Off 103
How the Experts Do It 106
Sailing Away from Home 110

Cybersailing With Modern Nav Equipment 113
Deviant Decadent DVD Dunces 116
Head Aches 119
Cruising in Home Waters... 124
Our Cellphones Inform Us We Are Dumb.. 128
Me and My Guitar... 132
The Global Marine Industry.. 136
Poverty & the Radar Screen of Life... 141
An Irreverent Look at the America's Cup.. 144
The Financing of Used and Abused Boat Gear 147
The Limitlessness of My Stupidity 151
The #1 Boat Maintenance Task... 154
Picking Up the Mooring, Fatty-Style 159
The Agony of Dried Snot... 164
St. Valentine's Day, Sea Gypsy Style!.. 168
The Writes and Wrongs of Slinging Ink 172
Write On, Peter!... 175
On Ports and Passages.. 179
Zen and the Art of Sailing... 184
The Perils Of Pearls 187
Showboating at the Boat Show 191
Hot Oil Massage, Fatty-Style... 194
Weather Wimp... 198
Appalling Apia Marina 201
The Worry Nets... 205
Getting Older 208
Another Sunrise in Paradise 211
Writing to Stay Afloat... 215
Afterword.. 222

Introduction
by Chris Kennan

There is something wonderful about receiving a letter from a friend you haven't seen in awhile. Do you know the excitement and curiosity you feel as you open the envelope? Well for those of us in the Caribbean, Fatty's monthly stories in *All At Sea* are just like that—a letter from a friend. Everyone is anxious to hear the latest mishaps and adventures from Fatty and Carolyn.

Fatty writes from the heart and it does not matter whether you actually know him in person. Once you have read a couple of his stories, you get a wonderful (and sometimes goofy) glimpse into his self deprecating world. Fatty in person and Fatty in print are one and the same.

The first time we met Cap'n Fatty, my wife and I had just taken a huge risk and bought a fish wrapper nautical magazine that needed some love and lots of experience. We had lots of love to give it but we were hopelessly short on experience. Our stable of writers and editorial content were so low in our early days at the helm of *All At Sea* that Fatty wrote two columns per month to make sure we had enough to fill our pages. Looking back, I can't believe how incredibly lucky we were to actually catch him in between circumnavigations of the globe. It was simply fortuitous.

We've come a long way together over the years. But the mentoring and support shown in those early days made all the difference in the world to us. Thanks Fatty!

As you will quickly find out, the true genius in Fatty's writing is his ability to make cruising seem so accessible to the average person. Reading his stories you can't help but think, "If this guy can do it, I definitely must be able to." It truly is an intimidating adventure to circumnavigate the globe. And with the multitude of authors preaching about all of the dangers—and the best way to flush the head while in a following sea—it's a welcome change to find someone sharing his successes and failures along the way in a humorous manner.

Enjoy this new book from one of our friends. After a chapter or two he is quickly going to become one of yours.

Chris Kennan
Owner and Publisher
All At Sea
The Caribbean's Waterfront Magazine

Preface

Chris Kennan, the owner and publisher of *All At Sea*, has earned my respect—as a man, as a publisher, and as an employer—against all odds. Let's put it another way: before I met Chris, I didn't like him. Actually, that's too mild—I didn't like him a lot. I was highly prejudiced against his profession. And I'd already refused to work for him numerous times. In fact, the only reason I met with Chris was to rudely tell him off.

Why? Because I'd solemnly promised myself to never, ever work for a Caribbean marine newspaper again.

I grew up aboard the schooner *Elizabeth* and have always loathed the shore. In 1967, at 15 years of age, I purchased my own vessel (*Corina*) and sailed away from 'civilization' forever—with a lovely little Italian girl from the south side of Chicago named Carolyn. In 1971 we built a 36-foot, 20,000 pound ketch named *Carlotta* and eventually sailed her to the Caribbean.

I was immediately dazzled by the Caribbean and the West Indian people. It was the first place I ever felt truly at home. It didn't matter if I was anchored off St. John, Jost, St. Barths, or Bequia—I felt I was in the coolest place on this watery planet.

My wife, Carolyn, and I were such orgasmically-happy hippies that we intentionally reproduced—the ultimate act of human optimism.

But I also realized my master-plan-of-life was only partially completed: I wanted to feel the same way about the entire planet as I felt about the Caribbean and I wanted to 'sea gypsy sail' the world for a life-time—not merely as a 'been there, done that, got the t-shirt' sojourn.

Now you might think, dear reader, because I grew up on a schooner in the 1950's that there was a pile of money somewhere.

There was not. My father paid $100 for the *Elizabeth*—and many intelligent people (my mother, for example) think he was ripped off. I had a wonderful childhood—despite the fact that we were stone-cold broke most of the time. Occasionally, of course, I'd complain. "I'm hungry, Dad," I would say. He'd try to ignore me. But if I'd persist he'd say, "Okay," and grab me firmly by the arm. We'd go to a nearby park. He'd feed me grass while staring me hard in the eye. "Grass fills your belly, son—you won't be hungry anymore," he'd say brightly. I'd try not to eat too much, but he'd urge me on with, "It is common to eat grass. It lessens hunger—which is what you were complaining about, wasn't it? So, here… have some more grass!"

When my father died, my generous sisters and brother allowed me to inherent his entire estate: an Airguide barometer with a broken indicator arm and his WWII sextant with a salt-clouded mirror. My father liked to travel light and was a wayward sailor to the end.

I'm not complaining. I was never truly hungry. I loved my father—and I still do. He was a great, larger-than-life, sailorman. And I had the best possible childhood I could imagine. But I didn't like the taste of grass and I didn't like the idea of ever having to someday feed it to my daughter. So I had a rather modest economic baseline that I didn't want to fall below.
So there I was. I had a good boat, a fine wife, and a lovely daughter—but totally empty pockets. And the grass around Yacht Haven on St. Thomas was beginning to look pretty tasty.

Now I hate to tell you too much of the truth, dear reader, but I suffer from a number of mental… er, conditions. One is delusions of grandeur. There's no other way to explain it. My previous job had been digging ditches (no wonder I'm always ranting against 'dirt,' eh?) and yet I had glorious visions of myself as the next Ernest Hemingway. So I decided to send Jim Long of *Caribbean Boating* (the sole boating newspaper in the Lesser Antilles) a story. The only problem was, I didn't know how to write a story—and I was utterly shocked how difficult it was. So, for the first few days, I just stared at the blank page and wept. Eventually I persevered. I finally managed to put pen-to-paper and made ten pathetic attempts to write a 'simple sea story.'

Each story was, at best, awful.

But a hungry man has no pride—so I sent them off to Jim Long regardless.

This was in the late 70's or early 80's and the St. Thomas chartering scene was truly exploding. You couldn't even walk down the docks of Yacht Haven—they were so full of people, dock carts, service peraonnel, dive masters, sea gypsies, racing sailors, con-men, outboard mechanics, rail riders, sail makers, dock boxes, movie stars… why, *The Momas and The Papas* were playing on the Long Bay waterfront… Paul McCarthy of the Beatles was wandering around Sub Base (looking for some rolling papers)… and Tristan Jones was drinking at the Bilge bar like, well, like he had a wooden leg.

Gosh, it was a happening scene!

Yes, the USVI's marine industry was truly exploding—and it was literally raining money. No matter how mismanaged a company may have been, any marine-related business around Long Bay was an instant success, even if the entrepreneur was completely crazed.

Jim Long wasn't just crazed; he was completely around-the-bend…and completely paranoid. His highly successful newspaper usually didn't even have an office or a manned telephone. Usually, he was the only employee. He wouldn't check his answering machine for weeks—and then only to erase it. Marine businesses had to beg for ads.

Jim Long was also highly suspicious of people. He acted as if everyone was out to get him. If someone walked up to him and asked him, "Do you know where I can find Jim Long?" he'd say yes, point out the back door and hastily slide out the front, thinking, "I outfoxed that jerk!"

Yes, I'm eternally and sincerely grateful to Jim Long for giving me my First Big Chance—but that doesn't mean I can't state the plain, unvarnished truth: he was a complete loony-tune.

But Jim Long was also smart. He'd seen how Richard Spindler of *Latitude 38* had made his marine newspaper fortune without writers. And Jim was eager to emulate him.

I, of course, knew none of this when I sent him my ten stories. All I knew was the man was illusive. He had the only paper distributed from Puerto Rico to South America—and was almost invisible on his home island. After about a month of silence, I decided to track him down at all costs and spent many endless days in 'hot pursuit' of the slippery Mister Long.

Finally, I trapped him in somebody's office and managed to get him on the phone. "Don't hang up, Jim!" was the first thing I screamed at him. "I'm Fatty Goodlander and I sent you ten stories…"

"Yes…" he said.

"…did you get them?"

"Yes."

"…did you… like any?"

"Yes."

"…would you like to publish one?"

"Yes."

"…which one?"

"All."

"…you want to publish all of them?"

"Yes,"

"…that's wonderful," I said.

Silence.

"How much?" I asked.

"How much… what?" he asked.

"…money," I said. "How much money do you offer?"

"I don't." he said.

"…you don't…what?"

"Pay," he said.

This shocked me. How was I supposed to become a professional writer without pay?

"Oh, dear," I said. "But you must. At least a token payment…"

"$35," he said.

I have no idea how he instantly came up with this strange figure. Probably from a speed limit sign outside the office window or some equally bizarre manner. And I was horrified at the paltry sum. I'd written ten stories over the course of six long months… $350 bucks was only pennies per hour… but, hey, you gotta start somewhere.

"Deal," I said.

"…click," said the phone as he hung up.

It wasn't until later, after I was completely addicted to the writing life, that I realized Jim Long had meant $35 for all ten articles—and we had our first major business disagreement.

But by then, I was absolutely enthralled by the literary life. I loved to put the words on paper, to tell stories, to watch people's jaw drop in absolute amazement. My favorite thing to hear back in those heady days was someone saying, with complete outrage, "You can't *SAY* that!" and me replying, "…not only can I, I did!"

At first, I thought Jim Long was an incredibly liberal editor—and a fine judge of words. Then I realized that he simply didn't read anything I sent him. He just forwarded it to a local redhead named Kathy Scarlett to be typeset and published as-is.

He desperately needed copy—and I desperately needed to spew. It was a match made in heaven—sort of.

I immediately realized that people thought my writing was funny—and began to explore the strange & exciting world of (mostly sick) humor. And I also quickly discovered that most of my fellow writers had the 'broomstick up the butt' problem of pompously lecturing their bored readers...instead of telling them exciting stories. I tried not to lecture. Since I knew I was a high school drop-out who'd begrudgingly entered the American school system at 10 years of age and eagerly left it in disgrace at 15... well, I didn't feel I should lecture anyone—and so refrained from doing so. I figured my job was to amuse and delight my readers—and I rapidly discovered that people are far more amused by a fool than a supposed expert.

And so I became, with full intention, the most *dis*-respected sailor in the Caribbean. I soon convinced even the dumbest of my readers that I was dumber than they—not an easy trick in many cases. Every time I sailed my boat into a reef, got punched in the nose, or DSQ'd from a local regatta; I wrote it down in loving detail.

So I enjoyed the writing side of the writing life immensely. Alas, the business side was totally gruesome.

It took days of arguing before I finally agreed to Jim's $35-for-all figure.

"Gawd damn it," I finally fumed. "Okay, Jim... what-ever-you-freak'n-say! Just gimme the 35 smackers and I'm outta your face..."

"Finally," he said smugly, "you're being reasonable."

I said nothing. He said nothing. Nothing happened.

Jim Long had a classic 'small press' business model in his neurotic head—that a newspaper was something which brought in money, disappeared it—and never, ever paid it out for any reason.

"Where's the money," I finally blurted out.

"I don't have it," Jim Long said.

"What do you mean you don't have it," I asked in outrage. "If you don't have it, who does?"

"Tony has it," said Jim.

"Tony who?"

"Tony at Tony's Fish Market," said Jim, "owes *Caribbean Boating* exactly $35 and I owe you $35 So you go get the money from Tony—and everybody is happy!"

By this point, I was very hungry—and the park grass was looking delicious.

So I rushed down to see Tony—who pulled his pants pockets inside out as I came bursting through the door. Tony didn't have any money…but, yeah, he thought my stories about being penniless in *Caribbean Boating* were so darn funny…he offered me some dead fish instead.

I didn't want to take it.

I took it.

Thus, my illustrious career as an 'international marine writer' was launched.

At one point, I asked Jim, "Is this how Hemingway got his start…. writing stupid stories, selling ads, and threatening to break the knee caps of struggling business men?"

"I guess," said Jim.

As elusive as Jim was, he would magically appear for a freebie. The guy could smell a hardboiled egg, for gosh sakes. If the VI government gave away only one fish pate to the press annually, Jim got it—by divine right.

The first year I covered the Rolex Regatta, sponsored by the St. Thomas Yacht Club, he only appeared to collect his free T-shirt. The following year, I demanded that I get the T-shirt—since I did all the work.

"Don't be ridiculous," he said. I insisted. He demurred. I demanded. He refused. I threatened to hand in my resignation. He called Judy Grybowski, the St. Thomas Yacht Club's press secretary at the time, on the phone. Tense negotiations ensued. His publication and my writing career were swinging in the breeze. Finally he hung up, smiled, and said, "Judy has agreed, in view of our sterling service over the course of so many years… to give us two T-shirts—one for me and one for you!"

I'll never forget the first time he gave me a roll of film. It was on the first day of the Rolex. "Pick your shots carefully," he told me. "This film is expensive."

I assured him I'd be careful—and asked him how I'd drop off the roll and get a new one for the second day.

"Are you crazy," he said. "This roll is for the regatta and the awards ceremony!"

Jim admitted he wasn't a writer but he did pride himself on his photographs. However, since he was a tad miserly and didn't like to have people blatantly staring at him… he generally took a lot of pictures of people's backsides—even famous people. My very favorite front page *Caribbean Boating* caption was "Don Street (facing away from the camera) looking at his famous yawl *Iolaire* (out of frame, just to the right)."

Yes, the quintessential *Caribbean Boating* caption accurately described what the picture should have been—if the photographer had exhibited even the slightest bit of common sense.

Oh, it was great training—working with such a tight, professional crew of journalists.

Jim Long not only loathed excellence—he was on-guard against it every second of his profession life.

"Do you know what will happen if we publish a great story about Foxy's Wooden Boat Regatta and illustrate it with a lot of in-focus photographs?"

"They'll love it and send us lots of letters of praise?"

"No, they'll expect it again. And again. And again. We'll raise expectations. We'll screw ourselves, Fatty… don't be stupid!"

This went on for years. I was never a minute late with my stories—Jim was often months late in telling me which marine supply store to loot for my paycheck. Even worse, he started issuing me strange missives. One note said, "A number of people are reporting to me that they find your stories funny. Do you intend this?"

The letters became more and more bizarre—telling me to do all manner of strange non-business-like things. I had wanted, of course, to quit *Caribbean Boating* by this point but was unable to because it was the only game in town—without competition there had been nowhere to jump-ship to. Eventually, however, a marine media did emerge in the Caribbean with such publications as the *Marine Scene*, the *Nautical Scene*, and the *Caribbean Herald*. And by then I had a radio show on WVWI Radio One and a column in the *Daily News* as well—so I quit.

Jim Long tried to rehire me. I refused. He offered me four times the money. I refused. He asked me why I'd quit—and I brutally told him that I didn't like getting weird instructional notes from an obviously demented editor.

"Okay," he said. "We're agreed. Four times the money and I'll never, ever communicate with you in any way—no notes, no phone calls, no letters, no *NOTHING*!"

That was fine with me—and so I went back to work for *Caribbean Boating* for many years on that bizarre basis. (Plus, of course, I continued to work for all the other marine media as well.)

But I learned an important lesson. It is the readers who ultimately sign a writer's paycheck… not the publishers. Jim Long was furious at me—but he rehired me because his readers demanded it.

I'm not sure why so many idiots, rascals, and con-men submerge themselves in the newspaper industry—but I'm sure they do. Perhaps we should ask Conrad Black, one time high-flying owner of the *Chicago Sun-Times* for the definitive answer. (Oops, he's in jail on embezzlement charges, isn't he?)

…perhaps it all started with William Randolph Hearst—who famously started an actual war so his newspaper could cover it.

Even the prestigious, Pulitzer-Prize-winning *Daily News* of St. Thomas ended up being owned—lock, stock & barrel—by an obvious Mafia-adoring thug, who has all the moral fiber of a moray eel.

The point I'm trying to make is that I've worked with a lot of publishers who were… er, less-than-honorable men.

This is unfortunate—and all too common.

Jim Long might have been crazy, but he was, in his own strange way, a man of integrity. When he left St. Thomas, he didn't leave someone else holding the bag. He paid his bills, mostly. He kept his promises, mostly.

Not all Caribbean publishers were so principled.

Example: years ago when the St. Thomas *Daily News* was still a Gannett Publication, a local (real estate multi-millionaire) entrepreneur started up a newspaper in competition. He hired me to the write a weekly marine column for it—which I did. He soon stopped paying me—but assured me it was just a 'minor book-keeping hiccup' so I continued to write for him—knowing he had many, many millions in the bank. This went on for a number of months.

He'd had no intention of paying.

I eventually discovered that he'd completely stopped paying all his writers—and just kept hiring new ones to replace them (whom he didn't pay either, just hired yet more).

I believe he thought of this as being clever.

I know I thought of it as fraud.

Eventually he owed virtually every single freelance writer in the VI money—and refused to pay any of them. All of them just threw up their empty hands in disgust—except for yours truly. I decided I'd either a.) get paid or b.) cost him ten times what he owed me.

I set about to methodically accomplish one or the other. I'm happy to say that within a few weeks I was paid-in-full by his attorney—the only writer and/or staff to see a penny from the bastard.

This made me proud.

I think it is very important for a worker—even a lowly writer—to be paid.

This puts me in direct conflict with many sleazy, fly-by-night publishers.

But I'm afraid I'm off on a strange tangent. Where was I? Ah, yes, charting the strange and bizarre course of various local marine publishing scams... er, enterprises.

Eventually *Caribbean Boating* went belly up. Ditto the *Nautical Scene* and the *Marine Scene* as well. But I continued to sling ink for various Caribbean publications...until a diabolical publisher intentionally stranded me, penniless, in the Chagos archipelago in the middle of the Indian Ocean.

Ouch!

I did not appreciate this. It was a sandy island and there wasn't even any grass to eat. I was ten thousand ocean miles from home, dead broke...and was owed over $7,000...which I desperately needed.

"Arggghhh!" as the pirates say.

It took me almost a year to sail back to the Caribbean (on an empty stomach) and plot my revenge. Let's just skip the ugliness and cut to the chase—I received every penny owed (thanks, in part, to the noble efforts of Gary E. Brown), and the fellow who had owed it to me decided to return to Europe where the pickings were a tad easier.

Why am I telling you all this strange and ancient history? Because a month later, back in the Virgins, I started getting various insistent messages from a new kid in town called Chris Kennan of *All at Sea* publications. He wanted me to write a Caribbean column for him. It was the last thing I wanted to do. I was done with Caribbean publications. I refused. Telephone messages and e-mails piled up. I ignored them.

Finally, a yacht racing friend named Kirk Boeger approached me on behalf of Chris Kennan. I politely turned Kirk down a couple of times. Finally, he came to me and said, "Fatty, as a personal favor to me—would you meet with Chris?"

I reluctantly agreed to.

The reason I didn't want to meet with Chris is because I thought he'd be like all the other fly-by-night pirate publishers I'd met—a grinning conman who would promise me the sky and ultimately leave me in a lurch. I was, happily, dead wrong. It was immediately apparent to me that Chris was a good guy, a sincere guy, and a completely honest guy. With Chris, what you see is exactly what you get. Not only couldn't I be rude to Chris—I immediately liked him—and Nicole too. Dang it! Instead of telling him 'never, ever,' I ended up working for him. And I'm now happy to report that Chris Kennan has kept every promise he's made to me over the course of these many delightful years of ink slinging. I believe in him completely: if Chris tells me something or promises me something—I know I can take it to the bank.

Plus, he's not even insane—or no more so than most Red Hook business folk are.

That's why I've dedicated this book to him and his growing family Thanks, Chris…

…thanks for not making my wife, my daughter, or myself have to go to the park and eat grass.

My pen is yours forever.

The Funny Thing About Being Funny

I didn't set out to be funny. In fact, I don't even know what funny *is*. I expect if I did, I wouldn't be. Writing marine humor is a curious business. There's no way to scientifically qualify it. And, alas, it has a lot to do with ego. To a large degree my oddly-fulfilling career as a sailing humorist depends on my ability to believe that what I think is funny *is* funny—and if you don't agree, you're an idiot!

The troubling fact is that some people—who appear otherwise sane—seem to agree.

I have fans. This makes me nervous. Nonetheless, I have carefully studied my geographically and culturally diverse fans and come to the conclusion they have only one trait in common: lack of judgment.

Recently I was chased through the streets of downtown Auckland by two former Caribbean sailors screaming "Electric honey!" and waving tattered-but-carefully-preserved pages of the Budget Marine catalogue at me.

"Kiss me full on the lips," one was shouting, while the other ranted, "Freedom is my drug-of-choice, too!"

Evidently they'd both had some sort of psychotic breakdown offshore—during which their already-bent sexual fantasies had merged with some technical writing I'd done for a local marine retailer. And they'd never recovered.

"Listen to this one. It is one of my favorites," said one fan to the other while reading from a fluttering catalogue page at full gallop. "'Hose clamps can be used to clamp hoses!'"

"Brilliant," cried the other, "he cuts right to the bone!"

Wouldn't this make you nervous? Of course! And I didn't even remember the "electric honey" line. Only by searching my hard drive, did I discover I'd used it on these very pages five plus years ago in an article about Chagos.

"Let's get together and have group sex with your wife and daughter," they shouted at one point, when they thought they had me cornered. "And we'd like our... our... well, we'd like your personal autograph in a personal place!"

Of course, I attempt to keep an open mind. I don't rudely punch people *just* for saying they enjoy my writing—but I *do* make a precautionary fist.

I mean, the *nerve* of some people.

Brooklyn Vito of *Wanderer*, an Amel 52, recently introduced himself with, "My wife says you're not as stupid as you pretend—but I disagree."

"Nice to meet you," I said lamely. "And I take it you are familiar with my work?"

I recently got back a manuscript submission (Carolyn calls them my "homing pigeons" because they always return) with a note from the editor which said, "Do you realize, Mister Goodlander, that trees have to *die* so you can write this dribble?"

Yes, rejection is stressful. Recently one of my stories was returned with "This is the worst story every written!" angrily scrawled across its cover page. To demonstrate to the editor that his remarks hadn't hurt nor discouraged me, I quickly sent him another story—to which he replied, "I need to revise my previous comment."

There are times when I think everyone is taking pot-shots at me—even my wife.

"The interior of *Wild Card* is a mess because my delusional carpenter husband thinks *this* is six inches," she recently said sarcastically with her thumb and forefinger barely apart.

The sad fact of the matter is that, even after 37 plus years of sailing offshore and living aboard, we have some issues—mostly about timing.

"Too slow," I shout at her immediately afterwards—as she says to me, accusingly, "Too fast!"

Yes, it is a shame when the marital arguments, no matter how short, last longer than the act.

Let's be totally honest, okay? Female orgasm is a myth perpetrated by women-libbers to make men feel guilty. That's a proven fact!

Seriously, the fact that my wife has any expectations at all—proves they're unrealistic ones.

But, damn, being married to her can be ego-bruising. "My husband is a realist with extremely low self-esteem," she recently told a friend.

"He'd have to learn a hell-of-a-lot to be merely dysfunctional," she told another.

"He calls nodding-off and drooling at the same time 'multi-tasking'," she complained to a third.

And she's always zen-messing with my head, "There are three types of people in the world, Fatty, people who can count and people who can't!"

How could *any* man put up with that?

I mean, I get insulted at the strangest times: I gave the eulogy at a funeral and as one of the pall-bearers was lowering the casket into the grave, he whispered, deadpan, "I thought you'd be funnier."

I was anchored in Tahiti when a large, palatial motor yacht went by. Its skipper remarked on *Wild Card* over his mega-watt power-hailer with, "Gee, she doesn't look *so* bad—considering how long she's been incompetently sailed!"

Even my daughter Roma Orion, light-of-my-life, got into it at the end of a recent phone call by asking, as I was informing her we wouldn't be back in the States any time soon, "Why are widely-accepted clichés like 'distance makes the heart grow fonder' so often wrong?"

My mother, who is 87 and blind, turned down my offer to visit her in California with, "Maybe in five or ten years, Fatty. Right now, I'm busy having fun with friends!"

Today I cleared out of Fiji for Vanuatu. As I entered the last government office, the open-mouthed custom's official was staring out the window at *Wild Card*. I told him that he was looking at my yacht and I wanted to clear it out. "Surely, sir, you jest!" he said. "Suicide is illegal in *all* the former Colonies!"

Thus I was a tad bummed as I returned to *Wild Card*.

"Don't worry," Carolyn consoled me, "You're just having one of those utterly miserable days when you get what you deserve!"

Sailing Away from the Dream Crushers

James Goodlander 1950's

According to my driver's license (happily expired), I'm 43 years old. I still remember some of my youthful years—though after the '60's, my memories get selectively fuzzy. In any event, I've lived over 35 years of my life aboard various sailboats.

I'm currently working as a marine journalist—since the gigolo trade often tends to be somewhat slow this time of year. I'm not complaining. It's a living. A large part of my job is, more or less, writing about how we boaters are just regular people, average guys and gals, just run-of-the-mill folks who happen to own a boat and like to sail.

In our culture (in the mid 90's) being too different from your island neighbor just isn't cool. It's bad for the sacred Bottom Line—especially here in the Caribbean. The smart money says that we boaters should just pretend that we're the same as—anyone else, any group or industry—anywhere!

The fact is, of course, that's a bunch of crap. We ain't just like everybody else, or we wouldn't be driven to live, love, and die under sail.

We ain't *better*—and in some ways we may be *worse*—but we damn sure are *different*.

At least I am.

I grew up on an old (built by Morse in 1924) 52' Alden schooner named *Elizabeth*. Living aboard and cruising under sail was rather unusual back in the early 1950's.

My father was, to put it mildly, a *"character"*. A radical's radical. A madman's madman. A wacko's wacko. He could charm the monkeys outta the trees—and manage to get arrested for disturbing the peace—within minutes of stepping ashore anywhere.

He was the Ultimate Artful Dodger.

Authority in any form—was antithetical to him. He loathed uniforms. He was against practically anything, anywhere that was at all "organized." He didn't consider himself an anarchist because he didn't like to be "confined" by such a "restricting" label.

Time and time again, he'd tell me, "Fatty, just 'cause everyone says that you're wrong doesn't mean you're right—but it's usually a good indication that you are!"

He had hair down to his as..., er... butt, a wildly electric beard, and he often wore floral wrap-around skirts. (He was 6'2", and an intense slab of solid muscle, *clearly* not the kind of fella you'd casually get flippant with concerning his personal appearance.)

He was an artist, of course. Commercial, graphic, or sign—a "painting-whore" for whomever would pay. He once handled the graphic section of the Bull Durham advertising account (a large prestigious account at the time.) Each time he'd draw the bull, the bull's... er... a certain part of the bull would get larger. This went on for almost a year. We couldn't believe it. Each time he'd do another drawing, our entire family would look at it, and say, "You'll never get *this* one past 'em!"

Eventually, of course, after he'd infiltrated the company's entire year's advertising campaign with the best developed, most monstrously hung bulls imaginable—he was fired.

We all went out for dinner, and celebrated his accomplishment.

He didn't send me to school much. "He weren't big on store-bought learn'n," as they say down on the farm. (I've gone to school a total of five years, which he thought was "rather excessive.") I was over ten years old when I first stepped foot into a class room.

Imagine my surprise when the students folded their hands at their desks and prayed aloud. I'd heard about "religion," and vaguely knew that the cultists whom it enslaved were snidely referred to as "Christians"—but I never thought that I would actually meet some!

I thought Christians were like—the American Nazi party or the KKK. In my child's imagination, I figured if I could get to a window, and signal a cop—he'd bust them all immediately! I might even get my picture in the paper. "Young Fatty Goodlander, on his first day of school, routs out secret nest of rabid 'Christian cultists'!" A beaming Mayor would give young Fatty "The Keys to City" as his proud father (neatly attired in a colorful skirt) proudly applauded.

Yeah, well, I had some adjusting to do....

You couldn't just be a cruising sailor back in those days. People wouldn't accept the concept. It just "did-not-compute". Everywhere we'd go, we'd attract massive media attention. An earth-mother wife, a strange man in a floral dress, three wild-eyed children, and a half dozen bizarre mis-fit wino/sailors just cruz'n 'long for the ride—a funky schooner—a few radical slogans about America being morally bankrupt, or Joe McCarthy and

Roy Cohen being gay, could really stir things up back then in the '50's.

When reporters would ask my father what we were doing, he'd say, "We're engaged in doing research for Tulane University" (or MIT, or Cal-tech) "concerning—well, here let me allow my daughter Carole to explain."

My oldest sister would then have to seamlessly continue the story, making up a multitude of specific facts as she went along, until she could foist off the continuation of the lie onto me or my other sister.

At the time, I thought it was just a neat game called "Lie to the Press Cleverly."

I didn't know that we were actually *at* school. (All the Goodlander kids eventually graduated with a BS from FU, and ended up owning pens which dribble out money in various amounts—though our professional fields vary widely—Carole the poet/teacher/author, Gale Orion the grant-writer, and me the shoddy journalist.

At 15, I purchased a 22-foot Atkin double-ender built in 1932, and took off for the High Seas. They often were. Three years later, and an equal number of thousands of nautical miles, I sold *Corina* in St. Petersburg, Florida.

At 19 years of age, I mailed away $25 for a set of Yacht Plans, and built a 36-foot ketch named *Carlotta.*

She wasn't much of a boat. But then, I wasn't much of a boat builder. The point is, she worked. She functioned. She existed.

My wife and I lived aboard her for the next 18 years. We cruised for over 30,000 miles within her. We raised our daughter aboard, just as I was raised. (Roma Orion is now 13 years old.)

We made it almost all the way through Hurricane Hugo before a 68-foot schooner dragged down on us, and *Carlotta* was lost.

A few days later I purchased a 38-foot S&S sloop for $3,000. It, too, was a Hugo victim. It was sunk, and had a 3 by 12 foot hole in the side.

Within the month, I'd repaired it enough to take second place in the cruising division of the Coral Bay Yacht Club's Thanksgiving Day race.

Since then, we've lived aboard *Wild Card* for more than six years, sailed to South America a couple of times, and cruised and raced it thousands of miles.

This stuff still can be done; the dream still can be real. Living *"The Life"* is still possible.

All you have to do is *do it.* Seize the day! Take the "tiller of life" in your own hands—kiss life full on the lips. Savor each day. Taste each new sensation.

Go for it!

My father used to rant and rave across the worn decks of our old schooner, *Elizabeth.* He would shake his fists defiantly heavenwards. He'd writhe out onto the bowsprit like a whirling dervish. His eyes would burn with all the intensity of the Blessedly Blissed.

"Don't let them get you, Fatty," he'd shout. "Don't let the Dream Crushers get you!!!"

"Who?" I'd asked, even though I already knew. I never seemed to tire hearing about the Enemy.

"The *Dream Crushers*, son!" he'd say. "They are so—*slick!* They'll pretend to be your friends. They'll ask you sympathetic questions. They'll get inside your head—find out your innermost hopes and dreams and aspirations. And then, they will tell you that you can *not,* absolutely can *not*—do whatever it is that you want to do! That you are too old, or haven't enough money, or are the wrong sex/color/height, or not educated enough, or too passive or too violent, too—something!"

On and on he'd go about the dreaded "Dream Crushers".

They never got him. He lived his life to the hilt—kissed it full on the lips. Even on his deathbed, he joked about the "over-grown patrol-boys."

"Puritanism is the sneaking suspicion that somebody, somewhere is having a good time," he'd joke.

I'm sure he's down there right now (I couldn't picture him being happy "up" there. He hated sappy harp music as much as Christians) literally giving the Dream Crushers hell.

To this very day, when I call my sisters, we often part with the words, "Don't let the Dream Crushers get you."

I try not to. For Daddy.

"I yam what I yam," as Popeye would say. I have no desire to pretend that I am exactly like everyone else. I have a different history, and I'm sure I'll have a different future. The sea has taught me many lessons—and I've even retained a few. I'm the kind of person that mothers tell their daughters to watch out for—and rightly so. I am in love (and lust) with life. I do not live my life seeking the approval of people whose opinions I do not respect, nor have I trained myself to be a "good consumer". I do not subscribe to the notion that "I buy things, therefore I am." I'm not into "sport shopping." I do not believe that my worth as an individual is related to the number of retail products I have purchased in my lifetime.

I just don't.

Sorry. (OK, I'm not *really* sorry!)

As one of our Founding Fathers quipped, "Eternal vigilance is the price of Liberty."

In other words, "Watch out for the Dream Crushers!!!"

The Ghosts of September

Culebra after Hurricane Hugo 1989

It is early in the morning here in Langkawi, Malaysia. It is still dark. We're about half way through our second circumnavigation. I'm holding our ship's bell in my hand—and reading off the names engraved on it: Bill Rich, Thatcher Lord, Ken Betts, Cid Hamling, Mary Pat Sica. Bill Henderson. Mike Sheen. Steve and Irene Macek. Jack Simmons. Fritz Seyfarth... just a few of the wonderful people who helped us in our hour of need. The date today is September 18, 2009. I'm also watching our ship's clock. It is 6:21 A.M. Only two minutes to go. I sigh. I shake my head to clear it. My eyes start to mist. It all seems like only yesterday. I glance up—and count down the seconds to 6:23. "...five, four, three, two, one... *NOW!*" I say aloud to my silent vessel.

Exactly 20 years ago, at the height of Hurricane Hugo, I lost my previous boat *Carlotta*. A 68-foot schooner named *Fly Away* lived up to her name and started doing just that in 150-plus knots of wind. We were in Culebra. She dragged her anchor. We collided. Our rigging tangled. She became sideways to the wind against my bowsprit. My four anchor rodes started popping like over-wound banjo strings. We were driven ashore. On rocks. Holed. *Game-over!*

Carlotta wasn't just a boat or just our home—she was the physical manifestation of our watery lifestyle. A sailor can't be a sailor without a boat. I'd built her in Boston from a few sheets of paper over the course of six long years. One pre-Hugo minute I was an intrepid captain and a daring sea-rover—the next instant I was a victim.

I hate being a victim.

It was as if somebody had removed the color from the sky. I and my family were still alive—but in a new, frighteningly-limited world. We were ashore. We were jetsam. We couch-surfed for a while, thanks to the compassion of wonderful friends—but living off the compassion of others is wearying.

I felt like I was shrinking. Hurricane Hugo lessened me. It temporarily crippled me. I felt less confident. I couldn't *quite* concentrate. My existence went from stereo to mono. I suddenly found myself speaking too loudly. My jokes began to fall flat. For the very first time in my life, I thought, "I'm unlucky." I was more than just homeless and broke—I was stunned. I felt punch-drunk. I began to doubt everything—including myself.

Natural disasters like Hurricane Hugo do these bad things to good people. They slap them in the face. They play '52 Pick-Up' with their entire lives. They not only knock them down—they repeatedly kick them while they're still in the fetal position.

It isn't pretty—especially when it is happening to you. It overwhelms you. You want to cry so much—that you break down and actually *do* cry. And then you feel both better & ashamed at the same time.

However, every dark cloud has a silver lining. I'd been coasting through life: as a sailor, as a husband, as a father—and even as a writer. Hugo shook me. It made me reexamine my priorities: did I want to be a boat bum or a circumnavigator? Did I want to be husband or just have a wife? Did I want to be a father or just have a cute kid around? Did I want to just dabble in writing—or dedicate my entire professional life to *The Art of the Sentence*?

Heavy stuff, eh?

One month after our vessel was destroyed by Hurricane Hugo, my wife, Carolyn, came to me. She had red eyes. "I don't mind losing our home, Fatty. I don't mind losing every single material thing we've ever worked for. I don't even mind not having any clothes or shoes—or any of that crap! But we're losing control of our lives, Fatty. And that scares me. It *really* scares me..."

There is a solution to most problems in life: hard work. It sounds simplistic and when we're young we don't want to hear it—but it is the truth. Yes, much of what happens to us is random. Chance plays a capricious role. But it is also true that character is destiny. We can't control what happens to us but we *can* control how we respond to it. And, generally, the harder we work, the luckier we get.

One day I woke up and decided to stop being a victim. I sprang into action. I decided that even doing the wrong thing was preferable to doing nothing at all. It immediately felt like a million pounds had been lifted from my shoulders. I stopped thinking about all that I had lost and started thinking about how rich I was. Most important of all, I got my butt in gear. I cast off my storm-induced inertia—and started, once again, to create my own destiny.

I walked the beaches of St. John in search of a free boat. I wasn't looking for a good boat or my dream yacht—just a reasonable vessel that I could 'win' without too much money upfront. I found *Wild Card* (a 1978 Hughes 38), holed and driven ashore on the rocks in Leinster Bay. I paid $3,000 for her salvage rights—and had to accept full responsibility to remove her from

National Park waters without damaging the environment—or pay to have the NPS do so.

It was a big risk for, potentially, a big reward.

I pulled it off. I managed to get her to the Independent Boat Yard on St. Thomas—where Pieter Stoeken hauled her immediately—knowing full well I had empty pockets and a mammoth rebuilding project ahead of me.

Fixing the big hole in her portside was the easy part. I managed to complete that itchy job within the first month. But her bulkheads were no longer attached, her mast step had been pulverized, and her engine was a rusted hulk. It took many years to turn her into a strong, storm-ready, ocean-sailing yacht.

Every penny went into the boat. Every spare second was spent either working on her or earning the money to do so. Up until 1995, I sailed her without an engine. Then we purchased a brand new Perkins M30 from Tom Gerker of Parts and Power in Tortola. This was a big step. I had a goal now—but I was too shy to admit it. In 1998 Carolyn came zooming back to the boat in our dingy…and was amazed to see an expensive Monitor self-steering gear on its transom.

"Looks like we're going somewhere," she said dryly.

What an understatement. Since that moment, we have sailed *Wild Card* over 50,000 ocean miles. We've circumnavigated. We've rounded the Cape of Storms, tasted the Roaring Forties, been repeatedly entertained by the Indian Ocean. The entire world is, literally, our oyster. And we've had the highest possible quality of life I can imagine—all aboard our modest little $3,000 craft.

There were two pivotal moments in my life—one of them was the launching of *Carlotta*. It was a wonderful day. I was bursting with happiness, with pride, with confidence. At 19 years of age I'd set out to build an ocean-going boat—and I and my wonderful wife had done so. I wasn't a dreamer—I was a doer.

The other pivotal moment was fifteen years later—when I lost her.

I thought, at the time, it was horrible-rotten-bad luck. But was it? In hindsight, I'm not sure. I now believe that losing my previous vessel—as dear & precious as she was to me—was really the first agonizing step in growing up. I was man-child before Hugo, and man-man after. It forced me to think. Certain sects in Tibet pray for major problems so they can learn from them. Hurricane Hugo was my watery Zen Master. Without Hugo's savage push, I might never have accomplished my life-long dream of sailing around the world. I had to bottom-out in order to realize my wealth wasn't my boat. My wealth was my health and my wife and my child and my own heart.

I'm lucky. I have a life partner. This is no small thing. Whenever I falter, she is there. She is my rock. Not only couldn't I have built *Carlotta* without my wife's help—I couldn't have survived *Carlotta*'s demise without her either. Nor could I have circumnavigated.

But life is strange. We humans don't know what is happening to us while it is happening. We're ignorant. We really don't know what is good luck or bad luck. We think we do, but we're often wrong. We win the lottery and think, "…good luck!" as the money destroys our marriage, takes away our health and lands us in bankruptcy court. Or our home is destroyed in a tornado and we think, "…bad luck!"

Maybe not.

Sometimes you have to lose 'everything' to realize that everything isn't terribly important. Material things mean little. Things are just stuff. We get tricked by consumerism into thinking 'stuff' is important—but it is not. Stuff is crap. Stuff is just brightly-colored baubles. Nor is money important. Money merely buys convenience—which isn't terribly valuable anyway. What is important is the stainless steel within our souls. Ours were tempered in Hugo. We are, strangely & ultimately, grateful.

Rigging the Facts on Freudian Sloops

Sailboat in the Philippines with ricebag sail

You might have noticed that different sailboats have different rigs. Once upon a time, things were easy—then the other caveman stood up on the log and opened his coat. Ever since, we've been arguing about which rig configuration is best.

Basically, all dumb sailors believe that the rig of their boat is the best because... well, it is the rig of their boat! And they are geniuses. So, it has to be the best!

This is stupid.

I feel this way.

But let's turn to science: ever heard of Freud? He was the first to point out the obvious, that sloop sailors are focused solely on their... penis. It is the solitary star of their show. Just listen to the language: how they 'erect' their mast, how they like to 'keep it up,' etc. Oh, sure, you can pretend that the terminology isn't sexually-loaded—but that's just denial. "Pole-tip up," they shout on the race course. They brag about how long they can stay 'hard on the wind.' Even the individual boat-bits smack of smut: spreader, cockpit, strut, mast*head*, etc. I mean, how many different disgusting ways can sailors use just the word lay: as in lay-line, lay-the-mark, lay-day, lay-of-the-land, etc. This starts from the very beginning: while lofting my 36-foot ketch *Carlotta,* I had to draw dozens of 'buttock' lines... hardly subtle, eh?

Even traditional sailors get into it by always 'thrusting' their bowsprits into Virgin anchorages, etc. I guess all that hemp cordage makes 'em somewhat kinky: why else would they have spankers?

Yes, maritime traditions change. Long bowsprits used to be called 'widow-makers' but are now referred to as the Johnny Holmes.

Even the Colin-Archer types—the traditional double-enders of Scandinavia—have joined in. "Our outboard rudders aren't the only thing aboard which are well-hung," a smirking Swedish sailor once told me.

Offshore sailors are the worst: always beating and taking a pounding and plugging away... on vessels named *Randy Tarr, Sin or Swim,* or *Dick's Playpen.*

If you think I'm making this up—check out the traditional sea chantey which begins, "T'was on the good ship Venus..."

Obviously, split-rigs represent a gender-conflicted sailor. Schoonermen are led by the immaturity of their 'younger, more boyish' spear-spar forward—while ketch sailors think maturely first—then 'get wild' with their sapling mast aft.

Multihullers are... notoriously confused. The only thing they agree on is to not agree with *anything ever done* on a mono-moron's boat. Cat sailors are, well, bluntly, bi. But even more bizarre is the obvious anger of the touchy, gender-blending, sea-spider aficionados. "I'd never sail on a fat-arsed lead-mine," huffed one tri-huller, "when I could be lightly skimming across the Pacific in a traditional Polynesian Fakkafakka design."

Some modern cats have such 'spar envy' of split-rig craft that they've put a mast in each hull and, thus, doubled the size of their erection... if not their boat speed.

Not all sailors of *multicoques* are into hyper-speed: some hefty hedonistic cat sailors prefer to savor life in the slow lane with "a beamy broad and a boat broad-of-beam!"

...then there are the *proa* sailors who are never quite sure which side of the bread their butter is on.

Yes, variety is the spice of life. One lovely Herreshoff design (named *Star*) in Nevis sports three masts. Obviously some Caribbean sailors think 'the more members, the merrier' when it comes to rigid protrusions.

Gaffers attempt to make up for their puny length with their long booms, stout gaffs, and noble topmasts. Certain women prefer these Neanderthal types; others complain they 'peak' too early.

One prudish British gal recently jumped overboard when her traditional Cornish sailorman commanded her to "sweat up the throat!"

Beach cat sailors are notoriously—chafe-resistant. And don't seem to mind sand anywhere.

Of course, the owners of many local racing craft are aging. This isn't openly discussed, just hinted at. For instance, I asked one silver-haired old Maxi duffer if he was going to do the Rolex Regatta. He just shrugged and said, "Depends."

...which was more about him than I needed to know.

I mean, sure the parties at the regatta on Sint Maarten are fine but afterward—well, *droop!* Ditto ASW (Antigua Sailing Weak).

Yes, we baby-boomers are aging. I had to tell one elderly cruiser heading for Trinidad that it wasn't famous for *bed* pans...

Of course, there are some positive aspects to aging. For instance, I've found that as my memory fades, my conscience clears.

We now wear name tags on *Wild Card* because at a recent cruisers party in Thailand, I attempted to seduce my *wife*. Yes, the island of Phuket is easily mispronounced. It takes awhile for some sailors to adjust. Recently a ketch pulled up to the fuel dock at Ao Chalong—and a little Thai girl in short pants and platform shoes pointed to the aluminum spar that holds the bottom of the mainsail and mizzen, in rapid succession.

"…boom-boom?" asked the puzzled owner.

"Four bucks," said the girl. (If you sail away with one, it's called 'Thai take-away' in modern sailor's lingo.)

Yes, there are a lot of things about sailors you might not want to know. For example, it is believed that early mermaid myths were spread by lonely sailors sighting bewhiskered manatees—I've been there, alas, while wearing my beer-goggles.

None of us are without sin. I suppose all long-time Caribbean hands have strapped the landlubbing hubby of some gorgeous blond into the bosun's chair—and sent him spinnaker flying in forty-knots-and-gusting for a couple of sensuous hours.

Ditto the ole 'wind-surfing lesson' trick which was so popular with single charter captains. (Hint: crank up Jimmy Buffet on the cockpit speakers so you can't hear his pitiful screams.)

Yes, I'm a romantic. And I love the sea. But I'm also a realist and I know it is hard to keep a sweet secret around a gossip-clogged waterfront. For instance, one young 'new-to-cruising' lady who sailed into our harbor recently blushed deep red when I commented to her on how active she'd been during her first week. "My God," she gasped, "how do you know?"

I explained to her about how sailors traditionally rise at dawn—and always reflexively check out which dinghy was behind which boat. "Solution?" she whispered in mortified shame.

"Can you swim," I asked.

Yeah, she's a regular Esther Williams now!

Avoiding Work

A wise man once said, "The problem with good ideas is that, if you're not careful, they can degenerate into actual work!"

How true! Extreme laziness might look easy, but it is not.

In fact, maintaining a high level of inactivity—especially year after year after year—requires considerable effort. Frankly, I'd give up avoiding work—if I wasn't so damn lethargic.

Confession: I recently allowed my "eternal vigilance" to slip and did some actual work on my 38-foot sloop *Wild Card*.

I know, I know... I'm loath to admit it, but...

...it happened.

It all started when my wife, Carolyn, purchased a rechargeable drill for my birthday. Luckily, both its batteries were dead, which was just fine with me. Almost immediately however, certainly within the next month or two, my wife asked me why I didn't charge them up.

"Well," I lectured her in my best know-it-all, I'm-the-man voice, "You see, it is *just not that easy*, my dear! NiCad batteries have a "memory" effect, which means you should not partially charge them, or recharge them when they are only partially discharged. Since I'm not sure *exactly* how long my next project will last—or even *what* my next project will be—well, obviously, I shouldn't just rush off to charge the batteries!"

The following day she returned to the boat with both batteries fully charged and an expensive sheet of half inch mahogany plywood. "Perhaps you might start on the galley shelves," she suggested sweetly.

Needless to say, the galley shelves have been a point of contention between us—for about five years now. They sort of rotted away from the hull. The instant I saw the problem, I immediately leapt into action—and propped them up with some rusty Campbell's soup cans. (I hate pea soup!)

After that, I told my wife it was completely up to her. "Yeah, only stow lightweight stuff on 'em—like marshmallows, bags of potato chips, sacks of Cheesos...."

"What about the cases of Heineken?" she asked. "What do I do with those? And the cartons of Mount Gay? Where should I put the racks of Slim Jims and the pickled pig's feet—you know, all the *cruising* food?"

Alas, I didn't hear her at the time...having already redonned my Walkman, while diving into the cockpit cooler for yet another delicious cold one.

"Ah, life is good here in the tropics!" I burped to myself. "Paradise is, indeed, just that!"

Needless to say, a couple of years later, due *totally* to her thoughtless repacking of the rotten shelves, they fell completely apart.

Worse, one of the larger bags of potato chips hit the galley counter top so hard, it popped off the soft-but-not-yet-totally-rotten front panel.

Thus, the purchase of the rechargeable drill, the acquisition of the plywood, and the beginning of matrimonial discord.

The first thing I did after I decided to truly get-to-work, was to procrastinate for as long as possible. (I am, I must admit, excellent at this!) I oiled my tools, sharpened the block of rust that had once been my wood plane, and attempted to determine which of the long skinny things with handles were my screwdrivers and which were my chisels. (Okay, so I don't coddle my tools!)

Eventually, damn it, I had to actually *do* something.

Working on a small sailboat on a mooring is difficult, especially in the heat of summer in Great Cruz Bay, St. John, Virgin Islands during a hot south wind. My boat was rolling from rail to rail in the greasy swell, and even Joker (the ship's cat) was having a tough time holding on. (He managed, alas, much to our varnish's detriment.)

But I didn't let the sickening roll stop me once I got cranking. I just tossed down the sheet of plywood, got out the drill, and drilled right through it.

...and the cockpit sole too.

"Did you mean to do that?" sneered my wife.

"Of course," I lied. "I'm gonna bolt an extra oak stiffener into the cockpit floor to prevent its excessive flexing."

Once I started actually making sawdust, a crowd of curious onlookers in dinghies gathered around my vessel. "I never thought I'd see the day..." muttered one particularly open-mouthed & amazed observer as I sweated.

To make matters worse, a few of my "friends" immediately left and quickly returned with video cameras, to better "record the event for posterity."

Next, while using my hole saw on a piece of wood that was too long to lay down on the cockpit floor, I managed to drill a two inch hole into the *side* of my cockpit.

"Don't tell me," my wife snorted. "You're gonna put a *really really big* bolt there."

"Don't be silly, my dear," I sniffed disdainfully at her. "That hole is for the new transmission temperature gauge I've been planning to install—something every offshore boat should have!"

The new drill/screw-gun was a big help, although it took me awhile to figure out its subtle drawbacks. (For instance, it is best not to attempt to attach picture frames to your main bulkhead with three long #16 galvy screws without pre-drilling, because it splits *both* the frame and the bulkhead.)

My wife was so pleased to see actual progress being made on the galley that she didn't even complain when I yet-again mistakenly Sabre-sawed through the cabin top while cutting a different piece of plywood. "Well," she said with a weary shrug, "We can always put in another Lewmar hatch for ventilation to fill the hole..."

Dastardly Diesel Mechanics

I once heard a rumor that there was a non-sadistic diesel mechanic in the Caribbean—but it turned out to be just that, a rumor. (How such outrageous rumors even get started is beyond me!)

Seriously, scientific studies have proven that diesel fumes rot the brain faster than, say, the Ebola virus mixed with anthrax.

Perhaps that explains the amazing hostility many mechanics exhibit towards their cautiously cowering customers. Maybe we can't chock it *all* up to petty revenge for their low social/verbal skills.

Of course, diesel mechanics vary—mostly between poor and worthless.

I prefer the "shady tree" variety. At least they're not pretentious. You *know* you're in trouble when they show up with a yard stick, crow bar, and a small sledge to calibrate your electronic fuel injection pump. You don't have to wait for them to confirm it with a, "Gee, I barely touched the outer housing with the sledge, and it cracked open like an egg! Why, it musta had a factory defect in the casting or sumth'n!"

The "factory-trained technician" types charge a lot more for even less. They seldom actually physically touch an engine any more, preferring instead to concentrate on such modern "profit centers" as billing for non-existent work, billing for non-existent replacement parts, and billing for non-existent problems that weren't fixed with parts that never existed.

"Being a modern mechanic is a much more *creative* job than it used to be," said Bottomline Ben of Blown Head Gaskets, Inc.

"That's right. We've gotten away from the actual 'dirt under the fingernails' aspect of the profession," said Ned Nerdy of Tele-Diesel Diagnostics. "We've got a computer in our office that hooks to a 56k flex modem. The boat owner just holds his cellular phone next to his diesel, and it completely graphs the whole thing."

"And what do you learn from those graphs," I asked.

"Well, usually, that he needs a new engine!" said Nerdy with a sly chuckle. "At least, that's been the case about 100% of the time so far."

Being a *marine* mechanic poses some special challenges, of course. "Just because it is a small job doesn't mean that I can't make a big mess," said Oil Slick Nick of Fly By Nite Flywheels.

"If I'm asked to change an oil filter on a really fine yacht, you can be sure I'll track some grime on the oriental carpets, wipe my greasy hands on the custom embroidered bath towels, and blow my nose on the silk curtains. And that's only for starters!"

Needless to say, power boaters have an advantage over blow-boaters. "With a stinkpotter, we've got to get his engine to run long enough to strand him far, far from home. A sailboater doesn't even get *that* level of incompetence!"

Of course, if a diesel doesn't run correctly, it is absolutely *never* the fault of the mechanic. "Maybe the battery is dead," he'll say if a piston rod shoots through the side of the block.

"Or perhaps you've adjusted your alternator belt too tight!"

Mechanics, of course, sing different songs at different times.

An engine that is "indestructible" when it is being sold to you, suddenly isn't guaranteed afterwards because you "ran it on too high octane fuel" when you walked by it after liberally splashing yourself with Old Spice cologne.

Yes, most marine diesel engine guarantees have loopholes you could drive a ferry boat full of sea-lawyers through. In fact, many marine engines aren't guaranteed for such things as being "run in a saline-tainted gaseous environment" like salt air.

If you buy a 900 hp turbo-charged diesel for your 17-foot runabout, and it only goes four knots at full RPM, well, then, "you're under-propped, that's all!" And it ain't the fault of the engine manufacturer.

Of course, the most successful marine mechanics gradually drift towards onboard gen/sets. "Let's face it," confessed one. "Even if, despite our best efforts, the diesel runs, we can still fiddle with the electronics so that the generator puts out 60 volts at 120 cycles!"

The engine manufacturers aren't shy about allowing their customers to know exactly what they think of them. For instance, if you ask a salesman why a brand new $25,000 diesel engine doesn't come with any real instruments on its so-called "instrument panel", he'll tell you quite honestly, "Because it's got idiot-lights—which are just *perfect* for you!"

It is, without a doubt, true that a modern mechanic has to know a lot more than his past counterpart. For instance, I recently saw a "technician" kicking a wrench repeatedly. "This is a torque-wrench," he explained patiently, "and I'm adjusting it for 22 foot-pounds."

Needless to say, you have to use only "factory approved" parts to keep your warranty in effect. If you, say, wipe down a Jap engine with a Kraut rag, you got the start of WWIII right there in your engine room!

I mean, what do they take us for—complete idiots? How come every time an auxiliary engine gets *lighter* (i.e., there is *less* of it,) it costs *more*?

Does that seem fair to you?

Of course, nearly all current engine manufacturers demand utter brand loyalty from their customers. If you want to get on the good side of the guy who sold you your engine, say something worshipful like, "I believe in Yammery Engines and Perkerbeke gen/sets, regardless of which of the seventeen different block manufacturers they happen to be using this week!"

Mechanics have no shame today. "You gotta admit it's quiet!" remarked one particularly callous fellow after the fourth time he visited my vessel and failed to fix the problem. "And vibration isn't an issue either!"

The best part is all the neat buzz words these imaginative gear-heads now use. "Do you know why they call this engine a 'green product'?" asked my mechanic recently. "I sure do," I said ruefully as I handed over my wallet.

All of which makes perfect sense, of course. Remember: German machinist Rudolph Diesel died utterly destitute. If you buy one of his noisy inventions—why shouldn't you expect the same?

Racing to a Halt

Fatty racing on Stormy Weather

The winter yacht racing season is finally over—and not a moment too soon. Once again, I proved conclusively to the entire Caribbean that I don't know how to sail fast—or even *slow* for that matter. Frankly, I don't think my fragile ego could take any more DFL's. (I was forced to tell my wife that DFL stood for the traditional British maritime saying of "Decent Finish, Lad!")

She believed me—which is, of course, why I married her.

Seriously, I was away from home so much this racing season that, towards the end, I even looked forward to seeing *her*! (Funny how sampling all those 'multi-cultural dishes' can make even home-cooking seem tasty!)

Hey—how'd we suddenly get from jib sheets to bed sheets?

Anyway, the horrible reality of Yacht-Racing-With-Fatty is that there isn't a boat in the Caribbean that won't sail slower if I'm aboard it. In fact, Team Caribbean could save themselves millions of dollars if they could just convince Russell Coutts to allow me to join his crew.

It doesn't seem to matter what racing position I attempt to fill—I have an amazing knack for failing at all of them.

Recently, I was a tactician on a large Swan. "What's the difference between Cap'n Fatty and a winch handle?" the semi-pro racing crew jokingly asked after the first race, then snidely answered in unison, "At least the winch handle has a *chance* of pointing in the right direction!"

In Puerto Rico, I was mast man—for the few moments that we had the damn thing. (It was the first mast that ever jilted me *before* I attempted to hump its halyards!)

Nobody even *thinks* of asking me to navi-guess anymore—not since I took that stupid flyer during last year's Antigua Sailing Week. (How was I to know that what appeared to be a 'dark & windy squall line to the west' was really windless Montserrat gently blowing its cork?)

Actually steering the boat is out of the question. Every time I attempt to 'get her in the groove,' a mark boat swings alongside and asks, "Are you aground?"

Needless to say, comments like this can adversely affect boat speed. The moment I grab the wheel, people often say stuff like, "Gee, we must have picked up some seaweed on the speedo!" Another thoughtless crew member asked, "Are all our anchors still aboard?"

I'm talking about S-L-O-W, real slow. Once, while racing off Alaska, I was passed by a glacier. (It was not, I understand, a particularly *fast* glacier, either!)

In order to find my homeport, I often have to factor in continental drift—now *that's* slow!

Upwind in the tropics I've been passed by fast-silting sandbars, downwind I've been overtaken by Styrofoam cups. Example: I was recently asked, while steering a large monohull upwind during a race in the BVI's, if we had rights while being overtaken.

"Absolutely!" I replied. "Who's gaining on us?"

"A jellyfish!" was the rather unwelcome reply.

Even being 'rail beef' makes me nervous... and being nervous makes me sweat... which eventually causes me to stink... and the unfortunate result is hell on those scent-sensitive sailors directly downwind of me. "Fatty to loo'ard," cried a large, odor-phobic heifer on the weather rail.

"Not back here, Fatty!" bellowed a member of the perfumey brain-trust in the cockpit.

This makes a guy feel kind of unwanted.

All this reminds me of a time I was sailing on *Heritage*, a 12-meter.

"You stink!" bellowed the sweating sewer man as I went belowdecks for a cold six-pack while he was repacking the light reaching chute. (Ever notice how some people, when they work, get rather irritable if you're smart enough not to?)

"Do you mean that literally, literarily, or sailing-wise?" I asked him, wondering whether he was offended by my odious pits, my sloppy prose, or my incompetent crewing ability. "All three!" he responded. "Now *please* leave before I have to inhale!"

Well, you can't win 'em all.

This recent racing season seemed to last an unusually long time. Towards the end—when I'd say something conversational like "Hello!" during an after-race party—I'd get the immediate curt response of "No,

Fatty, we're *not* going to buy you a drink!" During the final couple of regattas, my wallet was empty, my bladder was full, and what little there was left of my integrity was in total tatters. No matter how sincere I pretended to be, nobody believed me when I made simple statements like, "Gee, I think I'll have just *one more* before I head back to the boat."

I regret wasting my hard-earned money on those sea-sick patches. I chewed two of 'em—and still felt nauseous on the starting line! (Although, I must admit, I had some cool hallucinations!)

Another waste of money was that large economy-sized container of sun block. I gulped down nearly the entire bottle—and still burnt my face off! My face was burnt so bad that it appeared that I'd been staring directly at the hell-fires-of-damnation—which, in a sick sort of way, I had been.

Of course, every racing nightmare eventually comes to an end. I knew the racing season was over when the last yacht owner tossed my sea bag overboard, the last 'lady friend' proved she was neither by slapping me rudely in the face, and the last person that would even speak to me, shouted angrily, "No, Fatty, I will not lend you another five bucks!"

But, eventually, my body and ego will heal. They always do. I'm an optimist, and the drinks I cage are always half full, not half empty.

By next November, I'll be belly up to the St. Croix Yacht Club during the Mumm's Cup—singing out lustily while drunkenly waving a frothy bottle of Cordon Rouge, "The bubbles are my friends!"

And they will be. (At least until morning!)

Fatty steering Virgin Fire

Inside the Outboard Conspiracy

Carolyn with Baby Roma 1981

I recently attended a convention of retired outboard engineers (ROE) in Spiteful, Wisconsin. Needless to say, I had to sneak in. Security was tight. They were extremely paranoid that some deranged boater might infiltrate their annual meeting to seek violent revenge.

"Me?" I said when challenged. "I'm a water-proof flashlight designer who just happened to stop by!"

Once they realized I too was involved in the design, manufacture, and sale of a mechanical device that seldom actually worked within sight of the ocean, I was welcomed with open arms.

"Just how did the original 'outboard' concept come about?" was my first question.

"Well," said one Old Mangy-haired Coot (OMC), "It was a long time ago—back when inboard engines were just becoming fairly dependable. Of course, we were terribly worried. The last thing we wanted as an industry was to produce an engine that actually dependably propelled the vessel!

Anyway, a group of us engineers got together and decided that, since the least dependable part of a modern engine was its electrical system, we'd mount the engine just a couple of inches off the water *outside the boat*, where it would be continuously doused by salt water under pressure, and thus, seldom function as advertised."

"This *out*board concept gave us a second advantage as well," chimed in another ancient fellow. "By arranging to have the engine continuously doused with salt water, we were able to maximize our corrodibility factor. It took us a while to figure it out scientifically, but soon we had aluminum, bronze, and ferrous metals in close contact on the lower unit. It was great!"

"Yeah," laughed another. "That's why our early electric-start models didn't require an additional battery. Hell, they *were* a battery!"

"That's right," said a grizzly old dude wearing a pocket-protector. "And this was a real 'two-fer,' because with the electrolysis optimized, whichever metal parts didn't just get eaten right off the engine, soon seized together tighter than a Scotsman's purse."

"I was involved in the pump division," said yet another engineer with a sadistic smile. "Once we had the electrolysis down so that the lower unit was impossible to remove without twisting off the aluminum-seated studs, we designed a soft rubber impeller that wore out every six months!"

"That boosted the bottom line, like *big time*!" shouted a jubilant accountant in the back of the room. "We didn't make that much money selling the impellers by the six-pack. It was the lower units that had to accompany them, which truly revved up our suddenly bulging corporate coffers."

"Can you tell an outboarder from an inboarder by just looking at them," I asked. "Absolutely," giggled one of the few ladies present. "Just look at his right arm. If it is huge in comparison to his left, well, that's a right-armed outboard owner for sure!"

"How did you determine how long to make the starting cords?" I queried.

"That was easy," said the Old Mangy-haired Coot, who seemed to be the spokesperson for the group. "We did a lot of motion studies—and then made it just about four inches too short. So a normal man, after getting a little ticked off because the engine wouldn't start, would give its cord a mighty yank. So then, he would either break the cord or, worse yet, spin the recoil spring."

"Did you do scientific tests to determine the proper oil-to-gas ratio as well?"

"Naw," said one of the younger members. "We just used the oft-repeated 50-to-1 figure... about the same as the odds of one of those early engines actually starting."

"Those were the good-ole-days," mused another one of the retired engineers. "We even consulted a marine biologist to make sure our propeller blades folded when they hit a jellyfish!"

"Our success was based upon a multitude of small details," boosted yet another. "For instance, ever notice how those tiny screens on the raw water intake corrode so fast? And it is no coincidence that the tiny machined hole in the carburetor jet is exactly the same size as a grain of beach sand."

"I was involved in helping to design the first imported outboard from Japan," said the woman again. "I designed its cooling system so small, that it over-heated on its first test run. They said, 'It's *TOO HOT, SUE*' and I was so, so proud!"

"I moved here from Minnesota," said a Norwegian-sounding fellow at the convention. "I helped Sue on that original Japanese design. The Asian guy's name was Mister Ha, and his mother attended the test. When she asked if the engine was running hot, I had to tell her the truth, '*YAH, MA HA!*'"

"She wasn't convinced, but I told her that I could tell it was hot by the you-know-what in the thermometer. She thought I was a stupid German, so I played along by acting dumb. "*HUN, DUH.*" I told her dull-wittedly. ("What did I care if she thought I was *EVER RUDE?*")

"So I guess the true glory days are over," I said, and suddenly everyone in the room looked glum. Figuring it was silly not to kick them when they were down, I continued with, "I use a modern outboard engine every day, and it runs like a top. In fact, it is as dependable as a new car... maybe even more so! I think it's fair to say that they've really got the design of these two-cycle outboards down pat."

"Yes!" they shouted as group, suddenly all smiles. "Exactly! That's why we've decided to switch to four stroke engines. A totally new concept should create a totally new set of problems! It will take *years* before we're forced by the buying public to prefect them! In fact, we've already figured out a way to make the tiny little screw-down dip-stick weld itself to the engine block if it gets even a hint of saltwater on it!"

Fuel Docks, Blow Boats, and Other Natural Enemies

Sailboats and fuel docks don't seem to mix well—even here in the friendly Caribbean. There is, in my humble opinion, a number of sound, reasonable and logical socio/economic reasons for this sad state of affairs. 1.) Generally speaking, fuel dock attendants are absolute sadists. 2.) Marina owners are, for the most part, utter fascists, and 3.) greedheads, who are too nasty for the landsharks ashore or the blood-thirsty pirates afloat, *always* seem to end up betwixt and between the two opposing groups—laboring away irritably in some sleazy shoreside business while attempting to exploit both land-and-sea groups to the max.

Of course, fuel attendants, marine owners, and other such marine industry thugs might think (foolishly!) I'm a tad prejudiced in my views.

Ha!

"There is nothing worse than a blow-boater or a stick-boater," ranted one outspoken dockmaster to me when he was drunk(er than me). "They're always attempting to get sumt'ing for nutt'ing."

"They pull up to my dock in a half million dollar pristine sailing vessel and demand a half gallon of *clean* diesel fuel! And they want it *fast!* Then they ask for a couple of ounces of *clean* gasoline for their dinghy's outboard motor and a quarter cup of *clean* water to rinse off their bean sprouts. *Big spenders!*"

"If I haven't thrown them off the dock by this point, they ask me to pump out their 200 gallon holding tank for free, allow them to stay at the fuel dock overnight, and to ignore them plugging in their twin 220 volt 50 amp power cords ...so their wife can use her mini-book light to read her Bible by."

"I never *ever* allow a sea gypsy in the marina's restroom," he continued. "Not even if they begin squatting right there in the dock master's office! It's almost impossible to pry 'em out of a warm bathroom once they've settled in. Given half a chance, they'll bathe in the toilet bowl, drink the hand lotion right out of the dispenser, and eat so much of the free tissue paper that they'll throw up all over the sink mirror. I mean, I was truly shocked when those pink deodorizing pellets in the urinals started disappearing."

"That's a lot of crapola," fumed an indignant sea gypsy named Toothless Tom (off the S/V *Macho Moocher*) when he heard the above accusations. "Fuel dock attendants are notoriously anti-sailboat. They hate us cruising sailors because we don't burn 20,000 gallons of diesel fuel a day, stink up the atmosphere, degrade the ozone layer, or make quiet anchorages noisy with smog-producing generators."

"You wouldn't believe the trouble I've had with dock jockeys," agreed another cruising sailor during a recent interview. "I've had 'em toss back my docklines, flop my fenders on deck just a nano-second before we needed them, and attempt to wave me away with a loaded flare pistol. If I've got a little weigh on my vessel and need it to be snubbed off so I don't hit another vessel—they won't do it. But if there is no other vessel around, then they'll flick my stern line over the top of a stout stanchion real quick—and cleat it off in a jiffy... just for the sadistic joy of watching the stanchion bend like butter as the boat surges against it. In fact, during this stanchion-folding process was the only time I ever saw a dock attendant actually smile—and it was an ugly sight, I'll tell ya! Caribbean dock jockeys are simply outrageous!"

"Why, once I stopped at a fuel dock to see if they just might have a left-handed winch pawl for my 1922 Wilcox-Crittenden bronze flag halyard winch. And while I was carefully enquiring about the availability of this little part, my wife just happened to go ashore to reprovision, do the laundry, and refill our propane tanks. Well, the dock master got real, like, real PUSHY—like he could hardly wait to get us off the dock so one of those ugly Feadships that were circling could tie up."

"When my wife finally got back from her errands, just before we cast off, I naturally wanted to get rid of our galley scraps. But when we started to lug the large plastic sacks of dripping garbage ashore, the dockmaster suddenly started howling at us before we'd even schlepped a dozen of 'em across the pristine planks of his precious marina."

"No matter how nice you are to some of these crusty old salts," said another disgusted marina operator, "they end up thinking you've cheated them. One guy pulls up in a large ketch and asks me how his twin engines sound as I take his docklines. I tell him, "Fine, fine..." and then he balks when he sees the extra hundred bucks tacked onto his fuel bill for 'audio engine analysis! What the hell did he think I was gonna do—listen to his 'iron jibs' for free?"

"That's a perfect example of what I mean," ranted one of the sailing sea gypsies. "They're always slipping weird charges onto the bill. It is as if they have no shame! Once I was on a fuel dock, and the little store there wanted a small fortune for a cold six pack of Bud. So I walked across the street, and purchased a warm six pack of beer from a package store…and the marina guy wanted to charge me fifty bucks…just 'cause I cooled 'em off with one of his stupid fire extinguishers."

"Sometimes it seems like war," admitted one battle weary marina worker. "I've had chintzy sailboat guys attempt to photograph our charts, demand their money back because the ice we sold them melted, and threaten to sue us for 'breaking their mother's back' when they stepped on a crack. One real cheapskate on a beach catamaran asked how much a ham sandwich was, and then ordered a dozen bait worms. We were about to wrap them up, when he said, 'Don't bother. I'll eat 'em here.'"

"There's an old nautical saying," a retired marina owner once told me. "And that's 'Men and ships rot in port!' I believe that process of rot and decay is actually accelerated by the smell of diesel fumes, the whiff of gasoline, and the wafting scent of a dripping holding tank pump-out station."

"The only time I liked sail boaters on my fuel dock was around Christmas," the retired dock demon mused with a far away smile plastered to his wizened face.

"Christmas?" he was asked.

"Ah, yes," he laughed. "I always kept a carton of damp silverfish, a shoebox full of pregnant cockroaches, and a humane animal trap of ravenous wharf rats—as little secret 'blow boat' presents to sneak aboard in the Christmas season."

Insuring Yourself Against Idiocy!

Aftermath of Hurricane Hugo in Culebra in 1989

I confess: I don't have any marine insurance. None. Zero. Zilch!

In fact, I consider buying *any* insurance kinda stupid, like betting against yourself.

Needless to say, this makes some people rather nervous—especially on the starting line of a major international yacht race.

If my vessel is zooming around the starting line on an opposite tack from another speeding vessel, and we happen to be on a collision course, instead of laboriously attempting to figure out who has the 'technical' right of way, I merely shout, "I've got no insurance! I paid $3,000 for this damn boat, and I *know* I got ripped off! If we collide, hell, you can have the stinking thing!"

That makes 'em shear off quick, I'll tell ya.

It seems to me the greater number of insurance policies written, the greater the number of insurance policies needed.

Thus, I consider not having insurance an incredibly noble act of high moral courage. (It's cheaper, too.)

Example: Let's say I had a million dollars worth of insurance and somebody stubbed their toe on my boat. Naturally, he'd sue.

Let's say the same fellow stubbed his toe, and I *didn't* have insurance. The moment he inquired about the worth of my policies, he'd have an additional broken nose and two black eyes—and *still* no hope of ever collecting a penny.

I'm with the 'Like a Rolling Stone' Bob Dylan School of Asset Protection. "When you ain't got noth'n, you got noth'n to lose." says the song.

What could be simpler? There's another nice, sensible line in the classic song 'Me and Bobby McGee' that goes, "Freedom's just another word for nutt'n left to lose..."

That's true.

Have you ever tried getting blood out of a turnip?

Of course, some people do have physical possessions they don't want to lose. But what do I care about what happens to those materialistic greedheads anyway?

In addition, honesty and insurance don't mix well. Didn't some wise man once say "Truth is the first casualty of liability protection?"

I sincerely believe they call the worker/drones of the insurance industry "adjusters" because they're always attempting to "adjust" the facts to screw their policy holders.

Take the situation with the stubbed toe, for example. I'd claim that the deck of my boat was smoother than a (Bill Clinton) White House denial, and the plaintiff would claim it had more toe-catchers than a sea boot full of blue crabs.

That's why a legal contest like this is often referred to as a "lie-ability" trial. The settlement depends on which of the totally fabricated versions the jury prefers to believe.

Of course, the lawyers always go for the person with "deep pockets". Luckily, my pockets are as shallow as my intellect. (I'm a professional writer who gets paid what I'm worth—hardly a likely candidate for a profitable lawsuit.)

Have you actually ever read an insurance policy? No? I didn't think so. Few people have, especially those of us still awake.

Most marine insurance policies are as boring as Ken Starr's sex life. It's true! Many insurance policies are as long as a Russian novel and have even finer print.

They could just say, in large-and-friendly-block-letters, "If you lose your boat, we'll buy you a new one."

But they do not.

Instead they obliquely hint that they *may* pay, if you lose your boat at low tide on Mount Everest while the Queen Mother is ovulating—but, well, then again, maybe not! (And *surely* not if the accident occurred on any day of the week with the letter 'd' in it.)

I have a friend who pays over four thousand dollars a year for a yachty/snotty policy that excludes 1.) Named storms, 2.) Racing, 3.) Acts of God, 4.) Everything else!

The marine insurance industry doesn't like to hear any of this. Instead they slyly chant the sacred mantra of "shared risk," as if betting against yourself was something truly magical. Notice how they never mention the fact that nobody "shares" in the paying of your premiums.

Offshore sailors have little need for emergency medical insurance. If they can make it to the hospital, they generally don't need to go. Besides, nearly everyone in America (except maybe Bill Gates) ends up dying indigent these days, because the medical industry simply keeps the life-support systems going until they've pumped all the money out of you... and *then* they shut them off.

I love the insurance industry's unique perversion of common English terms. Life insurance should really be called "death" insurance. But, I guess such realistic labeling is bad for sales.

Advertising is tricky too, especially when it comes to group rates. Acme Insurance should say, "If large groups sign with us, we'll promise to give them back less money than they paid, but only after they die."

Instead, they whisper seductively about an "umbrella of protection."

Some localities even have "no-fault" insurance. This is a system in which the local government joins hands with the local insurance industry to prevent the local taxpayer from ever learning exactly who is to blame for such outrageous premiums. (Thus, no fault!)

Frankly, you're never gonna sell me life insurance. I'm simply not interested in paying for stuff I have to die for, and even then, don't actually get.

What about the wife and kid? Well, I suppose I could arrange to have a million dollars delivered to them when I finally croak off, but how can I be sure that it would make them *happy*? I can't be. And thus, I'm not going to bet my hard earned money on it.

Of course, we members of the marine community must take the lion's share of the blame for this mess. It was Lloyd's of London in the 1600's that started it all by insuring shipboard cargo. Eventually, like many bad ideas spawned upon the sea, it finally spread ashore.

My advice is to not fall for it. Remember: Only the most delusional of optimists believe they're gonna make a financial "killing" when they collect on their life insurance policy. I believe you're far better off investing in stout ground tackle, strong rum, and cheap Bibles—and not necessarily in that order.

Repowering

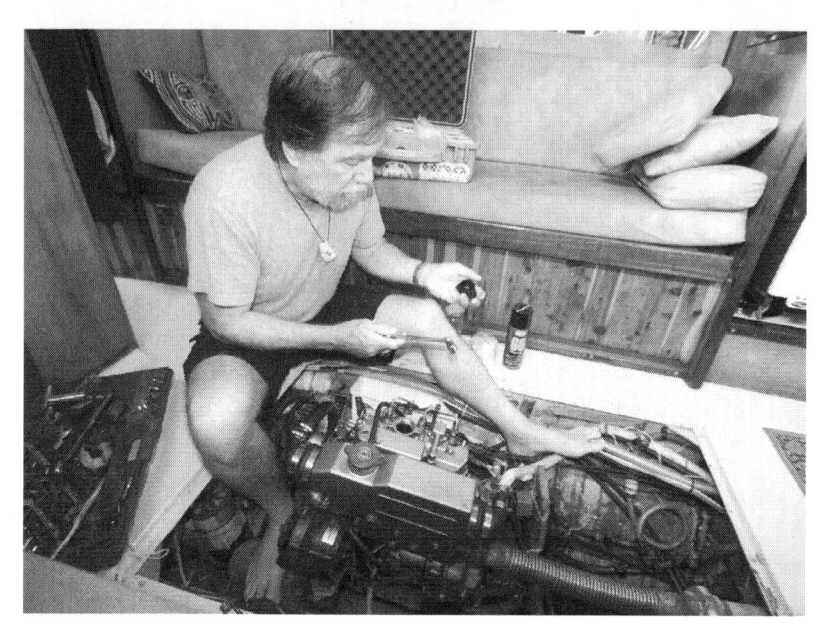

I am currently installing a new Perkins M30 diesel in my 38-foot sloop *Wild Card*. Since my vessel has been engineless for six years, I have to start this complicated, multi-faceted project totally from scratch—which has me, literally, scratching my fuzzy little head.

The nightmare started as soon as my check cleared, and my wife discovered that the IRA account *she'd* been paying into for the last 5½ years was really *my* "I'll Repower Again!" account. <GRIN>

Once the engine arrived at Independent Boat Yard on St. Thomas, things got *really* complicated. It would not fit where my old auxiliary had once lived. (Perhaps I should have measured first?)

Oh well.

The first task was having a crane lower the engine into the boat, and ten strong men shift it around inside the hull to see where it looked best.

It looked *great* on the port quarter berth, atop the galley sink, and in the head. But all three locations had, alas, "technical" drawbacks. It ended up living where all shipboard items destined to be neglected reside—in the deepest bowels of bilge.

The biggest problem that I faced initially was a fairly basic one. I wanted the engine to turn a propeller, and I wanted that propeller to be *outside* and the engine to be *inside*—and never the 'twain shall meet.

This tiny little detail entailed numerous shafts, struts, cutlass bearings, fiberglass tubes, bronze pipes, and stuffing boxes—all of which had to be machined within .003 of an inch of each other. That's some pretty fine tolerances, especially for the tropics.

Each one of the custom-made pieces cost a small fortune, and it was soon apparent that I was "getting shafted" in more ways than one.

As complicated as the drive train was, it was nothing compared to the installation of the exhaust system.

Ideally, marine engine manufacturers would prefer you to mount their engines as far above the waterline as possible, so any salt water that gets in the engine while it is running, drains out when you shut it off.

From their standpoint, the top of the main mast would be an ideal spot. But (remember?) we also want the engine to be connected to a propeller—and these are usually most efficient when mounted *underwater...*

See? Once again, *it gets complicated.*

Another factor is exhaust *back pressure*. When the guy who sold me the engine started to tell me about how truly complicated that convoluted subject was, I'd have gladly given him the engine *back* without much *pressure*!

All this isn't even mentioning the engine beds themselves. I don't know how other fiberglass boat owners have dealt with the problem, but I couldn't *believe* how many 16 penny nails I bent on my first attempt!

Of course, the agony of all of the above will soon pale in comparison to the ecstasy of being, once again, a stinkpotter.

I'll no longer be at the mercy of the fickle winds. Now I can handle my boat (obnoxiously) without their fickle favor.

I can't wait for the first time I power into a quiet anchorage, and befoul it with my noise and stink. Now I'll *really* be able to rip up some turtle grass with my anchors. My new three-bladed 15x9 prop should be able to *really* stir up some silty sediment. Heck, at full-throttle, I might even be able to create a little *shoreline erosion.*

Of course, I'll look down my nose at those poor cruising saps who sail on and off their moorings, because they don't have the *guts* to crank up their powerful engines.

Whenever I see someone maneuvering in close quarters under sail, I'll shout loudly to him, "Okay, pal, enough showing off already! Why don't you crank up the Iron Staysail, and spare us all that Dacron-flapping.

The best part of having an engine again will be regaining the respect of the local dock-jockeys. If you sail up to a dock perfectly, and ask for only *water*—every dock-jockey from Cape Horn to Cape Sable is gonna think you are a wimp.

It's like going into a crack house and asking for a glass of orange juice and some Vitamin C.

But if you pull into a fuel dock *fast* under power, rip out a dock bollard, and bend a couple of stanchions—and then bellow *"Diesel!"* The awe-struck fuel-pump-pimp will immediately say, *"Yes, Sir*! Right away, *Sir*!"

When I was engineless, I could not do a number of highly enjoyable harbor maneuvers I'd perfected over the years. Backing over my dinghy painter and entangling my mooring pennant were two favorites.

Now, the sky is the limit. And the best part is that I'll be able to get back into the harbor real quick, so I'll have plenty of time to crawl into the hot and stinking engine space, and "exchange fluids" with my newly beloved diesel.

Ah, yachting.

Born-again Stinkpotter

Wild Card *under power*

Yesterday I woke up and realized sailboats are stupid. I mean, most people have moved on. Truly. Let's put it another way: if Chris Columbus were alive today he would not be exploring the New World on the *Pinta, Nina,* and *Santa Maria*. He'd be lounging around the Jacuzzi aboard an Italian mega-yacht, hyper-yacht, giga-yacht, or VLP-yacht (Very Large Penis.)

Where were we? Ah, yes! The Ultimate Stupidity of All Sailing Craft. It is true. Only the truly "slow" still use wind as a method of watery transportation.

The sad fact is that I've been in denial of these obvious, blatant, and extremely well-known nautical facts for at least the last 45 years of "blow boat" living-aboard, and 100,000 miles of ocean sailing. But I'm starting to wise up.

Finally.

Here's how it happened. My wife and I were in Great Cruz Bay, St. John, and were invited to a Coral Bay raft up. So we powered *Wild Card*, our 38 foot S&S-designed sloop, nine-tenths of the way there. Then, just before we came into view of the raft-up, we shut off our diesel engine, hoisted up our sails, and came screaming into the harbor with a "bone-in-her-teeth."

"How was it on the south side," my sailor friends asked as I tossed them my lines.

"Not bad," I lied. "There were some nice lifts off Reef Bay and we tacked over when we got headed at Salt Pond. A single-reef and my trusty number three worked well in the eighteen knots apparent."

It was at that precise moment when it dawned on me that I was being a hypocrite.

Totally.

This hurt. After all, I'm a child of the 1960's and, thus, have ganja-vowed to always "tell it like it is," regardless of public opinion.

Now, I found myself to be a "closet stinkpotter" without the courage to admit the truth.

So I took a long, hard, objective look at The Wonderful Wacky World of Sailboats and concluded the following: they are about the most uncomfortable devices ever invented.

First off, they heel. And not just one way, but both! Example: we were on starboard tack for about a year while transiting the Pacific. Everything just sort of organically "mulched" over to the loo'ard (low) side—all our loose rhum casks, discarded underwear, old beer cans, stale pizza crusts, and cast-off wine bottles. They just sort of nestled down there. And what a horrible "broken-glass-crash" when we finally tacked over towards New Zealand!

This whole "heeling thing" is a pain in the butt—especially if you've ever visited the head at 45 degrees of heel while pounding to windward!

A deck leak on a civilized power boat mostly drips down, but a single cabin leak on a sailboat can drench tens of thousands of dollars in electronics within a few damn, damp moments, through the miracle of "effective heeling water dispersal!"

If all this wasn't bad enough, heeling is slow, and excessive heeling is even slower. So sailboats have very heavy (and expensive) lead keels to keep them upright.

Alas, heavy is slow too. So modern racing boats spend millions of dollars on lightweight hull materials such as kevlar, spectra, and carbon fiber, so they can carry their very heavy, very expensive keels around the race course even faster.

Does this make sense?

Actually, nothing about sailing seems to make sense. Why do people do it? Self-hatred? Masochism? Guilt? I now realize that Benjamin Franklin was exactly right when he said, "Anyone with enough intelligence to get thrown in jail would ever go to sea."

My wife, Carolyn, can't seem to understand why sailboaters have to spend so much money to suffer. "Can't we just sell our boat? And, when she sells, just take the cash and—buy crack? I mean, wouldn't it be cheaper? Less painful? Healthier?"

I dunno.

It's a judgment call, eh?

Why do people live aboard sailboats? They are usually very narrow and extremely low. (I mean the boats, silly). Many sailboats don't even have full-standing headroom—which is why so many old sailors are hunch-backed (from stooping) and balding (from scraping their heads.)

Which brings me to my favorite oxymoron (besides "military intelligence") which is, ready for this? "Hi-tech sailboat!" That's like saying "modern dinosaur" or "sophisticated log" or "up-to-date stone-age."

Okay, granted the first "yacht racer" was a relatively bright guy. He was drifting down a river with a few of his cavemen buddies. And while standing up to relieve himself, he expansively opened up his large fur vest and noticed a slight increase in boat speed. Okay, that was a huge "leap" of progress then. But why no advance since?

Sailboats hardly have any living space, storage space, or cargo capacity. Going anywhere takes forever and many destinations with shoal water and/or fixed bridges are off-limits anyway.

By any measure, sailboats are less suited for living aboard than powerboats. And yet 99% of live-aboard vessels are sailboats. And their wind-crazed, sun-addled owners somehow consider themselves smarter than their "gear-head" putt-putting counterparts.

Where is the logic?

The disadvantages of a sailboat are almost too numerous to mention. Take, for example, those very expensive "white floppy things." Yes, modern hi-tech sails are expensive. Anyone who says that "the wind is free" crap hasn't seen a contemporary sailmaker step from his Rolls Royce into his mansion/loft lately. Sails are truly awful things. They make noise. They tear, rot, rip, shred, and chafe. Worse, a sail is attached to a boom—a long, heavy, deadly bat that exists solely to 1.) Knock you overboard, 2.) Bash your head open, 3.) Both.

"Running rigging" is called that because any sensible person runs from it. I mean, it is always whipping around, fouling itself, and getting tangled. Jib sheets are the worst. If a headsail rigorously luffs for more than a couple of seconds, the jib sheets will tangle themselves into something resembling a "hanging noose," loop themselves over your startled head, quickly settle on your delicate neck, and slowly/slowly/slowly begin to tighten.

Sure, a power vessel might blow up and instantly kill its crew. But sailboats are sort of into S&M—slow, delicious torture.

It is not only the boats that are different. It is the skippers, too.

Powerboaters, for example, are free-spenders. Sailboaters are the cheapest guys imaginable. I've been on a 100-foot-plus mega-sloop worth mega-millions—aboard which the ultra-rich owner individually scissors each sheet of toilet paper into quarters, so as to "waste not, want not!"

Have you ever read a copy of the Seven Sleaze Cruising Association (SSCA) newsletter? Every entry says, "We're here, but it is cheaper somewhere else. So we're heading out!"

Yes, "east is east and west is west" and never the twain shall meet.

Sailboaters vaguely frown upon successful fishing, preferring to drag drab trolling lures so ugly even the dumbest of fish won't bite.

Powerboaters are exactly the opposite. They come down to their Bertram, Post, or Hatteras, sniff the exhaust gases for a couple of mind-numbing minutes, and then bellow, "Let's find a large aquatic creature, drag it around behind our vessel with a sharp hook, jab holes in it with our gaff, and then allow it to slowly suffocate in our cockpit while we photograph the slaughter!"

I mean, at least powerboaters are unabashed! Not so, their completely in denial "ragmen" counterparts. Many sailboaters pretend they don't have an engine, don't have a gen/set, don't have dis and dat—that their whatchamacallit literally doesn't stink!

What is it about sailboaters that make them so "holier than thou," and at the same time, so ill-suited for the role? I mean, the last honest sailboater I met (actually, the only one in a couple of decades) asked me, "At how many RPMs do you sail?"

Finally, an honest "blow-boater!"

The bottom line: my wife and I have decided our "retirement home" will be a powerboat. We are currently in the process of deciding which one.

"I'd like one with a noisy, smoky engine," my wife suggested. I chimed in with, "Yeah, a high-freeboard, tubby, diesel-gulping thing that leaves an extremely large wake."

"Yes," my starry-eyed wife gushed in sado-happiness. "That'll really shake up our old sea-gypsy friends."

"Rock and roll, suckers!" I cried gleefully as I high-fived her.

Two Grumpy Old Farts Spew

I try never to be serious. I think 'being serious' is stupid. I prefer being an eternal child. Perhaps Bob Dylan put it best: "Don't Look Back." And, like a child, I have no desire to tell others how to live. In fact, I try not to judge. I've learned long ago that my answer might not be your answer.

But I'm in a melancholy mood today.

Yesterday I had dinner aboard the *Mary Harrigan,* a lovely 64-foot, L. Francis Herreshoff designed wooden schooner owned and skippered by Len Hornick.

Len's quite a sailor. He chartered *Mary Harrigan* for over twenty years in Maine, Tortola, and along the east coast of the United States. Besides being a consummate seaman, Len loves boats. He's passionate about boats. In fact, boats are at the core of his long, eventful, salt-stained life. He's a sailor's sailor, through and through.

But he's also bitter.

"I don't like 'em anymore," he says. "Most boaters don't know anything about their boats, nor do they care. You can't talk to 'em about boats. They don't have anything to say—except maybe what part number they ordered yesterday or which circuit board will go missing in tomorrow's FedEx! So I don't hang around 'em. I just don't. I got no use for 'em. I anchor off—far off. So, yeah, I've mounted the Charlie Noble and cranked up the Shipmate—we're wintering in Marlborough Sound on the south island of New Zealand. Yeah, it will be cold, but yeah... it will be away from the maddening crowd too."

"You're an old fart, Len," I blurted out, and immediately regretted it.

My words hit him like a body blow. He reeled a bit and then begrudgingly agreed. "I wasn't always. There was a time I'd sail into a harbor, splash the dinghy, and visit with every boat in the anchorage—all three of 'em. Now there're a couple of hundred boats in that same harbor and I don't want to visit with a single one."

There was a strange look of both belligerence and resignation on his weather-beaten face. I didn't know what to say, and the silence hung heavy. Finally, my mind lit on one subject I *did* agreed with him on.

"When I was a young'n aboard my first boat, I ate, slept, and dreamt boats, boats, boats. And so did my best friends Dave Lovik and George Zamiar and a young Italian chick named Carolyn. We wanted to learn *everything* about *every* aspect of boats. So, we sat worshipfully at the feet of more experienced sailors, like giant sponges. We also read the 'Venturesome Voyages of Captain Voss'. We memorized pages of Kipling, pored over Conrad, and learned by rote the sails of a full-rigged ship. We learned knots and fancy rope work. We did canvas work—stood on our bow and learned the difference between a cranze iron, gammit iron, and the Norman cross. We sang sea-chanties, for gosh sakes."

"And," I continued, "when I built the ketch *Carlotta* with my bare hands, I did every single thing on that vessel that didn't require a metal lathe—every frig'n thing, save for turning the prop and rudder shaft!"

"I cast a lot of the bronze hardware for *Mary Harrigan* myself," cried Len with watery eyes as he pounded the galley table so hard he almost knocked over his gin bottle. "She cost me three times what they said she would—and I've gladly given her every penny since. What do I care? Woman have babies, sailors build boats!"

I interrupted him with, "And, I've spent months at Mystic Seaport and the National Maritime Museum in England. Why, I've held the actual log of Bligh's *Bounty* in my trembling hands in New South Wales. And I've knelt and touched the very spot where Nelson died aboard the *HMS Victory*."

"I've had thirteen boats—wooden vessels all," said Len. "One of my former wives said, 'Boating with you is—well, Len, you're simply not rational about it!' Did I mention she was an ex-wife?"

But I, too, was on a roll. "And I devoured every word written by Slocum! My wife, Carolyn, bought me an 1832 Bowditch, and I dog-earred it. Ditto, one of the original copies (only 500 privately printed) of Slocum's "Voyage of the *Liberdade*." Oh, how we laughed as we read aloud (naked and in bed) sections of Frederic A. Fenger's, "Cruise of the *Diablesse*" like it was erotic literature! I literally teethed on Eric and Susan Hiscock's books. Ditto Harry Pidgeon, Carlton Mitchell, and a living legend called Irving Johnson and his beloved *Yankee*. Why, when my father introduced me to Ann Davison (in the mid '50's, aboard *Gemini*) I was absolutely amazed to hear him say, 'This woman is more man than I'll ever be!'"

"I told Bud McIntosh I wanted more than just a boat," ranted Len. "I wanted something graceful and beautiful and strong and permanent and classic and noble and—a *real* boat!"

"And there were lots of other men—other boys—other Caribbean sailors, who cared about their boats and marine traditions as much as I way-back then," I rushed on. "Thatcher Lord. Paul Johnson. Bill Rich. Fritz Seyfarth. Big Jack Simmons. Fletcher Pitts."

"There's no reverence for maritime tradition anymore," lamented Len. "None!"

And I seconded that with, "A couple of days ago—on April 13, I happened to be walking past a boat and said to its owner sitting in the cockpit, 'Did you know that Olin's birthday is today? He's 99 years young.' And the guy said, 'Who?' I said, 'You're vessel's designer.' And the guy said, 'No, she's built by Swan!' and I said, 'Yeah, but I'm talking about your designer, Olin!'" He ducked below for a moment to check his ship's papers and then came on deck to say, 'No, she's designed by S&S'."

"Don't you just want to scream?" asked Len.

"And, on the same day, I'm talking to a guy on a double-ender about Colin Archer and William Atkin and such historic designs at the *Irene* and the *Eric*—and he blows me off with, "No, this is a Westsail!'"

The bottom line is: while accusing Len of being an old fart, I discovered I was one, too.

This was brought home even more forcefully the following morning as I pored over my semi-annual *All At Sea* 'care' package. I really enjoy getting the back issues. I like to keep up with what's happening in the Caribbean: how the KATS program is progressing, the local race results, who's screwing whom, etc.

But it also made me feel old. I remember Jeannie Kuich as a young flower-kissed fox protected by a Hell's Angel-type of guy named Mike. I first met Peter Holmberg when he barely knew how to row. I became friends with Peter Muilenburg just after he pissed off the President of the United States by sailing back and forth in front of the Caneel Bay Resort with "While Nixon Lazes Indochina Blazes" painted on his mainsail. I knew Les Anderson when he was *more* sex crazed than he is now! Hell, I knew Manfred when he was just beginning, and had only fathered a dozen or so children!

And we were all here in the Caribbean to get away from America, Europe, and South Africa—not to replicate it.

...or invest in it.

...or put a price tag on it.

It may come as a shock but many white folks came to the Caribbean and Hawaii *without* the intention of becoming real estate agents.

We were sailing adventurers, far off the beaten track. Our first question in a new harbor wasn't "WiFi?"

A few days later, Carolyn, as usual, put the whole subject into proper perspective. "Len says that when there were three boats in the harbor he loved to visit with 'em. Well, there are probably *still* three boats he'd love to visit with—he just can't find 'em among the three hundred. The world is getting more crowded, Fatty—more people, more boats, more cars. That's progress. Get used to it. In the early days of automotive design, cars were unique things too. People felt passionate about them. Now they're just ho-hum methods of transportation. Something similar is happening with boats. They are becoming—just things. Again—that's progress. Get used to it."

But some of us old curmudgeons don't want to.

"It's a crying shame that I gotta sail half way around the world to find a decent shipwright with wood shavings in his hair," laments Len. "We'll haul out in Whangarei soon—gotta take care of *Mary Harrigan* while I still can—before I toss off this mortal coil!"

Yes, Len, you must. It is your sacred duty. We sailors understand. You are her ship's husband. She depends on you. Fight the good fight, Len! Stand tall, me son.

The Romance and Reality of Single-handing

The reasons to single-hand are many: bad breath, bad sexual technique, and bad financial status are three of the most common. Let's face it, only a complete fool would go to sea alone if he could possibly avoid it.

Hell, I'd have *jumped* at the chance to have, say, Ken Starr aboard my boat last summer when I singlehanded it down to Trinidad.

I'm serious! We could have talked about cool stuff like—well, potty-training, shoe-shining, and which is the best type of cigarette lighter to use while, well, igniting certain gases. I'm sure there are some other "naughty" subjects that Ken might be fond of discussing as well.

That's right; compared to going offshore with only myself as crew, Linda Tripp looks like a fox. (I adore the way she snarl/smiles—just like an old dominatrix I used to frequent in New Orleans.)

But getting back to single-handing, it can be a drag. (Actually, I tried that too, but even my favorite gowns left me sadly depressed.)

Of course, single-handing isn't all bad. It has its good points. In fact, single-handers are notorious for their sense of style. Needless to say, most of them work pretty hard at it.

It isn't easy smelling like that, wearing those soiled clothes, keeping your hair that oily.

One old coot told me about getting hit by a blizzard just to loo'ard of Montserrat. I wasn't sure he'd actually sailed through its volcanic ash or if it was just his dandruff that scared him.

Conversationally, many single-handers are somewhat "challenged", if you will. It is not uncommon for one to say nothing for long spans of time, and then suddenly erupt with, "I've practiced crash-gybes off Cape Horn during a category five hurricane—and you haven't. So everything I say is true—and you are a F'n idiot!"

Of course, seasoned single-handers seldom socialize. However, just before the start of the 1988 O-Star Transatlantic Race, I saw a table of them huddled together at the Royal Plymouth Yacht Club. They weren't speaking to each other, just listening to the BBC news on their individual portable shortwave radios. "I get nervous if I go more than a couple of hours without hearing Big Ben," one confessed to me recently. In kindergarten, such single-but-group activity is referred to as "co-play".

Safety, of course, is always an issue. For instance, just before I hit the sack for 12 solid hours of "sawing ZZZZZs", I announce over my VHF radio on channel 16, "Pan, Pan, Pan! This is me. I'm now going to sleep for 12 hours or so. Keep a sharp eye out! I'm gonna leave my compass light on, so there shouldn't be any problem avoiding me."

This works. So far, anyway.

Needless to say, weight is an issue offshore. That's why we single-handers never carry razors, soap, deodorant...

Money is often tight, so we use discarded strands of old rigging wire to floss with, rusty wire brushes to comb out our underarm snarls, and spilled "Part A" West epoxy for "dress up night" hair styling.

Instead of foolishly attempting to keep numerous rolls of Charmin dry, we just use our old torn headsails ripped into one foot squares. (Ah, for the good ole days of *cotton* sails.)

Of course, safety harnesses are a must for the singlehander. I refuse to risk my life with some cheap "yacht quality" gear from Henry Lloyds. Instead, I want the stuff the pros use. Thus I buy mine in the Pigalle section of Paris, across from the Moulin Rouge, just under the neon "XXX" sign.

It is, I must admit, easy to "let yourself go" a bit too much while single-handing. Thus, I make sure I wash the dishes, clean the head, and shampoo my hair at least once a week when I'm in mid-ocean. (The fact that it's all the same container makes it easy to remember.)

The world is fascinated by single-handers. That's true. Everyone wants to study the lives of Joshua Slocum, Robin Knox Johnson, and Chichester to find a common denominator. (Hint: they didn't have girlfriends!)

Of course, while offshore, a single-hander has some pretty "heavy" thoughts. Three of mine were, "Gee, I hope my wife is still alive to support me," and "Gee, I hope my daughter gets a good job after college so she can *begin* to support me," and "Thank gosh my parents never attempted to instill any foolish work ethic in me!"

I had some fairly heavy religious thoughts as well. I remember thinking, "I wonder if God would be mad if I kicked the ship's cat across the cabin?" (Evidently not.)

The actual sailing of the boat is relatively easy. When a storm comes, I stay down belowdecks and listen to stuff break on deck. To keep from getting bored, I imagine what I'd do if I was actually a competent sailor. (This makes writing the obligatory Man-Against-the-Sea magazine story that much easier.)

The very best part of single-handing is the "needling rights" it gives you in relationship to other cruisers. "Yeah, well, I'm not scared to go offshore without a *sex slave*!" is a good opening line. "I mean, I prefer the immense joys of perfect solitude over the crass company of some pathetic person with such low-esteem they'd be willing to accompany me."

The biggest problem for many single-handers is stopping. "Wherever you go, there you are," is a powerful incentive to "keep on keeping on" for many globe-girdling sailors. It is easy while single-handing a tiny vessel on a big ocean to delude yourself into thinking you are truly master of your own micro-universe. It happened to me. There was a brief moment last summer—when I was far, far offshore. I thought to myself, "Gee, maybe I *ain't* such a bad guy!"

Needless to say, having such an extraordinarily absurd thought flash through my little pea-brain immediately drove me into the nearest safe harbor yelling, "Delusional! I'm delusional!" at the top of my frightened/lonely lungs.

Gybing into Nirvana

Part of the reason I like the cruising lifestyle so much is because it allows me to continue to do stupid things—to repeat my dumbest mistakes—to a new and unsuspecting audience. I mean, let's face it, falling into the same hole repeatedly can be booorrrring. But for first few times, well, it's a real scream watching an idiot prove he's earned his title.

In America, I used to do this merely by having failing businesses. In Boston I owned "Bozo Boat Works." Our corporate motto was "Cheap, but not chintzy. We don't clown around!" Needless to say, we received a lot of complaints for shoddy workmanship, public intoxication, etc. Regardless of how justified the complaint, we'd just smile sweetly and ask, "And what did you expect from a company named "Bozo Boat Works"—Einstein with a varnish brush?"

When I was in Fort Liquordale and attempting to hustle my fellow boaters at the Southport Raw Bar, my business card just read, "Fatty Goodlander, BN" (Boat Navigator, what in the hell did you think I meant?)

Many of my ex-friends who invested in my Cayman-based "Barnum & Baloney Floating Circus" idea have been incredibly tenacious. I can't believe that after all these years they're still searching for their long-gone cash!

My friend, Larry Pardey, has a similar sense of humor. There is a sign on the door of his shipwright shop in New Zealand that reads "A 3M Company" in large letters and below that, in much smaller type, "Mickey Mouse Marine".

But I didn't limit my business failures to just the marine sector. The moment I saw the overall literacy rate of the West Indies, I decided to form American Paradise Publishing—figuring I could save a tin* of money on proof readers. (*Tun? Toon? Ton?)

Basically, the story of my life is that I get bored with what I understand and am attracted to what I don't. This makes for a laughter-filled life—because my only other option is to cry.

Alas, I live in SE Asia now, where the people aren't nearly as money-conscious as in America. To truly screw up here, you have to do so much more cosmically than just being morally and monetarily bankrupt. Thus, I was faced with a perplexing problem; how to prove my idiocy in a serene Buddhist paradise like, say, Thailand?

Luckily, "spiritual enlightenment for the intellectually dim" is a growth industry here. Asians never seem to tire of fleecing Western airheads with fists full of cash and BDN (Big Dreams of Nirvana). I admire these "can't we somehow blister pack Buddha?" budding capitalists. They have no shame. I find it refreshing to meet young smiling entrepreneurs who aren't in denial—who openly embrace greed, gluttony, and self-indulgence, even in the name of the Awakened One.

Why shouldn't someone charging you $400 bucks an hour tell you rudely that your disgusting money is utterly worthless? Do you have a problem with that? If so, it just proves the point; selfishness causes suffering.

But let's back up. I recently decided to make a rare foray ashore in Thailand—and become one with Buddha.

I went to a Meditation Retreat at a place we'll call Swam Moke—in deference to any libel-lawyers they might employ.

I went there with deep misgivings. After all, I'm a jaded, rude, flippant guy who has skepticism tattooed on every strand of his DNA. And I've been around. I have a built-in, highly sensitive, media-tuned, globally-calibrated bulls#*t meter. So you have to have a pretty sharp pencil to out-scam this scammer.

The first thing that amazed me about SM was its efficiency, perfected by over 20,000 "spiritual fellows" who have passed through. I expected that there would be no mention of money in the beginning—all the better to hit you up for the big bucks later. I paid a key deposit for my room of 50 bucks, and went to see it. It consisted of a cinder block room with a cement slab, wooden pillow, and a mosquito net with more holes than a heroin addict.

I complained to the first monk I saw. "This is not modern accommodation. It's a torture chamber!"

"Yes," he said. "We want you to suffer. We hope you are very uncomfortable and believe that you will be. In fact, each day we'll make you suffer a little bit more. Don't worry my verrrry good friend; you will have much suffering by the end."

This took the wind out of my sails.

I dashed back to find the complaint department—only to see a notice on the wall with the rules. Rule #1 was "Absolutely No Talking For 10 days." I started to open my mouth, but 146 of my fellow "spiritual seekers" frowned. I then whipped out my reporter's notebook and scribbled, "Can I write notes?" A passing monk threw my notebook into the trash with a negative shake of his head. I then whipped open my tiny Vaio laptop and managed to type "Are you frig'n kidding?" before another monk slammed it shut and Frisbee'd it onto a high shelf.

Sigh.

I'd had no time to ask them what we were retreating from during the retreat. Nor did I know what we were supposed to be meditating on, when we emptied our self-centered minds to get "Mindfulness." Why is nothing spiritual ever straightforward? Why is the answer to every simple question, some mumbo-jumbo like, "It's the sound of one hand clapping."

The next thing I knew, people were being nice to me. I mean, I'd had a guy be nice to me back in the 1960's, but he was a hippie and high on drugs—at least, that's what I assumed. But now, people were being nice to me again and again for no reason. And I didn't even know who they were and they didn't know who I was.

So, since nobody was watching and I figured that it would never get back to my friends in the Caribbean, I was nice to a person.

It felt *very* strange, sort of like coughing up a golf ball—hell, a bowling ball! I said to myself, internally, "Wow, so that's what goodness feels like. For goodness sakes!"

Just about that time, a mosquito landed on my nose, and I started to swat it. My arm was caught by a Kung Fu monk who just materialized beside me. "Intentionally take no breath," he whispered and disappeared in a puff of dust.

I looked around for the smoke and mirrors but couldn't spot them.

I then decided they weren't allowing me to speak so that, during meditation, I couldn't leap upon the stage and make a fool of them all by saying, "Any monk who believes in telekinetics, raise my arm."

All of us were herded into a gorgeous open-air meditation center, and told to do nothing. Now this is exactly what I've been accused of all my life—doing nothing. Every boss, lover, friend, family member, and wife that I've ever had has repeatedly screamed at me, *"But you just do nothing!"*

Now I was to discover that I was doing "nothing" wrong. This came as a rude shock. Not only wasn't I really doing nothing, I wasn't even capable of truly doing nothing, which made me, even in my own book, a complete & worthless screw-up. This struck me as incredibly sad. My eyes started to leak. Tears ran down my face. Suddenly a monk was beaming at me, "Good suffering, good suffering!" he said in praise.

I smiled back—one of those creepy beatific smiles you see on religious zombies in churches and other areas of codified insanity.

Damn! The bastards were starting to get to me.

At 9pm, they allowed us to return to our rooms. I was careful getting into my mosquito netting and managed to do so without disturbing the milling crowd of hungry centipedes, millipedes, spiders, tarantulas, and scorpions that surrounded it.

There were only two horrible screams that first night—both from terrified people-with-their-pants-around-their-ankles frantically fleeing cobras. I kid you not, cobras abound! They come out of the rain and hide in the darkened, damp toilet stalls. The toilet doors sadistically open inward, so often the escapee brutally slams himself in the face—another clever way to "increase the suffering", I guess.

At 4am, a gong rang so loud that it levitated me out of my bunk. A few minutes later I was in the lotus position, doing my "silent meditation." This consisted mostly of me forcing myself not to scream aloud from back pain. After about an hour, when I could not move my frozen muscles at all, they sadistically announced it was time for yoga. For the next 90 minutes, they literally attempted to twist my spinal cord out of my body. They taught me the fish posture, and the cat, and the cow, and the lion. While I taught myself the "crying in a fetal position" posture.

Next, we attended a lecture by a Thai who obviously thought that he could speak English. I think the main purpose of this guy was to show us that, if you followed their system, you could be blissful *and* delightfully delusional. (The Thai guy, I must admit, seemed to really get off while not communicating with us.)

At 8am, we broke for breakfast. This consisted of—what appeared to be—yesterday's regurgitated rice soup. Actually, it wasn't too bad if you clothes-pinned your nose and managed to keep it down.

We all had chores—sort of forced slave-labor. My chore consisted of lighting five candles—which *sounds* easy. But I had to remember to bring matches, walk to the candles, remember not to burn myself, etc. It wasn't *so* easy. I'd have gladly bribed a monk to do it for me. But not being able to speak cut down on my attempts at moral corruption.

Then we had our main *Dharma* lesson by an old monk, who started off by confessing (who could make such a thing up?) that he lusted after Olive Oil, Popeye's girlfriend. Anyway, this monk, who lived in a hole in the ground and supported himself by begging from poor Thai fishermen, told us the answer to Life, the Universe, and Everything. That's right. He just laid it out. Simple as pie. Every question I ever had, this dude answered it—nonchalantly.

I was stunned. I've been in the presence of a "towering intellect" before, but this Tan Dhammavidu guy was over-the-top in cosmic-cool! He knew everything about everything—and how it all related to why... to why... to why I was just a complete idiot.

At this point, I began to worry. I'd come (okay, I admit it) to ridicule the place. And now I was weeping tears of joy, more orgasmically blissed-out than I'd thought possible.

Were they mixing LSD with the morning gruel?

Then we had lunch. I've racked my brain for something positive to say—and the only thing I can come up with is, "It was better than breakfast."

After lunch, I took a dip in the hot springs and noticed there were fewer people around than at breakfast. It was as if an invisible Buddha was eating them. "But that's impossible," I thought to myself, "The Awakened One is a vegetarian."

Obviously, I was coming adrift from reality.

I really got into the "mindfulness" (being totally in the moment) and had great fun doing "walking meditation" in the garden-like meditation area, while pretending to be a slo-mo zombie. With some fake blood, we could have been an out-take from the *Night of the Living Dead.*

At first, the retreat organizers gave us two meals and demanded we meditate for five hours. Then they ratcheted that up to one meal, almost no sleep, and eleven hours of "oh-my-god-my-back-hurts" meditation a day. People started going, well, crazy. They'd laugh, cry, keel over—and occasionally be taken to the hospital. (Of the 140 plus who started, only around 70 finished.)

But I'm an offshore sailor—suffering is nothing to me. I've based my life/marriage upon it.

By the Tenth Day, we'd been reduced to blithering idiots and they were hoping we were softened up enough to start hallucinating. (The only thing I started to hallucinate was the Golden Arches—I was that hungry.)

By the end of my experience, I'd reluctantly come to the conclusion that the people who appeared to be blissed out Buddhists with hearts of gold—really were. This was driven home when I discovered that I didn't have to pay any more money. My key deposit covered the entire cost! (About five dollars US a day, all inclusive.) They didn't even ask for a donation. And when I mentioned it, they said something like, "Yeah, maybe on the website is an address where you could send a check, if you wanted."

All the staff members were volunteers. They were the finest group of people I've never spoken with.

I was calm, utterly calm—calmer than I've been since—well, being a child. My potbelly had disappeared. The yoga had made me supple as a cat. I was filled with goodness-to-bursting.

The first person I met outside asked me, "How was it?"

"Awful," I said. "No, it was wonderful… awfully wonderful, I guess!"

"I'm confused," said the person.

"Me too," I said. And smiled—just like a blissed-out zombie!

Bad Marine Trends: Here, There, and Everywhere

The Good News is that 99% of what my wife, Carolyn, and I experienced during our recent trip around the world was good news! The world is a nice place, populated by mostly nice people, and you can have a good time almost anywhere if you bring the right attitude. Very few things we encountered turned us off or made us sad.

Let's put it another way: we believe in accentuating the positive and minimizing the negative.

That said, we did experience a wide variety of customs, trends, and experiences. And, of course, not all of these experiences were completely positive.

Since I'm often accused of "only telling the good parts of sailing offshore," I'll take this literary opportunity to mention some of the things, mostly fairly minor, which turned us off.

GUNS: The saddest thing we experienced during our circumnavigation was arriving back in the Lesser Antilles and listening to American yachtsmen endlessly discussing guns.

Guns, guns, guns!

We don't carry a gun. We don't like guns. And we certainly don't want to spend the rest of our lives talking about them.

If you carry a gun aboard your boat, fine. I don't begrudge you your choice at all. I respect it.

However, how in the *hell* did guns and piracy become the main topic of conversation on Hog Island, in Chaguaramas, or at Foxy's?

The most ironic aspect of "the gun issue" is that few circumnavigators in the Malacca Straits, South China Sea, Madagascar, or Africa ever talk about guns.

WEATHER GURUS: We love our local weather men and regional weather routers. The late David Jones routed us most of the way around the world. It was amazing how accurate his long range predictions were, despite the fact that he was in Tortola and I was in the Tasman Sea between New Zealand and Oz!

Southbound Herb, St. John George, and Alistair of Africa have all helped us at various times. We subscribe to Buoy Weather (computer generated day-by-day, advanced position-by-position, week-long e-mail forecasts—and we regularly get GRIB files via e-mail over our PACTOR III modem.

The bottom line is: we get more weather information and advice than we know what to do with.

All that is the good news. What is not good news is the growing belief that if you are careful and pay attention to this data, you can sail around the world without getting into bad weather.

We think this is wrong. We believe, instead, that if you are in the right ocean at the right time, *and* carefully consider your weather data; this increases your chances of a fair passage considerably. But it does not eliminate the chance of getting caught in a storm.

Basically we spent a solid year at sea in the four years it took us to complete the Big Fat Circle. That's 365 days or 8,760 hours. During such a long period of time, it is reasonable to expect being wacked by a major system offshore.

Here's our actual experience: we were hove-to about forty times during our circumnavigation. This is no big deal. If the wind stays above 35 knots for more than a couple of hours, and the seas have built to a decent size, we heave-to. It only takes a couple of minutes. Then we relax. Smooch. Dig out the blender. Read. Laugh. Sleep.

Carolyn often makes bread during gales. And then we just wait it out. In fact, some of our best moments have been those "snug as a bug in a rug" days while storm-bound in the Indian Ocean.

Three times during our circumnavigation, we were in severe weather: in the Tasman, off Madagascar, and coming into Cape Town. I define severe weather as a storm in which I'm truly concerned about the structural integrity of my craft.

The Madagascar blow was the only time in my life I was convinced that the slightest mistake at the helm would cause my vessel to pitch-pole or broach. Conditions were a constant 44 knots with higher gusts, and very steep "opposing current" breaking waves of 30+ feet.

The bottom line is this: all the weather forecasts and weather routers in the world can't help you survive a storm once it is upon you.

THE HERD INSTINCT: We don't sail in packs for a number of reasons. 1.) I'm not a joiner. 2.) I hate waiting. 3.) Group decisions are often late, wrong and/or political. 4.) Packs tend to stay together and not meet the local folks, and thus miss those wonderful, quirky adventures solitary couples often have. 5.) It offers a false sense of security. Take the Fastnet or Queen's Birthday storms as examples. Were boats able to help each other or was the "safety" of their proximity just an illusion?

When I'm in St. Barths and I hear a vessel come on Channel 16 to ask for a "buddy boat" to travel in company with to Sint Maarten—well, I can't help but smile. I mean, really!

THE SAILING OFFICE: I'm guilty of this. Since I make my living as a marine writer, I have very sophisticated communication systems aboard *Wild Card*: VHF, marine SSB, ham, e-mail—even a pricey SatPhone!

The plus side is that I can always make my living, anywhere in the world. And the down side is that everywhere I go in the world, I have to make my living!

The worst part is that now my bosses can get in touch with me—almost instantly. (This makes being stoned on kava in Tonga slightly less fun!)

If I missed a deadline before, I used to say, "Well, I'm sure I mailed it. If you don't get it within another ten days, I'll send it again!" This would give me plenty of time to actually write the damn thing.

Now my editor says, "Send it." And if I don't do so immediately, via the internet, there is trouble. ("The reason we call it a deadline is because if you miss it, as far as we're concerned, *you're dead*!" an editor told me early in my career. I've never forgotten his words).

The danger here is that we eventually won't be able to "get away from it all" while getting away from it all!

RELIANCE ON GEAR: People are beginning to think that if their gear breaks, it is defective or badly engineered. Not so. If a piece of sailing gear breaks, it is *the captain's* fault for 1.) not having the proper gear, 2.) not maintaining it, and/or 3.) for having too much sail up.

Again and again sailors show me broken blocks, bent travelers, and deformed tracks while saying, "Look what happened to this piece of junk! And I paid good money for it, too!"

While I think silently to myself, "I wonder why the idiot didn't reef?"

High winds usually aren't a problem at sea *if* you have the right sail up (or down). People who talk about all the gear they broke during a gale are really telling you they didn't reef early and well. You wouldn't drive a car with a sticky gas pedal, would you? Then why would you sail into a squall without reducing canvas?

ALL THE TOYS SYNDROME: There is a growing trend to think that you can have it all—all the conveniences of your Aspen condo—on your yacht. This isn't true unless your pocket book is nearly limitless and you don't live year-round on your boat (because so much time annually will be required to fix it).

Example: when we left South Africa we left behind a very wealthy friend on his mega-yacht. "I can't leave yet because my radar and watermaker are down—and my bow-thruster's shaft seals are leaking. Oh, and my refrigeration is on the blink too!"

"Sorry to hear it," I said as we left, wisely not having any of that stuff aboard *Wild Card*.

OVER RELIANCE ON EXPERTS: Again and again new boat owners complain about "the experts," and how they ain't. These well-heeled, trusting boat owners foolishly believe that 1.) Expensive marine gear doesn't fail, and 2.) If it does, you can hire someone to fix it.

Often, this is not true. While Europe, the States, New Zealand, Australia, South Africa, and the Lesser Antilles have a wide variety of skilled marine repairman, most of the world does not.

OLD RICH FOLKS ON LARGE BOATS: We've actually met couples in their late 60's or early 70's attempting to circumnavigate on very expensive, hi-tech sailboats longer than their age, 80-footers! The idea here is that, with the advent of electric sheet and halyard winches, in-mast and roller furling, twin engines and gen-set, bow-and-stern thrusters, and hydraulic anchor windlasses—well, that the size and strength of crew doesn't matter. And they believe that big boats have an easier motion—and can carry more Depends or whatever.

This is crazy. I feel sorry for these terrified old folks, as they helplessly drag sideways through the anchorage, regularly run aground, and often crash into docks.

This trend has to stop somewhere. What's a good rule: if you can't dead-lift the anchor, don't take it to sea?

Big boats aren't just big money—they require a higher level of expertise to run. You have to really plan ahead on a large vessel because by the time you realize you are in trouble, it can already be too late.

Many of these couples would be perfectly happy on a 40-footer and would save five or ten million bucks in the process.

SPEED CIRCS: Some hi-powered CEOs want to work full time *and* sail around the world. They hire a "shore team" to meet the boat so they can fly out the same day. The shore team then "does the heavy lifting" of getting the vessel completely provisioned and ready for the next leg so the CEO can fly back in for sundowners at the yacht club and leave the next morning.

True, you *can* circumnavigate this way—but you miss the people ashore, your fellow boaters, the countries. In essence, the entire cruising experience gets turned into something resembling—well, work!

Of course, everyone is different. If you happen to carry a gun, have all the toys, work profitably from your paperless web-connected nav table, love weather routers, and sail a mammoth boat longer than you are old—more power to you, *if* you are having a good time. If you aren't, I have three tried-and-true suggestions: simplify, simplify, simplify!

Bringing Fire to Curacao

Joe Colpitt on Virgin Fire *in St. John*

    I recently found myself with a few spare days between circumnavigations and so I decided to help Joe Colpitt bring his lovely 56-foot Gold Coast trimaran *Virgin Fire* to Curacao, Dutch West Indies.
    I like Joe Colpitt. I like him a lot. But he is, by almost any measure, an odd duck. He grew up in rural Oklahoma with a highly-abusive guy for a father—and a sedate future in the family oil-drilling business all neatly laid out for him.
    He was brought up to be mean, tough, and hard—a "man's man" so to speak. But it didn't quite work out that way. Joe rebelled by sneaking downstairs at night and, to drown out the drunken parental shrieks upstairs, listened to opera. "Sissy music" it was called in the oil patch back then. And he had strange, vivid dreams of being a seabird—a creature as far away from dreary Oklahoma as possible—continuously soaring above Mother Ocean, eternally free from the vexations of shore-strife.
    Yes, Joe is a strange duck, and delightfully so. He has since evolved into a sailor's sailor. A long-term live-aboard, he has also raced numerous multihulls across many a windy ocean. After apprenticing to famed multihull designer Dick Newick, he built a number of highly successful trimarans as well—once setting a transatlantic record which stood for many years (with Jody Culbert).
    Since the French are tops in ocean-racing, Joe learned French and toured Europe to learn from them. Once, when asked by a pretty French sailor if he was... well, it sounded like she asked him if he was 'a multi-cock man?' Joe smiled shyly and said, "Well, I've been called worse." That's Joe. He's sort of an Oklahoma cowboy with a strange watery, three-legged ocean steed—who, discovering that honky-tonks didn't like opera music, learned

to play the guitar instead.

One more thing about Joe: never mistake his meek, aw-shucks shyness for weakness. Once, we were walking down a road in England when some soccer hoons attempted to shove us off the road. I stepped aside with a sigh. Joe, however, wasn't paying attention. He got knocked into the ditch, shook his head to figure it out, and came charging up. In an instant the guy who had shouldered Joe was in the *other* ditch—in dire need of a chiropractor—and Joe was calmly asking the others "to dance," but they respectfully declined.

That said, Joe and I are getting to be old farts. So Joe suggested we invite a young fellow aboard "to do the work and take the blame if it all goes wrong."

Enter Brian Walden.

He owns the J/22 *Jaywalking* and used to run a small boat rental operation out of Coral Bay. Joe had no mercy on him. The minute he stepped aboard Joe barked, "Hank on the working jib and clap on the main halyard when you are done!"

Sure, Brian is an experienced sailor but *Virgin Fire* is a highly unusual, highly complex sailing craft. I could sense his initial discomfort. "Not the white floppy things," I said to Joe to ease the air. "Every time we hoist those things up we get ourselves in trouble!"

Yeah, it is almost never wrong to get people laughing, especially if they're new and stiff with each other.

Within a couple of hours Brian knew as much about *Virgin Fire* as I did... maybe more. He proved to be a fine offshore shipmate: willing, competent, and hard-working. Most of all, he never complained. Experienced sailors hate whiners. As far as we're concerned, one whine and you're overboard, as the saying goes.

Which brings us to *Virgin Fire*, the exotic sailing concoction Joe Colpitt designed as the ultimate 'fast cruising' yacht of the future. She is a trimaran, 56 feet long with 36 feet of beam. She flies an enormous amount of sail, and regularly touches 20 knots on 'fire hose reaches' and often turns in daily runs of 300 nautical miles plus.

And, while she is primarily intended as a cruising vessel, she is fast, fast, fast.

I had the privilege of sailing on her (along with Monkey Bill Henderson and SteveO Crumrine) when she won the overall multihull award at the hotly-contested Heineken Regatta. The victory was especially sweet as the French had sent a number of large multihulls to dislodge us, even an all-carbon unlimited Open 60 trimaran (formerly *Fleury Michon*).

Yeah, *Virgin Fire* scoots. During a recent Around St. John race she competed against a very fast, very expensive 62-foot hi-tech catamaran steered by famed multihull ocean racer Cam Lewis. And '*The Fire,*' as she is affectionately referred to, won by 42 minutes!

When I congratulated Joe on his amazing victory, he shrugged it off

modestly. "Naw, she's faster than us," he said. "I just got lucky."
Joe is lucky often on the race course.

Curacao, in the Dutch West Indies off the coast of Venezuela, is about 450 miles from St. John. It took us less than two days, from anchor-up to anchor-down. We just flew—like a large seabird in one of Joe Colpitt's early childhood fantasies.

The only problem was Brian. He'd make the strangest noises at the helm, as *Virgin Fire* would surf off a large sea and hit 'the high teens' on our speedo. "Oh" and "Ah" and "UMMMMM!"

Yeah, Brian sounded like—well, it was almost as if Joe and I were listening to a porno sound track. The guy was truly multi-orgasmic as he savored the smooth, turbo-charged adrenaline rush that is *Virgin Fire*.

And he was willing to learn. "How do you do it?" he asked me one afternoon as I napped in the cockpit.

"Cruise? Nap? Kick-back?" I yawned. "Well, it is kinda like meditating only much less work. I mean, it looks *so* easy, Brian, but, hey, there's more to it than meets the eye! Example: I've got more than one position for napping/relaxing/gazing-out-to-sea! For instance, this is Position A, and" (I shifted slightly) "this is position B. See how seamless and subtle the transition was?"

"Yeah," he said with a slow, dawning grin. "I think I'm getting it!"

The only negative of the entire trip was how soon it was over. *Virgin Fire* floats so effortlessly over the waves; I would have enjoyed another week or two of it.

Her gracefulness is utterly relaxing. I felt refreshed, renewed, and roaring-to-go at the end.

The moment that most sticks in my mind took place at three in the morning on the second night. Brian was just starting his two hour trick at the wheel and I was just about to turn in. But I couldn't. It was just too beautiful. I was in God's own cathedral. The stars, millions of 'em, were like a canopy of winking, twinkly diamonds set amid black. The phosphorescence on the loo'ard amma was too neon-blue. Our blue-white wake was a curling stairway to heaven.

Everything seemed too real, surreal, hyper-real.

I had to hold my breath...fearing to shatter the rare purity of the moment.

Finally I said, "It seems that offshore is the only place I can think anymore."

I could see Brian faintly illuminated by the red-glow of the steering compass. He said nothing. And I silently thanked him for it as I ducked below.

Christmas Afloat with Cap'n Scrooge

Roma Orion dressed-up for Christmas

Every December, my wife and daughter use the Christmas season as an excuse to reduce my vessel to a complete shambles.

They begin this gut-wrenching process just before the Thanksgiving Day holidays—so that they can achieve the maximum amount of irritation over the longest amount of time.

First off, they "decorate" my boat. They begin by draping silver tinsel everywhere belowdecks. It only takes them about three short minutes to fling more tinsel around the boat than I'll be able to clean up in three long months. The tinsel, of course, doesn't stay put. It immediately begins its implacable migration toward my bilge pump strainers.

This "annual family tinsel toss" is quickly followed by the ceremonial "stringing of the Christmas garlands." These garlands are brightly-colored decorative strings in silver, red, and green, and continuously shed their tiny plastic slivers quite prettily.

My girls intertwine these garlands around my overhead handrails (so I have nothing to grip), across the galley (so the plastic garland melts onto my interior varnish when the oven is on), and near the companionway ladder (so it catches on my sheath knife each time I exit).

Then they thoroughly spray, both inside and outside, my cabin windows and port lights with fake snow from an aerosol can. The solvent and/or propellant in the fake snow momentarily melts the plastic in the windows, and the whole mess must eventually be laboriously chipped off with a dull welding chisel. This leaves more than a couple of scratches in the plastic, I'll tell ya!

Back belowdecks again, they hang long strands of festive popcorn near the bookshelves—just to make sure that our shipboard roaches get plenty to eat during the holiday season.

Each Christmas card we receive gets Scotch-taped somewhere belowdecks. But they must dip the Scotch-tape in West epoxy first, because it adheres to my boat stronger and longer than any super-glue I've ever used.

They don't stop merely at passive decoration, however. Nooooooo Sirrrreeeeeeeeeeee! I've not mentioned the strings of 12-volt blinking Christmas lights along the lifelines, the illuminated Santa lashed to my stern rail, the glowing Rudolph perched on my boom, or the spreader-light illuminated Santa's sleigh on my foredeck.

Both of my shipboard battery banks last about 15 minutes after sunset during December. If I complain, I'm labeled "Cap'n Scrooge!" and "Cap'n Bligh!" and "Stingy, stingy, stingy!"

I refuse to encourage them by buying a Christmas tree. So they have a "Goodlander family Christmas tradition" of stealing them, branch by branch, from our shoreside friends.

It is so embarrassing to be invited into someone's living room, and when they leave for an instant to get the traditional eggnog and cookies…have your wife break off a large branch of their Christmas tree, slip a few fragile ornaments down her billowing blouse, and stash a couple of medium-sized candy canes under her commodious armpits, while your kid silently attempts to lasso the sacred angel off the top of their tree.

As Christmas approaches, my wife and daughter quickly escalate the abuse. "Let's bake some cookies, pies, and other horribly messy food-stuffs!" they gleefully sing out to each other as they start dumping cans of flour, sugar, and Crisco onto my pristine navigation table.

Even our ship's cat, which is appropriately named Joker, gets into Christmas—mostly by eating his holiday share of the "forbidden foods," such as tinsel and wrapping ribbons. He vomits up the ribbons and, at least partially, passes the tinsel. "Oh, gross!" screams my daughter, as Joker streaks past her with a little Christmas tinsel gaily trailing behind him.

By the time Christmas Day actually arrives, my boat is a (barely) floating disaster area. The bilge pumps are clogged, the batteries are as flat as my bank account, and the lenses of my port lights are about as clear as my conscious.

To signal the glorious occasion, my wife wakes up at dawn and puts on some Christmas "Steel Pan" music on the stereo. It sounds like an angry young man, pissed off about being forever mired in abject poverty, beating on a garbage can under the hot tropical sun—which is probably what it is.

Each year, I give both my girls something I know they will endlessly enjoy and truly treasure—an enlarged color photograph of myself.

This year, my wife gave me a large magnifying mirror so that I can better gaze upon my noble countenance without straining my aging eyes. My daughter gave me a review of one of my books with all the negative comments cut out. (Okay, so there wasn't much left of the book review, but that's not the point. It's the thought that counts, isn't it?)

Since my writing income doesn't allow us to, er, overeat, my Italiano wife often requests food stuffs from her Sicilian parents in Chicago. This year they sent her some Italian sausage, a bag of spicy meatballs, and some angel hair pasta.

It was, alas, kinda messy to eat with our bare hands. And the tomato juices kept dripping on the wrapping paper. But I couldn't complain too much because my family sent me a fruitcake. This caused both my girls to shout out gleefully, "How appropriate! They're all fruitcakes on your side of the family, aren't they?"

In the midst of all this, I had to sail my vessel to our annual Christmas raft up; where about a hundred people got to see that we really do live like slobs aboard our boat and that I really don't make up all these horrible things about my family—and that these lifestyle stories aren't sick exaggerations, but merely wretchedly truthful recitals of the dementedly demonic details of our dreary daily existence.

At the stroke of midnight on Christmas, I began cleaning up my vessel—attempting to get her back into "shipshape and Bristol fashion."

I used a machete on the tinsel and garlands, a shovel on the debris on the cabin sole, and a fire hose on the (highly sticky) galley area.

By dawn I was almost done, and at the end of my physical, mental, and moral rope.

As both my girls awoke, I hoped for a little genuine sympathy. But it was not to be. Instead, they giggled at my disheveled appearance, high-fived each other proudly, and sang out loudly in unison, "Let's decorate the boat for New Year's!!

A Lively Tale of Boredom

Brace yourself for a horrible shock: there are people in this world who are more boring than your average pipe-sucking cruising sailor.

{Gasp!}

No, not a sport fisherman! True, his fish tales are often yawn-inducing—but his personal wreck-of-a-life is anything but. Have you ever actually spent an evening with a local sport fisherman—smashing up cars, boats, and brain cells? I mean, when he isn't actively occupied in attempting to kill the last of some vanishing aquatic species?

I have—or, at least, did, back when I had a liver.

That's right! I got "Red-Hooked" into the Poor Man's Bar one evening. I went through two fights, one divorce, half a mental breakdown, *and* helped rebuild a Borg-Warner gearbox on the floor—all within the first hour or so.

No, you can say what you want about your average gnarl-fisted, fish-scaled, pot-bellied, ruddy-faced sport fishermen; but not that they're boring. They are not. They're colorful. Who else would have the balls—the, er, lead-weights to introduce their new girlfriend as, "my latest dock box."

Sure, a cruising sailor might refer to his wife as a sailbag. But he is almost always "out-cruded" by the fishheads at the bait shop.

Surfers? Yeah, surfers are boring in an ultra-hip, way-cool way. Ever ask a surfer a question? Waste of time, wasn't it? They'll intently stare out at the surf line, take a deep breath, slowly expand their chest, raise their arms majestically as if to indicate some magnificently "heavy" and obscure concept—then hesitate, deflate, sigh, and go back to staring morosely out to sea.

Jet-skiers certainly aren't boring. They are *very* social beings and always know the paramedics, ambulance drivers, and police officers of the area they "play" in. Some aren't too bright though, like the one who recently confided in me, "I've been finding a *lot* of dead bodies lately."

I personally find board sailors highly distasteful; especially now that my drooling wife regularly steams up our binoculars while muttering, "Rock on, rock-hard abs!" as they zoom through the anchorage.

Yes, sail boarding is a great way to stay in shape and exercise is something my wife could use more of.

"I'll buy you one if you want," I told her as a new carbon-fiber board with kevlar sail smoked past us.

"Yippee!" she said, "I'll take the blond, blue-eyed guy with the dreads!"

Tug boat skippers can be a fun bunch. I love the "I'll pull yours if you'll pull mine!" T-shirts.

Commercial fishermen are usually fun to talk to (on the VHF). I'll put it another way: their "fish stories" aren't what stink!

Kite sailors tend to be slightly smarter than their skateboard counterparts who get run over by automobiles—or maybe they were just lucky not to be told by their parents to go play in traffic.

Do you know why so many kite sailors have numbers tattooed on their foreheads? That's how many masthead anemometer cups they've destroyed!

Harbor pilots often know how to channel their humor, mostly into puns. Bareboaters are generally fun—with or without their swimming trunks. Sail makers? Well, they're sort of sew-sew. Many Caribbean marine mechanics are a few foot-pounds shy of a full torque. Shipboard electricians who cater to the fishing industry are usually hard of herring. That's why they shout, "Watt? Watt?" so often.

Yes, a lot of current nautical terminology is confusing, eh? Example: why are non-druggy people allowed on "head" boats? Are they called "cattlemarans" because all the fat passengers have such bovine expressions? Are all "six-pack" skippers drunks? Does the expression "fully-crude charters" mean they are never nice? Why do departing sailors say, "See yawl schooner or later!" Why do rich French racing sailors all buy "multi-cocks"? Why do sportfishing vessels call it a "fly bridge," when most of them are buzzing around the mate below?

It's confusing, isn't it?

Marine plumbers? Hey, I feel sorry for them. They take a lot of cra... abuse! "Why, I've had it up to here!" said one particularly despondent fellow as he pointed to his nose. "I'm tired of aspiring to be #1 in a #2 field!"

Yes, the pressures of marine plumbing, especially for its few female practitioners, are intense. That is why so many "marine monkey wenches" end up as substance abusers—mostly of inhalants. (How anyone could sniff—well, let's not go there, OK?)

Where were we? Ah, yes—identifying the worst of a bad bunch.

Term charter skippers are boring, true, but no worse than their day sailing counterparts. Both have grown lazy from having a captive audience who are forced to pay for the verbal abuse. (An S&M relationship if ever there was one!)

Divers? Well, I hate to pick on any group that is publicly acknowledged to be sub-intelligent. I mean, the whole "resort dive certification" thing is becoming somewhat of a joke. If you can learn to play patty-cake, then you can get your "Open Water" certificate within ten seconds—in the water basin of the resort's drinking fountain! (That's why the certification is phonetically pronounced PATTY, eh?)

Racing sailors are boring in the sense that you can never understand what the hell they are talking about. Mostly it is post-race "shouldda, wouldda, couldda" stuff; as in, "We shouldda tacked when Rudy Thompson did, then we wouldda finished before the wind died and, thus, couldda won the whole damn thing."

Most of the truly serious "race talk" is about their CSA (Crying & Screaming Abuse) rating. In a hundred boat fleet, 99 skippers think their rating sucks and one does not. (These are the "titans of industry" who rule the world? Golf help us!)

Ferry boat skippers? You'd think they'd be as boring as their routes, but you'd be wrong. They are not. They are a highly creative, hard-working bunch—at least when it comes to buying "black market" urine samples. (Is the USCG and Homeland Security really piddling around with finding Osama bin Laden's DNA in those little yellow jars?)

Who is the runner-up for most boring Jack-Tarr-of-All-Trades? Why, the pontificating circumnavigator, of course! Thank God they spend most of their time at sea!

No, the most boring person in the marine world is none-of-the-above. He is the marine journalist—that rheumy-eyed, salt-stained inkslinger who is too addle-brained and lazy to make it as a respectable obituary writer in the ole US of A!

Even my wife, who seldom agrees with me on any issue of substance, heartily concurs. "You're absolutely right on this one, Fatty," she beams. "And you've spent twenty-five professional years proving it!"

Empty Nesters

After 16 years, one month, and 19 days of frantic effort, my wife and I were finally able to convince our daughter to take some college courses at Boston University. I'm not sure exactly which courses she elected to take, but one course was entitled something like the "your parents want to be alone, so beat it kid" summer school course.

The bottom line is that after 5,894 long and difficult days of steadfast & stoic parenting, my wife and I were once again "alone together

Okay, okay, I'll admit it. At first we didn't know how to act. And then, after about an eighth of a nano-second, we remembered! YEOW! What fun!!!

The next few days were a sweaty blur. And more than once, some residents of our quiet little harbor rowed over to our rocking & rolling vessel to politely ask if we were slowly and repeatedly "killing the cat?"

Eventually however, dehydration, low-blood sugar, and human hydraulics forced us to stop—or at least begin resting between episodes. The spirit was willing but the flesh was weak.

But the fun wasn't completely over. We had an absolute *ball* breaking all the strict rules we'd made up over the course of the last decade and a half.

We shouted obscenities across the harbor, slept late, and ate crumbly food in our bunks. We talked with our mouths full, burped joyously, even loudly farted with pride! Yes sirree Bob! And that's not all. We mooned innocent bareboaters as they motored by in the anchorage, gulped our Cruzan rum straight from the bottle, and broadcast horribly sexist jokes over our VHF.

"What the hell do I care," I chortled to my giggly wife while hanging up the radio mike. "After all, I don't want to be a Supreme Court judge. I ain't gonna run for president. I ain't in line for the joint chiefs of staff."

"Hey, speaking of the joint chiefs...."

My wife immediately reverted to her "pre-mom" style of yacht attire—which is none at all.

I enjoyed being able to dig out my old *Playboy* magazines from under the forecastle's mattress, and read them openly, without having to resort to a blanket-shielded flashlight for my guilty illuminations.

That is, at least for me, the most shocking aspect of parenting in the regressive '90's—all the bizarre sneaking around you have to do behind your child's back. Modern youngsters can be so bright, observant, sensitive, intelligent, knowledgeable, and caring—well, frankly, it's enough *to really piss you off!* Luckily, I learned how to be sneaky, underhanded, and maliciously manipulative while sneaking around behind my *parents* back. But as a youth, I certainly didn't realize I'd have to use these highly-honed skills again.

Living aboard our boat suddenly became *much* easier. Why, just tossing overboard all the zit creams raised our vessel's waterline nearly an inch!

It saved a lot of time too. Without my daughter aboard, I didn't have to clean my bilge pump strainer daily of hairballs, bobby pins, or empty CK perfume bottles.

We tossed her tattered High School textbooks overboard, and "splashed" a few of her old Barbie dolls into the harbor for good measure. Ditto for her *New Kids on the Block* CD's, her fanzines about the *X-Files*, and those much adored Brad Pitt posters.

It was also great to regain control of our stereo equipment for the first time in years. She was barely at the airport before I twisted off the volume control while listening to *Satisfaction* by the Rolling Stones.

My wife and I immediately reverted back to much of our 1960's-style behavior—yelling "groovy!" about everything that "turned us on," giving each other soulful Black Power salutes, and making swine-type noises each time a USCG boat sped by.

And then suddenly it wasn't fun anymore. For the last 16 years, our daughter has been the main focus of our lives. She has enriched our marriage immeasurably—never a mutual burden, always a shared joy. The small freedoms we have had to forsake for her have been repaid a billion-fold. She has given us so much—so very much—it is difficult to quantify.

She has taught *us,* at least as much as we've taught *her.* She has literally made us young again. We've been able to see the world anew through her sparkling, unjaded eyes. She was, and still is, the human embodiment of our collective happiness.

She is the cement of our relationship, the rivets of our hearts, the keel bolts of our marriage.

And now she is gone—off the screen of our nurturing, parental radar. Over the horizon from our caring hearts.

Hugging a child to your bosom is easier than letting her go.

And it's scary. Some kids come home in a pine box—the innocent victim of the drunk driver, some faceless urban predator, the proverbial lightning bolt from the sky. Who can say what the future might bring?

And it is so difficult for my wife and me to accurately measure how well our child will be able to cope with the urban jungles of America. Our daughter is so beautiful, so intelligent, so nonchalantly witty, that it is easy to forget how fragile, naive, and trusting she can be.

Yes, we have labored mightily to teach her how to smile, to amicably chat, to openly love, to willingly embrace. But have we taught her how to accurately judge the character of her fellow man, to recognize their potential for evil, to realize that a shiver of fear can be her best tool for survival?

And so my wife and I (we've been together now for nearly 30 years) sit quietly in the cockpit of our vessel as the evening shadows lengthen. We seldom speak. Occasionally, we sigh. We are "alone together" with our private thoughts.

Time passes. Things change. The future arrives, ready or not.

And now we can suddenly imagine being wheeled into a nursing home—while clasping a cherished photograph of our child held out proudly in front of us, as if to magically ward off the further inevitable ravages of Father Time, who ultimately waits so patiently—to steal the dignity of us all.

"I love you," I whisper to my wife.

"She'll be fine," she whispers back.

Perverting the USCG Regulations

Where other sailors see adversity, I see opportunity. Take the recent USCG proposal to make the wearing of PFDs (personal floatation devices) mandatory at all times on all US-flagged vessels.

"You've got to be joking," my wife said when I informed her of the ramifications of the new proposed regulations.

"I'm not," I said earnestly. "It's just something that—well, as an actively married couple—that we'll, well, you know—we'll have to learn to, er, work around."

"Absolutely not," she said grimly. "No way!"

"Honey," I said. "If these proposed USCG regs go through, we're not going to have much of a choice. After all, the law is the *LAW*! First, it was safe boating, then safe sex. So this is really just a natural outgrowth of these two very laudable public-health concepts. We'll simply have to learn to wear our PFDs when we..."

"That's *SICK*!" she screamed, as she burst into tears and ran crying up to the forepeak.

I knew I couldn't let her natural revulsion stop me. Instead, I used it as a motivational tool. The very next day I was on the phone to the CEO of "Fred

Icks of Hollywood".

"You're proposing that we market your line of sexy what?" he asked in amazement.

"Lifejackets, Freddy Baby!" I repeated, hoping that for once, one of my 'get rich quick' schemes would pan out. "A 'Sexy & Seaworthy' line of erotic lifejackets."

"Let me get this straight," he began. But I interrupted with, "That doesn't matter. Regardless of straight or gay, you're gonna have to wear 'em!"

"I had no idea." he admitted.

"Well, luckily, I've got plenty of ideas," I told him. "When can we meet?"

Knowing that I wouldn't have a lot of time to make my sales pitch, I brought a couple of my hottest custom-made pre-production models to show Freddy.

"Okay," Freddy said immediately after I was ushered into his plush, black-light lit, leopard-skinned office. "Spill!"

"Okay!" I pitched, a tad nervously at first. "Lifejackets have been, traditionally, fairly utilitarian. They were intended to make you float—but not necessarily on a sea of ecstasy, if you catch my drift. In essence, they were sexless, boring, and as lumpy as a Republican housewife. But now all that's gonna change."

"Lemme see the samples," demanded Freddy impatiently. I could tell he didn't get where he was today by running on "island time".

"Sure, Freddy," I said soothingly as I whipped out my first PFD. "I call this the 'Naughty Navigator'."

"I like the waterproof black-polypropylene-lace," he admitted, "but what are the satin webbing and D-rings for?"

"They are used primarily in four ways," I lectured. "For a safety harness while on deck, a galley harness while at the stove, a masthead safety harness when she's hoisted aloft."

"Do you mean to say," Freddy quizzed, "that you're gonna be required to wear a lifejacket even when being hoisted aloft?"

"Absolutely," I confirmed. "Regardless of which way you go, a lifejacket will still be man-(or woman!)-datory. You'll have to wear it when you go up, and you'll have to wear it when you go down."

"I think I can guess the fourth use," admitted Freddy, proving that he wasn't totally stupid. "But I thought all sailors loved to engage in fancy rope work."

"Knot always," I responded punnily. "Many of our younger sailors prefer the ease of a good Nicro-Fico snapshackle over the time-consuming process of tying, say, Turk's Head wrist cuffs."

"Why does the next model come with its own bedspread?" asked Freddy.

"That's our 'Velcro Vixen' model," I beamed. "Perfect for heavy weather!"

"I could see where that could be an asset," Freddy mused.

"Please," I huffed. "Let's keep it clean, okay?"

"Sorry," Freddy said. "What's the next one called?

"This is our Mae West model," I boasted. "I think it will be quite popular. Notice the fact that there is no back or neck buoyancy to ruin its bouncy lines."

"Gee," said Freddy, "isn't it a tad—well, large?"

"Not by modern standards," I assured him. "And to allay any public safety concerns, we're hoping to have it approved by all three important endorsers."

"Which are?"

"Dr. Ruth, Dr. Tattersall, and the USCG!"

"What are the pointy thing-a-ma-jiggers on both what's-ma-call-its?" queried Freddy.

"They're man-overboard whistles," I said.

"Well, surely, this jacket wouldn't ever be worn by a man," Freddy scoffed.

"Well, you never know," I confessed. "Some single-handers have been known to put on 'make-believe TV shows' while in Deep Ocean."

"I didn't know you could even get television offshore," said Freddy, totally missing the meaning of my previous statement.

"Well," I said hastily. "Anchors aren't the only things that drag. But what do you think of my product line?"

"I think it is sleazy and disgusting and perverted—and I love it!"

Just then two large bouncers rushed into the office, grabbed me by my shirt collar, and tossed me out on the street.

A few months later, Freddy's company came out with my line of PFD's—and never paid me a single penny. It was a huge hit, and his stock soared; while my stock with my wife plummeted even lower than normal.

"It's not my fault," I whined to her. "I was completely ripped off! He totally stole my idea, I was totally scr..."

"Hopefully, while wearing your 'Captain Cupid' model PFD," she said, and smiled.

She's lovely when she smiles. "I've got my USCG-approved man-overboard pole with me," I suggested.

"Maybe we can ring our USCG-required ship's bell," she slyly acquiesced.

"We can try," I said, deliriously happy to be in compliance once again.

Customizing Your Boat

I don't want to brag too much—but I must confess that I have an amazing ability to transform a standard production sailboat into... into... into a rather remarkable live-aboard craft.

This is the absolute truth. Knowledgeable sailors throughout the Caribbean are always "remarking" on my vessel's—er, salty appearance.

"I dare say, Cap'n Fatty," said one astounded British Yacht Master, as he majestically motored his gleaming 72-foot Camper Nicholson alongside my delightfully dilapidated water (logged) craft in English Harbor, "you really can make a sow's ear out of silk purse!"

How true. My current vessel is a perfect example.

When I first acquired my S&S Hughes 38, it was a perfectly ordinary vessel. It could have been owned by a doctor, a lawyer, a real estate broker—or any other morally-corrupt professional, for that matter.

In fact, it looked so normal, so bland, so utterly "plain vanilla" that it made me nervous. I felt like an impostor while I sat at its chrome-plated, binnacle-encompassed helm—as if I was some rich-kid-punk whose wealthy daddy had bought him a boat to help his dear lad "find" himself.

Yeeck!

In fact, my new vessel appeared to be the kind of yacht you wouldn't want to throw up on. And what good would a vessel like that be to a guy like me?

So I immediately set about making my vessel an accurate reflection of my own inner personality.

First off, I painted it black.

Notice I didn't say "Awlgripped," I said "painted."

I didn't spray it, either. I used a Mike's Paint Store short-napped economy hand-roller to ensure that my topsides ended up with that wonderful "orange peel" effect that I admire so much. And I didn't use an expensive topside paint—just a cheap gallon of black "Resist-O-Rust" enamel intended for use on outdoor wrought iron furniture.

Perfect!

On all the exterior teak, I smeared cheap porch-and-deck enamel called "lumpy kaka brown." I applied it haphazardly with a throw away brush in such a shoddy manner that the shedding bristles of the rapidly thinning brush-broom helped to disguise the furry fact that I have never, ever "prepped" anything in my life.

Greatly encouraged by the fact that the blue-blazered "yachties" in my (formerly-friendly) harbor had begun circulating a petition to have my vessel towed away; I deep-sixed the sail covers. This allowed my sails to get that salty "urine yellow" appearance which is so highly prized by so many famous solo circumnavigators and various other socially-challenged boaters.

Of course, while painting both the topsides and the exterior trim of my vessel, I got a million tiny flecks of paint on my Plexiglas cabin windows. The quart of acetone that I splashed on the windows to remove the paint flecks didn't work too well on the paint, but it sure did a great job of clouding the plastic.

Another problem was the big brown drips of paint on deck. I solved this problem amazingly fast by simply steel-wooling the entire cabin and deck of my craft. I'm proud to report that within a couple of days, there was so much rust on my vessel that you couldn't even spot the formerly offending spots! (Ah, sweet success!)

Just to "gild the lily" so to speak, I briskly mopped down the deck and cabin with a gallon of undiluted bleach. This didn't affect the rust stains or the paint blotches—but left wonderful vertical "zebra stripes" on my black topsides under my deck scuppers.

As an added bonus, the bleach melted away some of the cheap bathtub-caulk-type-sealant crumbling out of my hull-to-deck joint, making my sieve- like vessel even leakier!

Speaking of leaks, I carefully dumped about a quart of "king of the roof" tar around each chainplate where it came through the deck, in a desperate attempt to seal them. But it didn't work. Neither did the tar ever dry. But the lumpy lumps of soft tar around the chainplates did gradually shrink—as I tracked the sticky tar belowdecks on my bare feet. (Yes, that's how those vivid footprints on the underside of the forecastle deck got there!)

Of course, I'm not solely interested in my vessel's appearance. I'm a modern man, and thus deeply concerned about our marine environment. I'm also a strong believer in recycling. In fact, I think everything on a boat should do double and triple duty. However, I found out that you can carry this noble idea too far when I plumbed my anchor wash-down nozzle to my holding tank and my normally cooperative wife suddenly refused to help hoist the hook.

Of course, Rome wasn't built in a day. It took months of solid effort to decrease my boats value by, say, forty thousand dollars.

If you want your vessel to be instantaneously recognized as the finely-honed floating debris of a confirmed sea gypsy—well, you gotta work at it. Such world-class sea-going shoddiness, at this exalted international level, requires constant vigilance. In the end, it's the subtle element that makes the crucial difference: the soiled underwear waving merrily from the forestay, those noisily slapping halyards, the amazing fact that each and every line on the vessel has a frayed "Irish Pennant" at its unwhipped end....

Ultimately, it's a matter of personal style. Some people get it, and some don't. I think of myself as having a sort of "black thumb" when it comes to basic boat maintenance. There is no marine problem that I can't make worse by simply working on it. And I'm highly confident if Elizabeth Meyer gave me her pristine J-boat *Endeavour* today, within a few weeks I'd have people wondering from which mud bank I'd salvaged that tired old hulk.

Yacht Racing Withdrawal

Stormy Weather racing in the BVI Spring Regatta

Well, the Caribbean racing circuit is finally over. The Heineken Regatta is but a dim, crushing, Dutch-tinged, garlic-kissed memory. Rolex is over. The BVI Spring has sprung. And Antigua Sailing Weak is now but an apt description of the moral strengths of its participants.

Yes, shore-side reality rears its ugly head once again. Soon local sailors will have to go back to sleeping with their spouses. Even worse, they'll have to check their business cards to remind themselves where they used to work and perhaps, still do. Even their diets will change: having a "Beckfest" in the morning won't be so cool any more.

No, the young girl laughing at your jokes won't be a rail-rider, bilge bunny, or racer-chaser—but your daughter.

No, your wife won't find the term "sail bag" funny.

Sad, eh?

Crossroads Eric won't be the only sober guy in English Harbor again until next year.

Yes, it will be difficult to convince your doctor you weren't on the losing end of gang fight. Only if he's a fellow yachtsman will he recognize your "boat bites" for the "purple badges of courage" that they are.

And, yes, it is easy to have some marital and financial "post-race" problems with your spouse when she discovers that all the money you told her you were spending on gambling, cocaine, and whores…actually was lavished on a new suit of high tech sails.

"How *could* you?" your angry 'better-half' will tearfully lament and then turn sado-cruel, "despite spending our retirement fund on a new Code Zero, still manage a DFL?"

"Well, while it is true that I *was* 'Dead Flip'n Last' in my class," you'll attempt to explain reasonably, "it was a very *close* last. I mean, last year, I couldn't even *see* my second-to-last competitor. While this year, there he was, right on the horizon. But, honey, it isn't strictly about *winning*. It's about sportsmanship, and all the Alpha-male lying and cheating that entails!"

Of course, there is a fierce-if-friendly rivalry between the major yacht racing venues. This year the vowel-challenged Dutch were particularly proud that one of their banks sponsored a global yacht racing winner—and it came to Sint Maarten to race. "We've got one of the Vulva boats," they proudly boasted—which was *very close* to being accurate.

St. Thomas brags it has "doubled" its parking for the Rolex Regatta by adding another space.

Tortola claims "less gun play," which is always nice.

Bequia is attempting to barge in with "better herb." And the Grenada Sailing Fest claims that no competitor will be verbally abused by the rude boys of Hog Island who doesn't deserve it—a noble aim, surely!

The St. Barths Bucket shows just how low a nice event like the old St. Barths Regatta can sink to—*if* regatta organizers foolishly allow participants to be gainfully employed. (Where is "moral-compass" Lou Lou Magras when you need him?)

Foxy still sponsors the Wooden Boat Regatta. But there are so few real "woodies" left, that young guys steering brand new Hunters while chewing toothpicks are demanding to enter.

Oh, for the innocent yacht racing days of yore when Les Anderson's "gafferoni" was considered a modern, hi-tech rule beater!

"I remember the first time someone suggested we shouldn't tow our dinghy during a 'fun' race," said one wise ole Caribbean hand, "which immediately made it less so. Then someone else mentioned rules. Were there any? Oh, dear, it turned out there *was*, and they were complicated—far too complicated to read with your beer goggles on. And, even worse, all the racing marks had to be completed in a particular order and left on a specific side—too, too much, really!"

It is amazing, really, how complicated mankind can make the simplest thing. For instance, picture a caveman standing on a log with his fur vest spread wide—and fast-forward to the Class A protest room on the final night of Antigua Sailing Week.

I know of which I speak. I've been stern-to the Ad Inn during the Awards Ceremony. If looks-of-envy could kill, I'd have been dead within seconds! (Perhaps putting the "Learn To Sail" brochures on our stern pulpit wasn't such a good way to show humility?)

But the fact of the matter is: racing season is over.

We lick our wounds. We plot our revenge. We contact our travel agent to see which rehab center is offering the best chance of bumping into Britney Speers. And we vow aloud to our spouses, "Never again!" while secretly promising ourselves, "Next year we'll win, win, win!"

Fat Family Reunions

There comes a time in any sea gypsy's life when he has to "go home" or be ex-communicated from his family. I gave these two options considerable thought before deciding—knowing how much money I could save in airfare, dental bills, bail, lawyers, shrinks—not to mention the added cost if I happened to bump into a half-bright IRS agent!

Our last "family reunion" involved cops, creeps, and at least one dead body.

One of my nephews attempted suicide by jumping out a window. He's not the sharpest knife in the drawer. It was a ground level window. At worst, he killed the flower bed.

Nobody seemed to have enough energy to bury the dead body. I carried it around for months.

I got arrested for—well, never mind! ("How do you plead?" the judge asked the following morning. "Pathetically?" I quipped. "What time is it?" he then nonchalantly asked the court. "Seven to ten," I quickly replied. "If you smart off one more time, Fatty, that's what you're gonna get!" he quipped back).

I've never liked a judge funnier than me.

No, I don't take these "back to reality" trips to America lightly.

I have to leave my wife, Carolyn, in charge of *Wild Card*. Her "preparations" are a tad disconcerting.

"Do you really need all those cases of Mount Gay?" I asked her. "And why the new six-inch red high heels? Isn't a 55-gallon drum of Stoli on deck, gravity feeding down through the mid-hatch, a bit excessive?"

"Well, you never know," she says gaily. "If *Wild Card* dragged or somethin', I wouldn't want to be short of party supplies!"

Of course, I'm never really out of touch anymore—which is a shame.

Daily, while away from the boat, I e-mail my wife Internet-generated questions like, "What's the 'No-Tell Ho-Tel' credit card charge about? And the deposit marketed 'lap dancing?' ...surely the surgery fees at Nip-N–Tuck were high... and what's the "Property of the Hell's Angels" tattoo charge?"

Needless to say, while in America I have to visit my daughter.

She's kinda—straight. She has a job, a fancy (non-stolen) car, and health insurance. Even worse, she has an IRA.

Her boyfriend goes to church.

"Where did we go wrong," cried Carolyn when she heard that last part.

It is confusing being a parent from the 1960's and counseling a post-millennium daughter.

Example: I didn't realize she was considering going to grad school when she asked me what I thought of "taking an MBA" at Brandeis University.

"Oh, be careful, honey," I warned her, "because a lot of my friends got screwed up on LSD at college!"

Needless to say, I attempted to keep my trip a secret from my fellow sea gypsies. Alas, I knew I'd failed when a "Fellow American In Need" rowed up to *Wild Card* and asked, "Could you bring me back a crankshaft for a FOUR-107?"

"Could you have it 'dropped shipped' to my sister's half-way house," I countered.

"Actually, no," he said. "It is still in the engine, which is still in the boat, which is still under the water. But I don't think it would be too much trouble for you to bring some tools and diving gear, tear down the engine, and hose down the crankshaft with WD-40 when it breaks the surface. Hey, I'd do it for you!"

"Anything else you want," I asked, dryly.

"Yeah, I was gonna ask you to bring me back a bottle of Old Spice cologne, but, hey, I don't want to take advantage of your good nature."

Most of my friends are like that—a handful of gimme and mouthful of "thank you much!"

Carolyn, too, wanted me to bring her something back and gave me a thimble to put it in. "All the WMD's the Bush Administration found in Iraq, please," she said.

"No problem," I said, "and there will be plenty of room left for the Vice President's humility!" (Actually, I gotta admire Cheney! I mean, none of the guys I shot apologized!)

Packing for the trip is another problem. I don't have any regular luggage, so I use the old bag from my mainsail instead.

This shocked a guy on the dinghy dock, when I told him I was gonna go back to my boat and rustle up my old sailbag."

"Yikes!" he said. "If my wife ever heard me say something like that!!!"

Yes, there's no getting around it. I have to go home—despite all logic and common sense.

By the time this story is published I'll be back in America with Morgoo the Magnificent (my younger brother), Blacksnake (my older middle sister), Ms Bligh (my oldest sister) and even the Sea Siren herself, my 86-year-old legally-blind mother. (It's easier to filch money from her purse now!) Uncle Foot will be there. Lovik the Lazy, too. Momo the Astrophysicist. Medicine Dog. Sea Otter. Even a German countess, newly inducted into the Goodlander clan, will attend.

There's only one thing for sure: although we might be in the same room, only a fool would refer to us as together!

Goodlander family reunion Pirate Party 2009

On Being Childish and Childless

It has been a summer of rude shocks, and I don't know which to disbelieve—the laws of genetics or my wife.

The fact is that our daughter Roma Orion not only managed to graduate from Antilles High School, she was the valedictorian of the Class of '98.

One of the teachers ruefully summed it up for the entire faculty when he muttered darkly, "Well, while normally the apple *does* fall fairly close to the tree, occasionally it might get hit by a gust of wind, or roll down hill, or *something*!"

Yes, it is rather difficult (even for me!) to believe that anything I've ever had anything to do with...might succeed anywhere, at anything.

Frankly, the only thing that *I've* been able to consistently achieve is a weird sort of semi-public, semi-comic, semi-amusing failure.

Actually, that's not strictly true. I've been able to maintain an astounding level of poverty, too.

Oh, well. So much for my accomplishments.

My daughter agrees. She says (jokingly, I hope) that the only thing I've taught her is "What not to do!"

In that sense, I guess I *am* a role model.

If all of the above wasn't astounding enough, I got a call from some idiotic telemarketer up in Boston, who is, I think, attempting to sell me some stupid magazine subscriptions or something. He's rattling on about tens of thousands of dollars—like I've just won the Irish Sweepstakes or the

Publisher's Clearing House Sweepstakes. Suddenly, I realize he's legit. He's from Brandeis University, and he's attempting to tell me that my daughter has been awarded their Presidential Scholarship, among other honors.

"Gee," I say, thinking fast. "Over the course of the next four years, this adds up to serious money, doesn't it?"

He agrees it does.

"Have you informed Roma yet?"

"No," he says.

"I understand that you've got a great School of Business at Brandeis," I say, "and that you guys have got some pretty sharp pencils."

He modestly agrees that they do.

"Then how 'bout sending me 15 or 20 grand cash, and just keeping this between me and you?" I ask, crossing my proverbial fingers.

There is a pause. I pray he's seriously considering my enticing offer— but to no avail.

"Surely you're joking, Mister Goodlander." he says, chuckling uneasily.

"Just ask anyone in the *entire Caribbean* if I'm joking!" I sob back at him, as I once again watch a small-fortune-almost-within-my-grasp slip away.

So that's the story. Roma is now at Brandeis University, attempting to learn how to pump the toilets.

"What about an allowance," she asked just before she left.

"Well, hon," I told her. "It's traditional for college students to send their parents fifty dollars a week."

She said she'd do her best, and I believe she will.

"Will it be cold?" she asked.

"Naw," I said, "Not really. If you feel chilly, just ask a fellow student to borrow their coat or something. And remember that wrapping your waist with newspapers can be amazingly effective during a blizzard. And you might want to slip a pair of galoshes over your sandals when it snows."

Roma has been a Caribbean boat-child all her life. Living in a New England dormitory is gonna be a bit of a change.

I remember once (back in the early '80's) drinking with Jean Luke and LouLou Magras at the Le Select bar in St. Barths, when some American tourists wandered in.

"Oh, God!" one of them said in disgust. "There's a baby playing in the dirt on the floor, right there in the corner under that table. And it's eating a chameleon!"

"Damn!" I said with a weary sigh. "And I *told* her not to spoil her dinner."

Once, when she was in second grade at Pine Peace School on St. John, a teacher noted that "everyone has to grow up at some point."

Roma's hand immediately rifled into the air, and responded firmly when called upon, "Not *my* Dad!"

I have a wonderful picture of her on the steps of a church in Hamilton,

Bequia, where she first attended pre-school. She was in the front row, and easy to pick out in the grinning sea of West Indian faces. "Your granddaughter," I wrote to Grandma and Grandpa back in Chicago, "is the one in the yellow shoes."

Once, we saw a charter boat breaking up on a reef. Its life-jacketed crew was terrified. Roma and I hopped in our dinghy, swung alongside, and leapt on deck. "Don't worry," five-year-old Roma said matter-of-factly to calm them. "We do this sort of stuff *all the time!*"

Of course, my most touching memory of Roma was on September 18, 1989, when our vessel began to founder in Hurricane Hugo. We'd told her a million times that evening, "Don't worry, Roma! We're gonna be all right. Don't worry!"

Then another vessel struck ours. Gaping holes in our hull and deck appeared, and water started pouring in, along with 160 knots of howling wind. I remember just how strangely calm Roma was, even though she was only eight-brave-years-old...standing there on that soggy, sinking port bunk with the softly gleaming varnish reflecting ever-so-gently on that vibrating bulkhead. Roma looked so bewildered and lost in her two tightly-wrapped PFD's...holding her man-overboard strobe in front of her, with her zip-locked passport duct-taped to her still-baby-fat belly. She asked in utter amazement, "Can I worry *now*, Dad?"

Yes, parenting is a trip. It is one of the few things in life that truly matter. It is a serious business, which is just another way of saying that it is so important that it must be dealt with laughter and love at every opportunity.

Roma's gone. We miss her.

Roma living and working in Amsterdam

The Savage Truth About
Big Fat Bon Voyage Parties

Generally speaking, members of the marine community of the Lesser Antilles are a diverse, cantankerous bunch of seadogs who seldom agree on anything. However, there are exceptions. Example: me. Almost everyone I've ever met seems to enjoy me going away. For instance, when we left on our previous circumnavigation, hundreds of people partied-hearty for days to see us off. However, our 'welcome back' party was attended by three socially-awkward individuals—two of whom (Oops!) I owed money to... and a third who didn't actually know me... but was in frantic search of a free drink.

I guess that says it all.

This time, since I announced that I'd be gone twice as long, double the number of people showed up at Nipa/Latitude 18 for a "Good-Bye to Bad Rubbish Bash."

Yes, it was a weird collection of sea-creatures. One of the largest tables was commandeered by The Felons. You could tell their most recent graduates by their stripes, prison pallor, and the fact they raised their hands for permission to go to the bathroom. Of course, their 'currently active' members were unable to attend—though I did get a number of Bon Voyage cards with the return address of Club Fed.

The Felons were a relatively fun bunch and very homogenous—all being named Herb. (I overheard them talking about Good Herb, Bad Herb, Primo Herb, Commercial Herb... and numerous other Herbs!)

I also learned another thing while eavesdropping on them: don't be prejudiced. I mean, I thought they'd be sort of hardened folks, but no, most of them were pussy cats. One of them nearly broke into tears when I snapped his photograph. "That's the first time anyone has ever taken a picture of me, Fatty—you know, without the numbers!"

Yes, it was a wonderfully diverse crowd that showed up. Everybody had a story and most weren't shy about spewing it. "Did I ever tell you about the time Jack Daniels threw me outta my dinghy?" asked one Lagoonie.

Another Lagoonie was haranguing everyone about being 'rideless' because his dinghy overheated attempting to made it up the hill between IBY and the East End, and, more bad luck, his car had immediately sunk when he drove it off the dinghy dock. "Some days you just can't win," he said gloomily.

We were having a gay old time watching the wild and crazy geriatric crew of *Zulu Warrior* gyrating on the dance floor. Yes, it is always trouble when the *Zulus* go on the warpath: I remember once in the 1960's when they got thrown out of the Bitter End... not an easy task in those days... and now they were at it again.

Yeah, I knew it was going to be trouble when I spied the *Zulu* skipper pounding down a six-pack of Geritol... while sneaking shots of Jagermeister in between! Finally, I captured the *Zulus* and introduced them to my 'pink topsider' friends. "Ah," said Brucey, "so she's a dyke?"

"No," I said, attempting to clarify things. "Her husband is a Dyke. She's an Inga!"

"Whatever!" he lisped, then turned to me and asked, "Buy me a drink, sailor?"

"Well, no," I said and pulled my (custom-sewn, additional) empty pockets out to prove it. "Actually, I'm so broke I can't even—pay attention!"

"That's alright," he cooed in my ear. "I can't even *think* straight!"

"Carolyn," I shouted at my wife across the room, "Help!"

This took place a matter of days before we shoved off on our second circumnavigation—which was a big topic of conversation during the party.

"Where are you planning on visiting," asked Independent Pieter.

"Well," I said, putting on my 'serious circumnavigator' face and dropping my voice an octave. "I think we'll avoid the islands we borrowed money at during our previous circumnavigation and, hopefully, go to islands that have wealthier folks who are even *more* gullible!"

Judy and Her Brain (sp?) were there. She's off the charter yacht *Small Bear*. She used to be the executive director of the VILC (Virgin Islands Libidinous Charterers) but has calmed down now that the tide has turned, century-wise.

Anyway, she and her Brain are talking about circumnavigating season-after-next and, thus, were quizzing Carolyn on the finer points of provisioning.

"After filling the boat with Cruzan," Carolyn said, "stuff cans of Dinty Moore wrapped-in-socks to prevent the bottles from rattling in a gale."

"I never thought of that," Judy said, and then turned to her Brian, "see how useful it is to get advice from *real* circumnavigators?

Davis Murray was there, singing "Rum is the Answer, What is the Question?" and "Junk in the Truck." His Pillsbury Jam band also included Chicago Conrad and Morgan-the-Magnificent on Pan. (During the Police Riot of 1968 Conrad and I were tear-gassed by the same canister. Ah, the sweet memories of our rabble-rousing, radical youth!)

Many people asked me "When do you shove off?" I gave each one my stock reply: "Next week!"

Actually, of course, I planned on staying as long as the Fat Farewell Parties continued. I mean, why sail away when they're still buying you free drinks?

The Reverend/Captain showed up. I'd lost track of him in Oz (Australia). He'd once been the captain of the notorious *Miss Piggy* of AYH. One time on a delivery from St. Thomas to Florida, his GPS went out and he was (alas!) forced into Antigua (for Sailing Week) and Jamaica (for Sunsplash)... before (lucky, eh?) finding the loose wire.

He'd become a mail-order Rev to break into the marriage business... but that fell through because he kept offering to test-drive the bride. (This wasn't a problem when she refused, but was a *very big problem* when she agreed!)

So he ended up keeping his Divinity Degree with his skip's papers—hoping that local Customs and Immigration officials would not see fit to charge any harbor dues to a vessel engaged in His business!

This, too, was an economic failure, but resulted in him being known affectionately throughout the Caribbean as the Reverend/Captain. (Not to be confused with Ed Hamilton and the Ministry of Rhum—a totally different hustle!)

Where were we? Ah, yes, my Blow-Out Blowing-Out-of-Town Party.

Thai Tom was there, reliving his wild Phuket R&R daze as a globe-trotting petroleum engineer in Borneo. Tugboat Tom had a lovely lass with a great... attitude... in tow. Timmy Carstarphen was duck'n and a'weaving. "Stemhead Dave" Dostal took a few minutes off from chopping holes in *Rob Roy*. Marine artist Les Anderson showed up with a girl who could remember her name. ("...just give her time," Les said, "she'll get it, yessiree!")

Kiwi Brett, one of the Caribbean sailors most noted for his cheapness, surprised me by giving Carolyn and me some used docklines. (It was a nice gesture, even though they were far too short to be of much use).

A couple of other people slipped me ten or twenty dollar bills to "...buy your wife dinner in the Pacific." But, hey, I figure what she doesn't know won't hurt her!

I didn't sit down once the whole evening, instead mingling with our guests while muttering, "Gee, it is hot in here... sure makes a sailor thirsty!"

Plus, I didn't stand still because there were a number of 'prior business associates' of mine attempting to bend my ear about ancient history and other unimportant stuff. "What happened to my money? Did you co-sign that cashier's check as Admiral Obese?" shouted one. "Do you have my wife's e-mail address?" shouted another. A third just abbreviated his remarks with, "I told the IRS you were an SOB on LSD. So now you're SOL!"

A lot of our guests were puzzled by why we wore our heavy weather gear—many mistakenly thought we were just being stylish. But it wasn't that. We know our friends, and just wanted to be prepared. "You go chat with the guy drooling in the corner," I told Carolyn, "I'll touch base with the spitter at the bar!"

Yes, it was a fine evening. A few of our guests said they got home alright, and the majority said the mosquitoes weren't too bad on the beach. (The tropical sun is *such* a dependable alarm clock!)

Of course, we'd still be there, and still be having the Final, Final, Absolutely Final, Last Going Away parties—except that the VI government stepped in.

I received a tip from a friend/informant at the Department of Licensing and Consumer Affairs, that if I had one more going away party—and didn't actually leave the Territory—I'd be arrested for fraud.

"Well, that's it," I told Carolyn. "It looks like we're outta here on the next tide!"

"...you mean, we're gonna..."

"Yes," I shouted aft to her as I hauled up our anchor, "we're going to go somewhere else to wear out our welcome!"

Getting Off On Shoving Off

I've read enough dusty cruising books to know exactly how you're supposed to begin an offshore voyage: careful planning, careful preparation, and careful execution are just a few of the prudent ingredients for a trouble-free passage. "Plan the sail and sail the plan," the cruising experts wisely say. And it is difficult to argue with such wonderful logic.

However, I'm not a "reasonable" person, so argue I will.

First off, I've found that the "experts" seldom go to sea. Second, I've found they often don't know what they are talking about. Third, I find that, generally, free advice is worth exactly what you pay for it.

I mean—only a fool would waste their time giving advice to an idiot like me, right?

Here's the hard reality of it: Shoving off isn't easy. It requires a lot of TLC.

"Ah," you say. "You prepare your vessel with Tender Loving Care, eh!" No. TLC stands for Treachery, Lying, and Cheating.

First off, politely ask all the people to whom you owe money, to meet with you—about a week after you plan on leaving. (This will cut down on distractions during your preparations.)

Landlubbers often don't understand the whole concept of being a sea gypsy or leaving on an extended cruise. I've found that it's best to make up some stupid story to tell them, no matter how foolish or illogical it may sound.

"I'm going to Haiti to look for a job," is a good one. Or "I'm going to Trinidad to ward off hurricanes by attempting to drink all the rum in South America!" is another of my favorites. Married men sailing away from their wives often use the tried-and-true "I've heard the women of Venezuela have loose morals, and I'm going to do everything humanly possible to find out if that's really true!"

Of course, many sea gypsies like myself spend the vast majority of their money on booze, broads, and—I, er, forget what the third one is. Anyway, this means that we often don't have all the expensive offshore safety gear we'd like to have.

But, happily, the fact of the matter is that there are a lot of rich yachtsmen in this world who have tons of marine safety gear, which they just don't, alas, have to time to use—because of their crushing corporate work load. They would truly love to have their safety gear field tested by a real sailor in real sailing conditions, but are just too timid and ashamed to ask.

So, to help out these "too-much-money, not-enough-time" guys, I just "borrow" things like EPIRBS, PFDs, MOB poles, strobe lights, life rafts, and flare kits; on the pretext of "seeing how they'd mount on my boat". Then, I conveniently forget to return them before I depart. (I don't steal them. Once they cease working, I send 'em back!)

I've never been able to afford nautical charts, but I get around that by having a globe aboard, and using a magnifying glass for coastal work and a microscope for entering harbors.

Of course, I'm not one of those "type A" guys who have a specific destination in mind when I shove off. I'm usually headed for, say, the next bar—assuming that it isn't to windward, of course.

Provisioning isn't a problem. I eat mostly beans and rice offshore, spiced by an occasional roach which might blunder by.

Everything on my boat does double-duty. For instance, I keep both Don Street's and Chris Doyle's cruising guides on a convenient shelf in the smallest cabin of my yacht—right alongside my porcelain throne. But I sure wish they'd make the pages of their books softer, I'll tell ya!

There are lots of other ways to cruise on the cheap. If my main sail rips, I tuck a reef into it if the tear is near the bottom. Or I instantly convert my boat to a gaffer if the tear is near the top.

My electrical needs are small. If I have enough 12-volt power to run my

Pina Colada blender, I'm happy.

It's best to check your batteries before heading offshore. If, when you take off the caps, you see a fluid, that means your batteries are "full of juice" and you'll have no problems.

Courtesy flags—absolutely! If anyone gives me 'em, I fly 'em in appreciation.

I don't believe in anchor lights, since I'm familiar enough with the gear on my foredeck to be able to work in the dark.

Ditto, radios. I simply don't believe in them. First off, many Search and Rescue agencies are more intent on getting another plant leaf plastered on the side of their vessel than in saving lives. Also, while many 'Good Samaritan' type people are interested in life-saving in general, very few are interested in saving me.

That's right; I've had many enthusiastic rescuers suddenly lose interest when they realized it was ole Cap'n Fatty himself shot-gunning out yet another mayday call! (When the USCG asks for your name and the name of your vessel, that's so they can weed out another one of my "Help I'm out of Coco Lopez and nutmeg" distress calls.)

Insurance. This is one thing I don't skimp on. I prefer the lubricated ones, in the blue foil.

The bottom line is: people won't miss you unless you go away. (Alas, in my case; not even then.)

Shoving off is tough. You have to get stern with yourself. I say to myself, "Okay, Fatty! It is now time to stop being an incompetent fool ashore, and begin to be one offshore!"

This somehow reassures me. But it might not have the same effect on you.

The important part is, like the ad says, "Just Do It!"

Cast off—even if it means telling your friends to kiss off! Cut your umbilical cord to civilization! Go fer it!

Remember: you're not just sailing into the future; you're also sailing away from all those desk-bound creditors!

YESSSS!

How the Experts Do It
or
A Perfect First Leg

Somehow I became, despite all logic and common sense, an "internationally respected marine expert." How? Well, I think it was a combination of four things:

    1.) I was blissful—in the "ignorance is bliss" sense,
    2.) I didn't know what I was talking about,
    3.) I didn't know that I didn't know... and, frankly,
    4.) I didn't care.

Let's put it another way: the only two jobs I've ever had were ditch-digger and marine writer. And the ditch-digging tended to cut into my drinking time. Thus, I ended up an "award-winning marine journalist."
    Stupid, eh?

You have no idea how stupid! Example: the last two weeks of my life.
    "Shouldn't we... er... work on *Wild Card* a bit before we sail her around the world again?" asked my long suffering wife, Carolyn.
    Carolyn is like that. Always nagging. A worry-wart. And, worse, a complainer: "The boat is out of water/diesel/rum," she whines. "I don't have any shoes" she laments. "Could I have five dollars to provision for six

month across the Pacific?" she begs.

Yes, it is always "a drama" with that woman.

Sometimes she makes me regret I am, as one Old Flame delicately put it, a "raging heterosexual."

"Don't insult the vessel," I yawed back at Carolyn as I fluffed my salt-encrusted pillow and resumed my after-lunch nap. "*Wild Card* is fine. Tip-top! Bristol! Cherry! Lloyds A-1! Way-cool!"

Frankly, my vessel looks like a bomb went off. I never do anything to her—except deep-six all the crap that falls outta the rig—because I'm too busy telling other people how to maintain their pristine Hinkleys, Swans, and Little Harbors.

"What story were you working on between your mid-morning snooze and your afternoon nap," Carolyn recently asked me.

"An article on gold-leaf," I muttered.

"I didn't know you'd actually ever gold-leafed anything," she said.

"Well," I admitted, "you might be right. But, hey, it can't be that hard, can it? I mean, you just smear the gold-leaf over your genitals."

"I think, my dear," Carolyn said gently, "that 'fig-leaf' is what you're thinking about."

"Really?" I said, mouth agape and hand-on-chin in consternation. "Perhaps more 'diligent research' is in order, eh?"

"Yes," she said, "and, anyway, it is time to get up."

"What?" I said. "But I'm just getting comfortable napping!"

"But you wouldn't want to miss dinner, would you?"

"No, indeed," I said briskly, as I swung my feet onto the cabin sole. "You know how goal-oriented I am."

Where was I? Ah, yes. The last few weeks of boat-nightmare.

We left St. John on our around-the-world trip and got as far as Christmas Cove—about two miles away.

"Not a long passage," Carolyn noted, "but a good one."

"It was rough in the middle," I reminded her. "Some of those wavelets were sort of sloppy. Current Cut is aptly named. I didn't actually deploy our Para-Tech sea anchor, true, but don't think I wasn't considering it!"

The real reason we pulled into Christmas Cove was because our exhaust system was leaking.

"That's allowing poisonous gas to get belowdecks," I told Carolyn. "We can't have that. Brain damage can result."

"You're handsome, kind, and a good wage-earner," she said to me dreamily.

"Drat!" I said, "Too late!"

There was a tiny pin-hole in the galvy exhaust pipe. But, alas, the entire section turned to rust-dust when I touched it with a putty-knife of wet Marine Tex. (Couldn't they make the Marine Tex mixture less stiff, for gosh sakes?)

Thus, because of the ridiculous stiffness of Marine Tex, I had to replace my entire exhaust system from transom thru-hull to diesel manifold.

"There!" I shouted triumphantly as I wiped my greasy hands off on a copy of The Watchtower magazine which I carry for just such a purpose. "Thank you, Lord! Now we're ready to sail around the world!"

"Aren't we gonna sea-trial the repair," Carolyn asked. "I mean, take a little ten minute shake down cruise?"

"Ye of Little Faith," I scolded her. "Honey, when I fix something, it's fixed. F-I-X-E-D! As in, like, forever! Cast off, okay?"

Alas, I was wrong. Slightly. Well, okay, a lot wrong. The brand new Fat-engineered exhaust system leaked worse than the old one. In fact, it had more leaks that the White House! Fumes poured out one end, saltwater leaked out the loose joints at the other. This required reassembling the entire mess twice. The final time was at sea becalmed off the north coast of Columbia, while slowing drifting sideways through a fleet of mid-sized, blacked-out freighters being loaded with drugs.

"Are you sure we're safe here," Carolyn asked, as we wrestled with our monkey wrenches. "I mean, I know you say the deck guards on the boats around us are waving welcome. But I could swear they're waving us away with those Uzis!"

"Hey," I told her, "don't be prejudiced just because their faces are covered in scars, topsides riddled with bullets, and their vessel's name is written in duct tape. After all, we're rabid capitalists too!"

Finally, we fixed the exhaust system and went putt-putting away. To celebrate, I decided to have a drink, placed it on the coffee table/engine box, and tossed in an olive.

It tossed the olive back out.

"What the hell?" I said.

"Yeah," Carolyn concurred. "Ain't the boat vibrating a bit more than usual?"

It was. Very much. Being in the boat with the engine running was like attempting to live within—a paint shaker!

"Damn," I said as I threw open the engine compartment and observed the engine attempting to jump off its beds with each piston thrust. "We've got a loose engine flange mount."

This required re-aligning the engine. We do this as a team. Carolyn places a .0005 inch feeler gauge between the prop flanges while I hit the engine with a ten pound sledge.

"Did it move," I asked her.

"Yeah," she said. "About a yard. But I think to ultimately get the engine to stop vibrating excessively under load, we're gonna have to move it less than a yard at a time—say, even less than a foot at a time."

"Hey," I pouted, "I can't help it if I'm all-man!"

Finally we got it aligned. Hooray! And the exhaust still didn't leak. Yahoo! We felt we were pretty-much home free—until we looked at the temperature gauge.

It was leaning to the right, and Carolyn didn't like it.

"Hey," I said, "Sure, it was middle-of-the-road when I installed it during the Clinton administration. But it is an American instrument on an American yacht, and Dubya is president now, and everything is leaning to the Far Right!"

"Don't be silly, Fatty," she said. "When was the last time you replaced the impeller?"

"Let's see," I said. "New Zealand, maybe? I mean, it was definitely after the millennium!"

Carolyn wouldn't accept any mealy-mouthed excuses and forced me to "whip out" the impeller.

"It looks okay to me," I said as I handed it to her. "Both blades are still attached."

"You idiot, Fatty," she screamed. "It is supposed to have six blades, not just two! It is a miracle the diesel ran at all! Why did you wait so long to replace it?"

"Laziness?" I mused. "Cheapness? Stupidity? All-of-the-above?"

Finally we pulled into the Canal Zone and were soon belly-up to the Panama Canal Yacht Club bar.

"I'll have a Jack Daniels, *por favor*" Carolyn shouted at the bartender, "and a Shirley Temple for the wimp I'm with!"

I was just about to dream up a scathing & clever retort when I was stopped in mid-formulation by a fan.

"I just wanted to tell you, Mister Goodlander," the smiling yacht-attired guy said, "how much I enjoy your marine articles, especially the technical ones."

I felt Carolyn slump beside me, and heard her mutter, "Mister Goodlander?"

"Thank you," I told the guy, and then added brightly, "after all, most voyages fail before the boat ever leaves the dock. Preventive maintenance is the key, really, and by preventive maintenance I mean...."

I didn't allow it to stop me, but I could hear Carolyn shouting loudly at the bartender, "Make it a double, *Senor*, and bring me a pair of earplugs too!"

Sailing Away from Home

Maori warrior in New Zealand greeting visiting cruiser Ron Newell of s/v Rontu

We've been gone from the Virgin Islands for over six months now, and I'm starting to feel it. Like when I telephone back to St. John, "Fat who?" they ask. "Are you sure you have the right number?"

My own mother is the same way. When I ring her up—say, every millennium or so—she says, "Who? No, I don't want any diet pills!"

America is beginning to fade. Sure, people tell me stuff like; the president is mad because he can't torture people; but, hey, I don't believe them.

I attempt to keep up. I buy *Playboy, Hustler,* and other American cultural mags. But still, I feel the social fabric of America gradually slipping away from me.

Thank God for DVD's! If not for the *Sopranos,* I'd have completely lost touch with New Jersey!

And 50 Cent's new movie *Get Rich or Die Try'n!* is, in many ways, the perfect American Export for the Third World.

But some of the news items seem too ghoulish for even a gullible person such as myself to believe. I mean, nobody really stole Alistair Cook's bones, did they? (Wow! What a "Letter from America" that would make on the BBC!)

There's a lot of stuff I can't figure out. How did Bob Dylan, who was famous for forty years for not uttering a single coherent word, suddenly get so chatty?

There was actually a paragraph in his latest book that, if you read it a few times, made sense. And I saw a teaser for Martin Scorsese's new DVD bio on the net in which Dylan muttered something like "Where's my socks?" which was, again, completely understandable and not obscure.

Boy, you can't depend on anything or anybody anymore!

We're currently cruising in New Zealand. It is funny how much of the local news parallels the international.

For instance, there is a sizable minority of people here who feel they've been ripped off, marginalized, and discriminated against. While the majority can't seem to figure out why they are whining and complaining so much about being merely ripped off, marginalized, and discriminated against!

But when you are cruising-without-end, year-after-year; you do, indeed, start to have a slightly "bent" perspective on world affairs.

I mean, if the French Quarter really wanted more FEMA funds, couldn't they rename themselves the Freedom Quarter?

Solutions like this seem so easy—when you are 10,000 miles away.

Of course, since I'm a bit of an infamous fellow I often get interviewed by foreign reporters as we circumnavigate. Sometimes the subtle meaning of what I say gets, well, "lost in translation" so to speak.

"Do you often have friends visit you aboard *Wild Card*?" I was recently asked by an inquisitive Kiwi National Radio journalist. So when I blurted out, "All my friends have visited me!" Well, only people who know me well would realize that means never.

The trick is, for a true sea gypsy, not to get too lax. I mean, I have to (darn, I hate work!) occasionally make sure my checks are being auto-deposited via the internet, my fan club knows how to accept donations on my behalf, and (lucky me!) young girls know where to e-mail those naughty pics of themselves!

Yes, it is "attention to detail" where most yachties fall short. How do you make sure that any stray money finds you—but no bill collectors?

It's a challenge, believe me.

There are medical issues, too. I'm getting older; there is no question about that. For instance, yesterday while watching my wife hoist our dinghy aboard, I got eye-strain!

Darn.

My job is taking more and more of my time; especially the photo-journalist part of it. Doctoring all my pics with Photoshop—adding hair, whitening my teeth, reducing my "waste" line, unsagging my buttocks, uncrossing my eyes, drying up the drooling—all takes oodles of hours, I'll tell you!

Oh, it is easy to believe an ocean-jaunting, ocean-jotting writer like myself has the Life of Riley. But the reality is a tad different. Sure, I've got buckets of money stashed all over the boat, but no; it never seems to be the right currency!

Most people have no idea of the problems I face. Take my passport, for instance. It is bulging with stamps, visas, and worse. Did you know many countries have stamps for bail-jumpers, deportees, dead-beats, womanizers, and tax cheats?

Neither did I.

Ditto, my vessel documentation. I'm astounded by the number of countries that reject my ship's papers merely because the expiry date of 1998 has been XXXed out—and the current year written in with crayon. (Gee, I hate government burly-crats, don't you?)

And things expire! I just had to renew my FCC SSB license—and my VHF license—and my EPIRB license—thank God my poetic one didn't expire as well!

Seriously! It cost me $155 US to "internet renew" all the above, and the end result will be that somebody I used to know, like, a hundred years ago, and conned into telling me their address (probably when we were drunk) is gonna get a little note in the mail that says, "Thanks, Fat Man, for the cash!"

Who knows what address the FCC is using? My old reform school's PO Box? That half-arse Half Way House in Brooklyn? The hot-sheet hotel in Bangkok? General delivery, Cali? The bartender at the Whip & Chain in Amsterdam?

The sad fact is: Governments the world over want you to live somewhere. Basically, they want your cell number. And if you don't give 'em one, they get suspicious. (Yes, I realize "cell number" has one written and one spoken meaning—that's why I reject both.)

Part of the problem that I have as an "international marine writer of some repute" is that people are always meeting me, who have grown to know me through my writing. They are either too slow and/or too illiterate to realize I'm not a nice guy!

This is troubling.

Every time I pull into a dock in South America, Asia, or Africa and someone yells, "I love your writing!" Carolyn mutters underneath her breath, "Loser!"

But, life flows, and so it goes. We sail on. And on. And on. Occasionally, we bump into land masses and wander ashore to amuse the locals. Bits fall off our boat and we glue them back, sort of. When money is needed, I scribble.

And, occasionally, people in uniform ask us questions and we do our best to answer with a straight face.

It sounds crazy. But for us—this is maturity.

Cybersailing With Modern Nav Equipment

I've recently "gone modern" with my navigational equipment. In fact, I've installed *"The Skipper"* charting device on my shipboard laptop PC.

Many of its features are absolutely dazzling; for instance, its nautical drink recipes. Click on St. John (Virgin Islands), and it tells you the proper ingredients for a Pina Colada. Click on St. Johns (Nova Scotia), and it instructs you on making a hot toddy.

Ain't computers wonderful?

What I mean to say is—that mariners shouldn't consider porn the *only* reason to buy a computer.

As I get older, I enjoy interfacing with my computer. (Of course, when I was younger I was a more "hands on" person than I am now—thus my daughter.)

There are three main ingredients for successful computing: your hardware (computer), software (computer program), and wetware (brain).

I figure, well, two outta three ain't too bad. Although I must admit that I found it kinda funny that my new computer has *twice* as much memory as my old machine, while my wife has only half the memory she once did! (I've told her this joke a million times, but she *still* doesn't remember it.)

When I purchased my computer, I told the salesman it was for a marine application. Besides jacking up the price about a thousand dollars, he asked me, "Is your bridge humidity controlled?"

I told him, fibbing slightly, that it was. (Occasionally sheets of salt spray, minor bilge sloshes, and small waves crash over my nav station—but they're in God's control, not mine.)

Here is an important cyber-savvy tip: don't use the standard Windows95 operating software for a marine application. It can't stand up to the salt air. Instead, buy Microsoft's Porthole96, version 3.1.

The main reason I purchased the computer, software, and GPS interface for my nav station is so that I can be guaranteed of never losing a boat again. (I may sink it on some rocks, but, *by God*, I'll know exactly where the damn thing is!)

A lot of the features on "The Skipper" are optional.

For instance, I have no need for the "Drug Smuggler" option, but it does give good advice. (#1: When in doubt, flush! #2: Don't leave any copies of Hunter Thompson's books in plain view when the USCG boards your vessel. #3: Even if your boat is ferro-cement, don't name it something stupid like *Stoned Again*, etc.)

The software even has ethnic and cultural toggles. For instance, if the sun is extremely hot and you are British, it tells you to put on a hat. If you are American, it tells you to put back on your sailing shorts. If you are French, it requests you put sun block on your whatchamacallit, instead of putting back on your sailing shorts. If you are Dutch, it suggests that you to ask a mate to get the sun block.

The whole idea here is for the computer to be "user friendly." Amazingly enough, even the Caribbean models are.

Another useful feature is the log: every day while south of 20N and east of 65W, my log automatically is updated to read, "Got up, got drunk, went back to bed!"

The shipboard inventory control feature is another computerized marvel. For instance, within 44 minutes of typing the words "toilet paper" into my computer... it told me I had three slightly soggy sheets aboard, at inventory control point r3~f44333. Within the hour, I'd discovered in my software documentation that inventory control point r3~f44333 was the nearly empty spool just to the left of my (alas, odious) Groco toilet bowl.

Thank gosh, for Bill Gates, huh?

The software program even prompts you for routine maintenance tasks. Daily it tells me to "polish head seat," weekly to "pump head," monthly to "change shorts," and annually to "throw overboard IRS form 1040."

It also includes a "people and places" note-taking area to keep track of all the new friends you make while cruising. Mine reads, "Lusty Laura; Le Select, St. Barths" and "Tipsy Tina; Yacht Haven, St. Thomas" and, unfortunately, "Tina's Husband, nick-named, incorrectly, Tiny; Roy L. Schneider Hospital, ER!"

I'd love to be able to review the "StormTraker" (V4.0) option for you, dear reader. But my own copy appears to be defective. At least I *hope* it is defective. Because no matter where I place my yacht on the North Atlantic chart, all the major hurricanes seem to steer a rhumb line course straight for it!

Perhaps the best part is that the software helps to steer my vessel when I'm not at the helm. "God damn it, Carolyn!" it bellows at my wife via an extremely loud .wav file, "More to port!" Or, "Starboard, you salt-stained sea-swine! *STARBOARD!*"

It does a number of other diverse tasks, too. Wanna know the difference between deviation and variation? One is a small men's magazine, while the other is frowned upon even more!

Tide? Separate colors and don't use too much bleach for the best washing results.

Current? For instance, all you have to do is keyboard in the current date, and the *very year that you do so* will be displayed in large block letters on your computer screen!

Fall overboard? If you've a long enough phone extension, just dial up your local ISP (internet service provider), log on, type in the USCG's complete HTTP address—and then terminate your original float plan! Easy, eh?

The system also helps to keep me up to date on important, significant geo-political happenings. For instance, how many Caribbean yachtsmen know that the Prime Meridian has been moved to the town of Redmond in the State of Washington? (At least, according to Admiral Gates it has!)

Many computer programmers have a delightful sense of humor. For instance, my nav computer, once submerged beyond ten feet of depth, will sing out brightly, "Game over! Game over!"

How do I know?

To find out, e-mail me at MEFATTY@WASTINGTIME.NET or visit my web site at HTTP://DONTBEFOOLEDSTUPID.COM

Deviant Decadent DVD Dunces

Instead of watching movies, Fatty learns kava pounding in Fiji

Tonight are the Academy Awards and I have a horrible confession to make: I like to watch movies. I know, I know—I'm supposed to be a rugged offshore guy who has escaped from the brain-numbing media madness of America. But the sad, sick truth is—(sob!)—I like James Bond.

Weirdly, circumnavigating on a small sailboat is a *perfect* lifestyle for the movie-maddened and/or flick-afflicted. Virtually every cruising boat has a DVD player these days, and now swapping these are as common as wives used to be in the 1960's! (Why can't I resist writing stuff like that?)

In Fiji, a first-run movie that is so new most New Yorkers haven't seen it yet, costs 85 cents. This seems strange, as the disk it is written on costs a buck each at the local office supply.

Of *course* I worry about copyright issues. In fact, whenever I purchase software in a Third World country I have the salesperson assure me they're going to give some of the money to Bill Gates. With movies, ditto Spielberg. Yes, I think everyone should do their part. (As the royalty-receiving author of four books, I also advocate fire-bombing libraries—because, well, I like to be both intellectually consistent and legally fair!)

We happened to be in Bangkok once when a US trade envoy visited. The result of this was that the Thai cops had to rush down to the six story mall that sells pirated movies and software—and sternly ordered them not to do so for the next couple of hours. The venders, taking the long view, complied. However, being good Buddhists, they also had the entire mall "disinfected" from evil spirits the next day because of the unfortunate, atypical law enforcement pulse.

Now I'm not saying *all* boaters watch pirated movies. Josh Slocum didn't. There may be others, too.

In Fiji, they really go all out. They not only "strip" the region code off the DVD's, they often offer "shrunk" versions as well. Thus it is possible to get 12 TV shows (of lesser quality) on the same DVD for the same price. (Yes, capitalism is weird in the Third World.) This figures out to less than a dime a *Soprano* episode—or mere pennies per wack job!

Many primitive communities watch DVD's communally—to share the energy costs of the tribal generator. Needless to say, they are proud of how "modern" they are, and always invite foreign visitors to join them. Thus we often watch episodes of *Desperate Housewives* or *Sex in the City* with large groups of popcorn-less, HBO-less tribal peoples—and have to explain the jokes.

This isn't easy—just try explaining what a "metro-sexual" is to an outback Aborigine! Former cannibals consider *Six Feet Under* wasteful. *Law and Order* fans are puzzled why there is so little of either. *The King and I* (either version) can still get your boat confiscated in Thailand. It's gotten to the point that I only watch Kung Fu movies in such communal situations; movies in which a kick-in-the-crotch doesn't have to be culturally parsed.

No, it isn't easy explaining some movies. I've stopped sharing one of my very favorite movies (*Memento*) because Asian people keep insisting it is broke. ("It is *not* broke!" I shout at them, and sigh when they politely reply, "Yes, broke-broke, Cap'n Fatty Boy! Play same-same over and over again—broke-broke, yes?"

Grrrrrrrrrrrrrrrr!

The Wire is another one they find puzzling. "Who is good guys?" they ask. "It's Baltimore," I reply, "there *are* no good guys!"

"But who are law-breaking, drug-sucking murderers?"

"Everyone!" I moan, "That's the point!"

Entourage is another HBO production they have trouble with. "Nothing ever happens—just yak-yak-yak," they complain. "And what is famous movie star famous for?"

"It's California," I regionalize, "where wise-cracking and/or following the career of Paris Hilton are *both* considered legit professions. Besides, lots of people in America today are just famous for being famous—not for anything else."

Yes, Hollywood is a powerful myth-generator. I've been asked a few times why America just doesn't send Sylvester Stallone or the governor of California to Iraq and be done with it.

There is no question it's a topsy-turvy world. My sailing buddies Lin and Larry Pardey are making more on their DVD sales than on their book royalties. I mean, who knew the path to "modern sailing stardom" required knowing how to diagram a sentence *and* apply saltwater resistant make-up!

And there's a lot of confusion about the entertainment industry in the Third World. Example: when I tried to tell them about Vice-president Al Gore's *Inconvenient Truth*—well, they asked if the movie actually showed him having sex with Monica Lewinsky. "No," I sputtered, "you got the wrong guy. This was our *vice* president!"

"Oh, yes-yes, so-so sorry," they say. "The VP who shoots the guy in the face and makes the pellet-face guy apologize. They show the actual shotgun blast in this *Inconvenient* movie?"

It is enough to make you cry.

"No, the plot of *Grey's Anatomy* isn't taken from the book, for gosh sakes!"

"They don't call it *LOST* because that's what happened to the plot!"

"The mafia has *nothing* to do with opera," I whimper, "and stool pigeons aren't found either in parks *nor* bathrooms!!!!!!!!!!!!!!!!!!!!!!!!"

Of course, occasionally Third World viewers surprise you with the accuracy of their savvy insights. Example: at the end of *Blood Diamond* when the dark fella gets to keep the stone, wear a tailored suit, *and* gets a round of applause from the Brits; an African friend of ours laughed, "Now *that's* Hollywood!

Head Aches
or
There are no Plumbers at Sea

Roma with the Snot Club Regatta Bowl

    Holding tanks are, for better or worse, a reality. We have one aboard *Wild Card*—plumbed for a variety of ecological, practical, and legal considerations. I wish we didn't. However, we do. Thus we have to deal with it. However, living in a confined space with a holding tank isn't easy nor fun. It's nose-wrinklingly tough. The sad scientific fact is that every living thing produces waste. Or, to put it more sailor-succinctly, "s**t happens."

    Wild Card is a very small, narrow boat which cannot comfortably carry a lot of weight—which is why I'm not exactly overjoyed at the prospect of occasionally having 20 gallons more effluent aboard than fresh water.

    I mean, I like irony as much as the next sailor but when my wife,

Carolyn, says, "The bad news is we're out of water, the good news is we have ten gallons of urine." I'm not exactly laughing.

The saddest part is that in "de outer islands of de Turd World" where we like to cruise, the diesel fuel we buy is often—well, it occasionally appears to be, dirtier and more polluted than the stuff in our holding tanks.

"Could we save money by cross-plumbing them?" Carolyn quipped.

I shot back, "Cut the crap!"

The vast majority of holding tanks are made of that white plastic stuff that is completely watertight—but not, alas, odor-tight. Evil marine scientists have formulated a special "odor-oozing" plastic to accomplish this. The bottom line: if you are not sure exactly which your spouse is doing in the head, time to replace the holding tank and its hoses.

Sound is another problem. If a shaft-bearing in one of our 12-volt cabin fans corrodes and starts to shriek, we don't oil it, we transfer the noisy unit into the head. This is much more convenient than carrying a small transistor radio that suddenly blares the BBC at odd moments.

There are, of course, legal considerations. In many countries there is a "zero discharge" policy. I abide by this as best I'm able. But not all ocean rovers do. "Arrest that mammal," I shouted to Carolyn as I peered suspiciously at the white-splotched wake of a passing whale. "Can't he visit a pump-out station like the rest of his species?"

I'll never forget the first time I—well, "availed" myself of a pump-out station's services. I was ditch-crawling the ICW and it was a Sunday afternoon at the fuel dock. Lots of week-end warriors were there to gawk at the passing yachts. For some perverse reason, the large hose was clear plastic. People gathered around, curious. Once I started pumping, a guy peered at the hose closely, pointed a finger that moved slowly with the flow, and said smugly, "Corn!"

"Oh, gross!" Carolyn lamented as she stomped belowdecks.

Some countries allow overboard discharge offshore. This requires a toxic octopus of hoses, valves, tees, and clamps. Usually, a large diaphragm hand-pump is involved. Here-again I'm not exactly sure how the evil scientists do it, but somehow they orient the pump so that any diaphragm leak—gets you in the eye.

Yes, you can use an electric impeller pump for this purpose, but I don't find them dependable—especially for "golden-oldie" cruisers. If you insist on using a pump of this design, lubricate it daily with prune juice, once removed.

And it is absolutely amazing what unexpected "marine-thingies" manage to sadistically leap into the head. Of course, to prevent this we try to remember to leave the toilet seat cover down, but it is easy to forget. Obviously, for ventilation, we keep the head hatch open as much as possible. Of course, I wasn't thinking of any of the above while I recently furled our mainsail after a day sailing. I searched around the cabin top for the lost sail-tie—one of those "Sea Ties" that consist of a shock cord with one end a loop and the other a wooden toggle. Nor did I recognize the white cord peering out from the toilet bowl flapper. I just gingerly bent down and grabbed the cord with crab-claw-fingers and a strained grimace, and pulled. And pulled. And pulled. Until suddenly the hardwood toggle became unjammed—and sling-shotted itself into the center of my horrified, dented, brown-dripping forehead.

"I had no idea a human being could make such retching sounds," Carolyn laughed later.

I supposed we've all got our war stories. Landlubbing guests are the worst. You'd think telling them "Only if you've eaten it" would be plain enough, but, alas, no. I've learned a lot about, well, "female absorption" the hard way. It is amazing the non-eatable items I've fished out: bottle caps, reading glasses, and the odd French letter.

I've been forced to become a paper expert. Needless to say, "water soluble" is preferred, but some seem as fragile as gold leaf. They fall apart in the briefest of transits. Others look just as delicate, but are actually made out of thin stainless steel sheets. Half the sheets can still be on the roll and the other half of the sheets trailing forty feet astern in deep ocean.

Why is it that, if there's a deck leak that is unable to fall upon your pillow or bunk it will be directly above the toilet roll?

And why, on a boat with everything corroding shut, do the toilet paper dispensers seem to run friction-free on Teflon bearings to pool all the sheets silently on the damp floor?

Make no mistake: these rolls are precious! I mean, to sailing wives they are—well, "strategic war material" in worth. Discarded dock lines just won't do. I'm serious. I mean, you have to occasionally be careful around otherwise honest cruising friends.

We spent four and a half months in Chagos in the middle of the Indian Ocean. There are no stores in Chagos, no inhabitants, no nothing—just toilet-paper-hoarding yachties. Sure dinghy gasoline, booze, and sugar are in high demand. But it is a roll of toilet paper that is the real coveted trade-good. I mean, name your price! Yes, it is amazing what some visiting multi-millionaires "hide in their handbag for later use" in Chagos.

Just before dinner parties aboard *Wild Card* I'd unroll to the sixth sheet and write with magic marker, "Don't be greedy, please!"

Cruising Mexico is "special case" and most marinas now have at least one store on the premises that sells nothing else. Look for the sign with the word "Montezuma" or "revenge" in it. This wasn't always the case. In fact, it wasn't long after Carolyn and I first sailed into Cozumel in early 1970's when I heard her lament forlornly, "Oh, where is Mister Whipple when you need him!"

Ever wonder why holding tanks are built of such flexible plastic? This is so they can balloon. I kid you not. It is amazing how much pressure build-up an athletic crew member can achieve with a hand-pump with an eight-inch handle. And, oh, what a horrible "dull popping" sound is heard when the weakest hose clamp finally fails and the fire-hosing-in-confined-space begins.

I'm reminded of the two ship-retched guys I met in Trinidad. They'd just lost their old wooden boat in a gale, and were even more shattered than you might expect. Being a professional marine journalist, I felt compelled to record their story.

"As the seas built, she started leaking worse and worse," said the weary, wild-eyed captain. "First the port garboard seam opened up and then the aft horn timber started squirting. Anyway, soon our engine and batteries were underwater and we were both forced to bail for our lives with buckets. We managed to keep her afloat for a long time, but it was tiring. We only had one flashlight left."

"It was around midnight," chimed in the second guy. "It looked like we might not see the dawn. I was scared, real scared. So I muttered something like, 'What could be worse than this?'"

"Just then, a large white disgorging object worked its way up from under a bunk and burst to the surface of the sloshing water. It was like a stinky white whale—waving its broken-hose holding tank coupling like an effluent-dribbling fluke-from-hell..."

"I'm sooooooooo soooorrrrrrrrrrrrrryyyyyyyyyyyyy!" sobbed the crew.

This whole subject is weird. Why are they called joker valves? Is this some "sanitation engineer's" idea of humor?

I once owned a boat with a top-of-the-line Wilcox Crittenden head. It was a huge thing with a large bronze base and long, strong pump handle. It was called, grandly, "The Skipper." For real! Imagine how I felt each morning as my crew would announce with a sly, smirky smile, "Well, time to show "The Skipper" what I really think of 'im!"

I replaced it with a smaller, more modern "Head Mate" in revenge.

Needless to say, most effluent—er, affluent yachtsmen pay someone else to deal with—such crappy jobs. In Fort Lauderdale, that chap was a British yachtsman known as Robin. The name of his business was "The Head Hunter!" Yes, any sailor with a survival instinct would immediately begin, consciously or not, to "work his way to weather" of Robin when conversing with him.

But Robin was cheery fellow and always raking in the money. "Sometimes I'm up to 'ere in it," he'd say with hand under his chin. "And sometimes I'm up to 'ere in it!" he'd say with his hand quaking just under his crinkling nose.

Which brings us to how marine toilets got their nautical name. Some say it is because old sailors use to go forward and lean it over the side while hanging onto the anchor davits. Eventually, they built a "privacy screen" around this area at the "head" of the boat.

Maybe so.

However, recently Carolyn and I were dinghying out to our vessel and happened to notice a tradition-loving single-hander sitting in the cockpit of his carvel-planked sloop that was named something like *Cedar Bucket*. He must have been daydreaming. He was just staring off into deep, vacant space. And we must have startled him as we came alongside. His jaw opened in amazement and his head—all we could see was his head—just sort of got yanked forward into the cabin, as if on a string.

"Ah," said Carolyn, as the light dawned, "that's why!

There's always the bucket...

Cruising in Home Waters

The Lesser Antilles are our oyster—even after sailing around the world. There is nowhere else on this watery planet that compares as a cruising ground. It is as if God and Walt Disney got together and said, "Hey, let's create a paradise for sailors—heaven-on-earth for the cruising yachtsman!"

We just spent a year wandering between Trinidad and St. Thomas—and had an absolute blast doing it.

We love Trinidad. It has a unique, exciting energy. Trini's work hard and party hard as well. They are a proud people, with much to be proud of. Carnival is almost a religion there. Steel pans are everywhere, as are clever, world-class Calypsonians.

As sailors they are fierce competitors on the race course, and firm friends at the parties.

Their society, though imperfect, is a shining example for the rest of us in the eastern Caribbean. No other island nation has a more diverse ethnic mix of Africans, East Indians, and Chinese—all working together for a brighter future.

Right now Grenada is suffering, but she will soon be on her proud feet once again. I love the whole south coast of that Spicy Island. And my wife, Carolyn, particularly adores the markets in St. Georges.

The Grenadines are like a string of pearls arcing northward. We could have spent the entire year right there and never got bored. Sure there are crowded anchorages but there are also dozens of empty ones as well.

Where?

Well, I don't want to spoil it for you as "The Hunt for the Perfect

Anchorage" is one of the main joys of Caribbean cruising. (Hint: work to weather of the bareboats. Once you get off the rhumb line, you could be back in the 1800's!)

It is impossible for me to say which our favorite stop there is: but both John Smith and Paul Johnson can make a rhum bottle evaporate in a most delightful, Carriacou way!

Bequia has always been a favorite stop. Tom and Sally at the *Caribbean Compass* are wonderful people. Come to think of it, so is almost everyone else on that delightfully laid-back island.

Carolyn and I spent many an afternoon hiking: to Spring, to Friendship, and beyond—utterly delightful!

Every time I glance at the *Friendship Rose* I remember why, 30 years ago when I first sailed "down-island", I called out to Carolyn so excitedly, "We're home!"

St. Vincent and Young Island are an exciting side trip if you're careful. Just stay away from the obvious "bad boys" smoking ganja and you'll be fine.

St. Lucia is blessed with the Pitons, Marigot, Castries, and Rodney Bay. Wow, lovely spots all!

I love Martinique and all of the French West Indies. Fort-de-France is my favorite large city in the Antilles. I love to drop my hook amid the dashing ferries off the city. And I love to look at the lovely restaurant ladies washing their pots and pans in the harbor, while their customers nonchalantly stand next to them peeing.

St. Anne? Anse Mitan? St. Pierre? Delightful! Yes, whenever I'm down a quart of garlic I sail into Point Du Bout and inhale!

Dominica is certainly dramatic ashore and afloat. The waterfalls and rainforests aren't to be missed—neither are the Caribe/Arawak villages.

Antigua is always interesting. I've been going there so long that I can remember when Desmond Nicholson was young, foolish, and pinching girl's bottoms! ("The rascal!" Carolyn said in appreciation.)

Soon after arriving in English Harbour, I always touch base with Jol Byerley to find out who is dead, indicted, or just out of rehab. It is so difficult to keep up with that delightfully naughty group of Blissful Brits.

I remember when a penniless Carlo sailed into Falmouth Harbour on a broken-down plywood boat he'd built on the muddy shores of a river in Rome—hoping to daysail for his supper!

I even like Jolly Harbour: all those fat German ladies playing volley ball with the skinny West Indian guys, laughing. "He says that a little cushion is good for the push'n!" they say as they are chased down the beach like bikini-clad elephants.

St. Barths was the coolest place on the planet back the 1970's—what little I remember of them. Buffett was caging drinks at Le Select. Fast Eddie was the most angelic man/child I had ever seen; the only bartender so young he had to stand on packing crates to serve his customers!

LouLou was a revolutionary radical back then—mellowed now, but no saner! Chris Chapman, Speedy John Everton, John Luke, and Harry the Rasta were all hardcore regulars. Sailor Chris Bowman had Bob Dylan jammed into a corner at Le Select—lifting his wallet and brain cells at the same time. Eric Taberly was aground in the harbor, and famed French ocean racer Phillip Poupon was going to tow him off—just as soon as he finished his Petite Punch!

And the Pirate Queen—that was where I first met Sylvie, the Pirate Queen. She owned a boat called *Life's a Beach* and was touring the Caribbean in search of whales.

"Whales?" I asked.

"Yes," she replied with a sexy growl, "men with forty foot tongues who can breathe through the top of their heads!"

She bit off my clothes (the first and last woman ever to do so, I'll sadly admit) within hours of our "lust-at-first-sight" meeting.

Oh, what fun I've had with the Pirate Queen over the years! She's utterly unrepentant! That wild night in a fancy French restaurant when she attempted to show us her magic trick of yanking away the table cloth—three times—was amazingly unsuccessful each time! (I just managed to get her out of there before the gendarmes arrived by pretending I was the cash-laden skipper of the ocean racer *Heavy Metal*!)

Oh, yes! There's always some bizarre aura surrounding the Pirate Queen! That crazy lesbo Nurse with the bladder problem she brought aboard my Uncle Foot's mega-yacht; that time she basted her famous Whiskey Chicken in gasoline and then tossed it into the sand (okay, she was drunk) in Virgin Gorda; and don't even get me started on the night she terrorized that poor defenseless American Colonel, who got so confused he forgot he was out of uniform. (Yes, totally out of uniform!)

Oh, St. Barths! What a crew! Mad Murphy! Raquel Welch. Les Anderson. Elizabeth Ashley. David Wegman. Treat Williams. And I'll never forget Timothy Leary's wild & crazy wife and that bizarre night she rented the subchaser for her birthday party and then—whew!

I didn't know what decadence meant until I sailed into Barths!

Sint Maarten is another island I remember with great fondness. Robbie Ferron was trying to scrape up enough money to buy some outboard head-gaskets in quantity, Bobby was attempting to drive pilings for his new marina with a large sledgehammer, and only a few boats were anchored in the Lagoon—all hanging out at Khim Sha's for Chinese food on Wednesday nights.

Anguilla? Well, Johnno was a character then and now. Caribbean song-writer Bankie Banks was just about the coolest dude alive back then, when his "What Do You Want, Inspector" drug song blared from every West Indian radio! (Gee, wasn't the "Big RA" a cool radio station? I mean, I actually went to St. Kitts to dine on "mountain chicken!" Oh, the power of advertising!)

The truly amazingly thing is that the Lesser Antilles are real. They exist. Still. Truly. A sailing yachtsman's paradise, bar-none! You can have just as much fun today as I had yesterday—and thirty years ago!

All you have to do is go—just do it. Chop your anchor line. Point your bowsprit seaward. Hoist the mainsail! You'll have more fun than you can possibly imagine—guaranteed! Adventure isn't just a possibility during such a trip, it is an absolute certainty.

And it always will be.

One more thing—say "Hi!" to the Pirate Queen for me!

Sylvie, the Prate Queen with her consort Bill and Rosclot the cat

Our Cellphones Inform Us We Are Dumb
or
The Titillating Joys of Techno-Phobia

My goal is to be the freest American sailor on this planet. Yes, freedom is my drug and I mainline it. To put it another way, there are three things I'm interested in—freedom, freedom, and freedom.

Get the picture?

Call me crazed, obsessed, and single-minded. Call me generationally-stubborn, even.

Freedom!

Of course, as a flower child of the late 1960's, I'm also worried about *selling out*. Yes, that was our big fear as starry-eyed hippies of yore, that we'd eventually become greedheads and "sell out to the Man."

Oh, what an awful thought!

Of course, the 1960's and flower-power have faded for most members of my generation. We're all older, and "The Movement" is now more closely associated with elderly bowels than young radicals. I mean, today a Weatherman is—well, a guy interested in weather.

Sad, eh?

To paraphrase the radical singer Gil Scott-Heron, the revolution not only "wasn't televised" it just—wasn't.

I, however, have steadfastly endeavored to stay true to my counter culture roots. But most of my friends have "moved on," which is, of course, just another way of saying they sold-out.

I'm not sure why this is. Perhaps they didn't—er, self-medicate themselves enough?

Take my wife, Carolyn, for example. She's not worried about selling out. In fact, she recently told me, "It's 2008, Fatty, and—face it!—there are no buyers!"

But I continue to soldier on. I mean, I'm still a true-blue Pinko-Commie-Fag. I still give the peace sign with a hopeful grin. I still say "far-out, man!" I still know all the lyrics to Alice's Restaurant. I still believe in Abbie Hoffman—well, right up until he slit his wrists, anyway.

Of course, being an aging, buttock-sagging hippy means that I can't work for anyone—because gainful corporate employment is restrictive.

In fact this whole "not working" concept led me to an entire lifetime of abject poverty—despite, or because of, living in the Land of Plenty. To compensate, I moved to the Third World where everyone is as poor as I (though not by smug choice.)

Thus I have missed out on a lot of techno-enslavement—which is how I think of many of the "modern conveniences" of Western shore life.

For instance, it used to be that you'd go into the corner grocery store, grab a dime soda, slap a dime on the counter, and waltz out. Not anymore!

First off, the "corner grocery" store is now ten miles away through dense traffic. And you'd best have electro-locking doors on your Lexus or you might get car-jacked. Second, the two dollar soda doesn't have a price tag. And inflation might have raised it to three dollars by the time you get it to the counter. To save time, the non-English-speaking carbon-life-form behind the counter will use a scanner to "input" it into the "system." But that seldom works the first time. So they try scanning it in another dozen times—slower and slower— this-way-and-that-way. Until finally, the clerk is forced to punch in the fourteen digit product number *and* their 12 digit employee number *and* the store code *and* the manager's Zodiac sign. But, of course, one of the numbers is inputted wrong and the entire sequence has to begin—painstakingly—*again*. So that, finally, about 20 or 30 minutes into this POP (point of purchase) pantomime, the clerk puts your now luke-warm soda into a plastic-bag-intended-to-gag-a-sea-turtle and says listlessly in Iranian, "Next!"

It used to be that retail businesses did their *own* inventory. Now, however, through the time-saving convenience of modern computers, we have to do it *ourselves*—for hours—each time we want a soda.

This is referred to as "progress" and "time-saving convenience" in the business community.

Where was I? How do I get off on these bizarre rants?

Ah, yes! I was explaining how I became a poverty-stricken sea gypsy in the Third World and missed out, thankfully, on a lot of high-tech advances.

Unfortunately, I *did* eventually have to work to earn a living. I know, I know... It seems far, far below my tie-dyed, bell-bottomed, Nehru-jacketed dignity—but that's how the deal went down. So I began writing. And this (somehow or another) led me to the Sultanship of Brunei and an international radio spot.

Actually, my radio career was almost derailed by a mis-communication before it left the audio station.

"But I'm not *in jail*," I responded in amazement when a hip Washington, D.C. studio executive said, "We'll call you on your cell."

Of course, I figured it out—eventually. Many of today's phones don't have wires. And they're mobile. Thus, they're technically called mobile or wireless apparatuses. However, since most of their "early-adapters" were incarcerated at Club Fed and thus needed smuggled-in mobile or wireless devices to continue conducting their criminal enterprises—they became widely known as cell phones, through the glories of hip-hop culture. (There is an urban myth that they were originally called "cellular" phones because street people used to hide them in stalks of celery while strolling down the avenue—completely untrue!)

Anyway, my wife, Carolyn, and I suddenly found ourselves forced to buy mobile/wireless/cell phones—that we needed like a hole in our heads.

For one thing, we're never apart. For two, we have no friends. For three, the only reason strangers have contacted me for the last decade or two, is to complain about articles like this.

In addition, it was immediately apparent that we didn't 'give good phone.'

Plus, Carolyn won't allow me to be alone. And the only reason I wanted to be alone—was to call her on her new cell phone.

I'd say, "I'm gonna go ashore and take a shower," and she'd say, "I'll go with."

Damn.

If she gets into the dinghy *alone* to go ashore, I call her just after she's pulled the starter cord. She has to stop, shut off the outboard engine, search her purse/bag/pockets (drifting though the anchorage all the while,) find her phone, and *not* drop it into the water in the bottom of the dinghy, turn her phone on, hit the "talk" button and shout "Is that you, Roma?" (Our daughter is the only one besides myself who has her number).

But, alas, it is only me and she ain't pleased—not at all.

She has no phone manners!

She shouts, "(Expletives deleted)!"

Texting is no better. I sent her an SMS message which read, "DONT B L8 2 ***K." She texted me back. "Not romantic enuf, you pervert!"

The last time we were at the Royal Brunei YC together, she was like a shadow. I could not lose her for a nano-second.

Thus, I slipped away to the head (the only place she can't follow) and called her from there.

"Disgusting!" she said. "You have to call me for a *reason*, Fatty!"

I had no idea.

A reason?

Damn it!

So the following day I hiked a solid hour under the glaring tropical Brunei sun and called her from the local little grocery store. "I'm at the grocery store. Do you want me to bring you back anything?"

"Yes," she said. "Five pounds of sugar, please."

Needless to say, I was taken aback. I mean, I wanted to call, sure, and I knew I had to have a reason. But five pounds of sugar weighs five pounds. And I didn't want to carry it at noon at 6 degrees of latitude.

"I'd rather not," I said. "That's too heavy. How 'bout I buy us a candy bar—and eat both halves here?"

"You call me from a store on your new cell phone to tell me that you *don't* want to carry stuff," she said. "That's—that's—dumber than stupid!"

Thus we had I first "mobile" argument.

I guess that's progress.

Me and My Guitar

Fat with his Tongan fans

"I'm home schooled," I often tell people. Then I start spinning them a typical Fatty sea yarn with, "You see, I grew up aboard an old 52-foot Alden schooner."

The last part is true. The first part is false.

I wasn't home schooled. Nor did I attend much "regular" school either—just a year here and there as we cruised aboard our family schooner *Elizabeth*. The bottom line: I only went to school ashore for five or six years—and I slept through much of that.

Which isn't to say I learned nothing in the halls of academia: I did—how to cheat, for example.

I always think of cheating when I hear the term "useful education."

And this is where I first got involved with journalism. I was a cub reporter as a freshman at Gage Park High—and took that last part quite seriously.

Since I was a reporter I had access to the newspaper's darkroom. When I printed pictures and turned the darkroom light on, a light outside the door said "PRINTING, DO NOT ENTER!" In fact, in order to prevent people from ruining our pictures and exposing our expensive photographic paper, we locked the door.

And, because it would get hot in there and there were dangerous chemical fumes, there was a huge ventilator fan which sucked out the air. Yippee!

There was even a convenient sink to throw up into, if you were so inclined. It was the only place in the school where a student could lock a door, and not have to open it immediately at a teacher's request.

Ah, it was heaven in there at times—many times. Why, I instructed a *number* of developing girls...er, a number of female photographic apprentices in the art of developing photographs!

And all I had to do was pen a few stupid stories now and then! (The only article I remember was featured on Page Two of our April 1 issue. It filled the entire page with the headline "Everything I Know About Sex" and my byline of Gary Goodlander. The rest of the page was blank.)

Where was I? How do I get off on these sick tangents?

Ah, yes, I was explaining how I ended up an uneducated oaf. Example: if I'd have attended school more often, I'd have entitled this article "My Guitar and I" which certainly sounds a little more nose-up-in-the-air.

But I didn't.

I flunked journalism. I flunked English. Hell, I flunked gym!

One teacher told me, while reading one of my assignments, that I had a dangling participle. I checked to see if my fly was open.

And so, I figured that I couldn't be a writer because writers had to be intelligent and know stuff.

See how foolish I was back then?

So I decided to become a songwriter instead. I mean, if Dylan and Jagger were making it—sheesh, why not me?

I dashed out, bought a guitar, learned three cords. I waited for the money to start rolling in.

I'm still waiting.

But while patiently waiting, I discovered that writing songs and playing music filled a giant creative void in me—and that girls liked it!

Yes, a guitar-plucking, pimply-faced, long-haired, morose-looking teenage boy is almost as popular as a football jock—and much easier to be, for a guy like me, who finds it difficult to carry yet a third ball down the field.

I don't know why girls find guitar players attractive, but I'm more interested in the effect than the cause. And being a songwriter—why, I could "whisper sweet nothings" in their ears until... until... we were both so tired we had to lie down.

So for five or six years as a young man, I played guitar—and had duets—with great passion.

However, once I started writing for a living, the driving "need" to play ceased. And music gradually faded from my life for about 25 years. ("The happiest years of my life," sighed my wife, Carolyn.)

Then I bumped into Joe Colpitt in the Virgin Islands. He's a boat-builder, designer, and offshore sailor. We hit it off immediately, mostly because Joe was very quiet back then—and I didn't want some idiot attempting to get a word in edge-wise while I was around. Nothing worse than having a couple of solid hours into building a monologue, and some jerk ruins it with an inane comment like, "Aren't your vocal cords tired yet?"

Anyway, one day Joe Colpitt said, "I think I'll buy a guitar and become a singer."

Now, I hate to admit how sick and sadistic I can be, but I blurted out, "Sounds like good idea, Joe!"

Strangely, however, Joe soon learned to play well—and to croon too.

I was shocked. All the stuff that Joe seemed incapable of expressing in words was pouring out of him—to rave reviews!

He really was earning "Money for nutt'n and the chicks for free!"

Now, fortuitously, just a few months before this, my wife had started saving up for a mammogram. Needless to say, this seemed a tad one-sided to me and rather gender-biased to boot. I felt that, perhaps the money might be better used for something we both could participate in—something that I could play and she could stare up adoringly at.

Anyway, I, too, soon bought a guitar, relearned my three cords, and started writing songs again.

And I, too, was really amazed at how passionately people felt about my music. Why the West Indians in the audience practically rioted when I played "Dark Meat" for the first time at Latitude 18 in Red Hook, St. Thomas! (Of course I'd have rather earned their *applause* but, hey, I figure I'll have to work up to that).

But the real pay-off was personal: playing the guitar soothed me. Instead of coming home and kicking the cat across the boat, I'd just boot it a couple of yards or so.

And it can be a real ice-breaker for a cruising sailor. For example: within minutes of starting to play music in primitive Vanuatu, I saw Chief Tommy's jaw drop and heard him utter under his fermented breadfruit breath, "Fatty long-long!" (In pidgin, "long-long" means crazy).

Yes, there's no faster way I can convince someone I'm off-my-rocker than to play "Big-butted Mama" and "Handy, Handyman!" back-to-back.

Of course I have some strong ideas about music and song-writing. Like, "Don't learn more than three cords." Because if John Prine can earn a million bucks with 'em—so can I!

And my musical skills really come in handy. If we're having a party aboard and our guests won't leave; just a couple of off-key, super-draggy stanzas of "Sad-eyed Lady of the Lowlands" have them *pole-vaulting* into their dinghies!

Right now we're in Brunei, hanging out with the Sullens... er, I mean.... Sultans!

Every time I go ashore, I bring my axe. It is really interesting, culturally, to play with/for Muslims. I mean, they sorta always thought rock & roll was the devil's music. Here's living proof!

I've been hinting around with the princes (The YC is full of 'em, each with his own jumbo jet) that I'd like to be invited to the Palace for a sleep over with the Sultan's harem. But no luck so far.

I even added, "I'll bring my guitar," as a sweetener. But still no luck.

I try to accept this gracefully, but it ain't easy. I know the Palace has 1,700 plus rooms. Why, the dining room alone sits 4,000! But they're small in stature, the Brunies. The dining room would probably only seat 3,500 porky Westerners.

Anyway, we play a lot of music ashore. I'm learning quite a bit. Some things truly amaze me. Like, when I play Jagger's "Sympathy for the Devil"—how fast the startled women in head-scarves can run while holding their ears!

An Irreverent & Perverted Overview of the Global Marine Industry

Fatty holding Stone Money in Yap

My wife, Carolyn, and I are currently in Micronesia, 38 years into our blissful honeymoon cruise. (Yes, it is true. We're still in lust.) Anyway, as radical American urban youth of the 1960's, we were both involved with the SDS (Students for a Democratic Society) and, thus, interested in revolution. This evolved into our adult passion: revolving around the earth again and again. The best part of endlessly circumnavigating is, of course, the exchange of cultural mores: learning from one destination, teaching in another.

For instance, here in Micronesia everyone takes drugs. That's right, everyone, including all the cops and government officials, chew betel nut constantly. It is sold everywhere—in every store, grocery hut, and gas station. No one in the entire country would *think* to go more than a few minutes without stuffing more dope into their happily-bulging cheeks.

It rots your teeth. You have to spit/drool slimy-stuff constantly. It turns your whole mouth bright red, as if you've been drinking blood. It cost ten cents to get high—that's right, 10 US cents!

Frankly, I find it sort of fun and refreshing to walk into a country's Department of Customs—and realize I'm the only guy there *not* high on drugs!

But that's not why they call Micronesia paradise.

Actually, the "micro" part of the name indicates how hard they work. They're basically lazy people—which is, perhaps, why I love them so dearly.

But, like everyone else on this striving, dissatisfied planet, they want to progress—no matter how disastrous the path. Since I come in contact mostly with sailors and marine-folk, they're often interested in the global marine industry. Thus, recently in Yap, I was visited aboard *Wild Card* by three Young Yuppie Yappies in Nappies interested in a youthful entrepreneurialship: a potential inboard engine mechanic, a sailmaker, and an electrician.

They wanted me to help & guide them. But it was difficult. They are in awe of technology & magic (pretty much one-and-the-same to them,) and I am not. There's a lot of subtle stuff going on—stuff that all world-weary Westerners instinctively know but never speak. How could I convey this complex information in easily digestible, trans-cultural form?

Plus, I didn't want to appear pompous. And I prefer to sprinkle a dash of humor into even scholarly musings.

So I wrote them the little essay below—just dashed it off with a chuckle, in hopes it might spur them on. As I handed it to them, I told them the Universal Truth of the Industry, "It is easy to make a small fortune in the marine sector—just start with a big one!"

I recently wrote a "sweeping, in-depth dissertation" on modern marine diesels for a major marine magazine. Imagine that! The strain of me attempting to appear both informed and intelligent was *truly* immense. Yes, it was *very* scary. I not only was supposed to have my "facts straight," I was supposed to arrange them in some logical order—neither of which I'm particularly good at.

Competency is a concept I've never mastered. The closest I've ever come, is to be able to convince a few gullible people (like you, dear reader) that I know what I'm talking about—even if they can't seem to puzzle out exactly what it is I'm saying.

And I was forced to leave out of my "complete modern marine diesel dissertation" the central fact of the matter: the sick concept that every sailboater knows in his heart, but is afraid to put down on paper. The very reason that modern marine diesels exist—is to bedevil cruising yachtsmen the world over.

Yes, it is true.

I recently interviewed (on an off-the-record, without attribution basis) a red-nosed German diesel design engineer on this very subject.

"There are two schools of thought on why we design marine engines that don't run. School #1 says that, since we have to work all day in stuffy offices filled with ugly secretaries and flickering computer screens, and yachtsmen don't—that we hate them and thus take our sweet revenge."

"Ah," I said. "Envy, lust, boredom—three powerful human motivators."

"But School #2 takes a far more sophisticated, spiritual view," he continued. "That we marine engineers are really *helping* the cruising yachtsman realize what a great, fun lifestyle he really has. That we're the yang of his yin! I mean, where do all you guys sail to? Paradise, right? And how do you define paradise—as the opposite of hell? Then how would you know how paradisiacal paradise really is—if you didn't have to spend half your life squatting in the bilge covered with grease?"

The intellectual ramifications of his argument were so vast—I was temporarily at a loss for words.

"Yes," he continued on. "Rich people basically want to buy convenience. Plus, they're lazy. But we know from Einstein and his General Theory that, relatively, the amount of happiness in the universe is fixed. Yes, you can convert happiness into mass and mass back into happiness— but only with a powerful release of energy. But short of that, rich people *can't* actually have any more fun than the middle class. And, to achieve this desirable and delicate social balance, the simplest way was to formulate the theorem: more money equals more internal combustion engines, which equals more problems!"

I must admit I was amazed. Sure, I knew diesels tended to perform erratically, but I had no idea that their global malfunctioning was—well, cosmically correct!

"Now you're starting to understand," the fellow beamed at me. "But it isn't that our engines are merely 'undependable' as you put it. They are far, far more sophisticated than that. Any-old mechanical device can just stop running. But have you ever noticed how modern diesels always leave you in a lurch? That they suddenly grind-to-a-halt when you are on a dead lee shore, shooting a rip-tide inlet, or throwing it into reverse at the crowded fuel dock? That's because of modern micro-chips, onboard computers, and interfacing. Almost all marine diesels manufactured since 1999 have this capability. They monitor the depth meter, detect sea-state, sense rudder movement; and, coupled with the skipper using the 'F' word and his wife the 'S' word and the grandmother shouting, "Oh, my God... the children!" Well, *that's* when an "intelligent" diesel poops out! Smart, eh?"

Needless to say, as a journalist of integrity, I needed to confirm this information. The first guy I asked was a grease monkey at a gas station in San Francisco.

"Well, I ain't that familiar with diesels," the pump jockey admitted. "But I think the reason diesels have the word 'die' in them is because they don't got no spark plugs. The way I figure it, if you want to start sum'thin, spark is the way to go!"

Once I confirmed the fact that diesel manufacturers actually had, in a desperate attempt to reduce manufacturing costs, discarded the spark plug entirely—well! No wonder!

I rushed down to my British mechanic in Bali (Indonesia), Stinky Potter, for further confirmation. "Tell me about diesels," I said, and pointed to a poster on his wall that showed a turbo diesel and a regular one. "For example, what's 'naturally-aspirated' mean?"

"That's the simplest way of sucking money from the owner," Stinky Potter said. "Turbo's can suck out more money faster, but the coins can damage the blades. It's a trade-off, speed for dependability."

I realized I was getting the plain, unvarnished truth from this guy, and thus felt as virtuous as a reporter from the National Inquirer. "What's a 'complete' engine rebuild require? And does the old engine really end up 'better than new,' as some repair shops maintain?"

"Well," he said, evasively, "I'm not supposed to discuss that. But the fact is, we put a *complete* list of all the internal parts on the invoice, even if we just Scotch-tape over the hole in the piston! Here, let's go back into the shop."

Stinky led me back into a dark work area where large, extra-Y chromosome types in furs where beating on engines with sledgehammers. "Yes," Stinky shouted over the din, "we find employing cavemen is cost effective. Or, to put in another way, a mechanic who can damage as much as he fixes is—well, worth his weight in gold!"

Stinky instructed Halgar to stop working for a moment and tell me what he was doing.

"I'm pulling the head," said Halgar. "This is the most important step, psychologically. Let's say an owner comes to us with a diesel that has been switched to an empty fuel tank. We tell the owner we must 'pull the head.' If he agrees, well, like they used to say in the 1960's, we're 'in his head' and have control over his mind—and his pocket book soon follows!"

"What's that contraption on your wrist," I shouted at Halgar, pointing at what looked like an over-large dive watch.

"Oh, that's our billing timer," said Halgar proudly. "Our prices have actually remained fairly constant over the years, only the units have changed. We used to charge by the hour but now discover it is more cost-effective to bill by minutes, seconds, and nanoseconds!"

"For example," he said as he checked his wrist, "your question just cost someone $800 smackers."

"Tell him what you do at the end of a rebuild," yelled Stinky.

"We 'mic' the engine. That is, we use a microscope to see if there's any more money to be squeezed from the project."

"So the tolerances are close?" I queried.

"Yes," he said, "as close as we can get and still have the customer pay."

Stinky Potter continued to lead me on a tour of his facility. Next up was the Estimator's Office.

"How do you do it," I asked their nerdy-looking "numbers" guy, "How do you know how much to charge in advance?"

"Well, it's all computerized today," Mister Morenmore said. "For example, does the yacht owner wear a gold chain? Have a wife more than 50 years younger? Buy Viagra by the barge-full? Have a cod-piece sewn into his Sportif's? Drink designer water? All these factors are assigned numerical values and then combined."

"Wow," I said, "It sounds like a science."

"It is," beamed Miser Morenmore. "In the old days we just sort of guessed—by dreaming up the highest number we could, then adding some zeros to it."

"Are there currently major differences between modern diesel manufacturers?" I asked Stinky when we were back in the showroom.

"Well, there used to be. BM was a bit too aptly named; now they're not so much crap as Generally Malfunctioning. The price tag of a Perky sure gets your attention. The Vulvu is aimed at women, as you'd expect. The Nipstammer is popular—if you like your RPM's higher than Hunter S.

Thompson. Caterpillars have crawled up a bit. The Sob engine had trouble marketing itself. I wonder why? Luggers have a reputation for being over-propped."

I must admit I was astounded by it all. In fact, I thought it was unique to salt-stained wrench-twisters. Then I went to a sailmaker in Hong Kong and asked how *his* industry was progressing.

"Absolutely super," he gushed. "Why, we've made wonderful strides recently! For example, Dacron sails used to last a long time and be cheap. Then we discovered 'exotic materials' and our profits skyrocketed. I mean, we tell an owner, who isn't sure within three or four *yards* where to place his boom while racing—anyway, we tell him that having a quarter-of-an-inch less stretch on his luff is important. And he buys it!"

Ditto, marine electronics.

"The whole NEMA thing was a stroke of genius," said our Aussie informant. "I can't believe boat owners allow us to connect *all* their instruments together into a New Electronic Malfunctioning Administrator, which then can make various electro-bits 'crash' depending on the ebb and flow of the sailor's bank account. And those new 'Electronic Chart Plotters.' Wow! A wealthy sailor can now know exactly where he is— every step along the way to the poor house!"

Yes, this "pay more for less" trend isn't just limited to the marine industry. The idea for coin-operated autopilots, for instance, trickled down from land-based vending machines. Ditto these new ultra-expensive weather routing services that will air-lift you from your vessel if they're wrong. Or the new Internet-based radar units that can automatically toggle between the LCD screen and full color porn. Or marine Sat Phones, with 900 numbers already installed on the speed dial. And stern-mounted WiFi antennas taller than your mast.

It's a Brave New World, all right. Why, modern technology might even help shipboard marriages someday! Or, to put it another way, my wife was recently ruffling what little is left of my thinning hair. And I asked her amorously, what she was doing? She responded coldly, "Looking for the mute button, Fatty."

Poverty & the Radar Screen of Life

A funny thing happened to me recently: I had too much money! I know, I know, this is the least likely 'bad' thing that you'd expect to happen to a penniless sea gypsy such as myself—but that's how life is, always throwing curves. And it wasn't that I earned more money, just that I spent less.

You see, Micronesia doesn't offer much in the way of shopping opportunities. They are, truly, micro. So there isn't much to buy. And people will give you anything you point at—even their spouse. So spending becomes somewhat of a challenge.

Mostly what they have here in the Nor-west Pacific is stuff left over from WWII which, alas, doesn't include ATM machines. (What were the Allies thinking—not bringing ATM machines. Stupid, eh?)

Anyway, after three months of cruising Micronesia, we pulled into Yap, a port with an Internet connection and (as soon as I got up-to-speed on porn) I checked my bank accounts—wow, I was rich!

Immediately, I sensed a problem. You see, my wife likes to see a dentist once a year, wear shoes, buy soap. In essence, I realized that if I didn't loot my bank account, she certainly would—on useless stuff like prescription eyeglasses, food, and—well, female stuff!

The problem isn't so much that she spends money but, rather, that she's addicted to it. I mean, she is insatiable! Take food, for example: if you feed her breakfast, she wants lunch. You give that meal to her, damn—she's already planning on eating dinner—and this is all-in-the-same-day!

Now, in Micronesia there are (sort of) US post offices. I mean, they're pretty good—only about half the stuff gets stolen as it passes through Guam. So I figured this was a good place to have stuff shipped in. So I went to the post office and began to copy down the address written in large, two-foot high letters on its entrance—when the clerk at the front window rushed out to caution me—and the some the sorters from the backroom did too.

"So sorry," said the clerk, "but address is wrong!"

"The address on the post office is wrong," I said in amazement. Perhaps, I didn't hide my incredulity too well.

The people of Micronesia are, like everywhere else, somewhat micro-proud. So the clerk defended his country's honor by saying, "Not all wrong! For instance, zip code of 96943 is right, and the word 'Yap' is spelled correct. So, mostly, it's right, sir. It's just the other numbers and words—well, there's a problem!"

"Then why not change the sign?" I asked.

"Only sign we have," was the answer. "And, besides, everyone here knows it's wrong. We sent 'em a letter and told 'em!"

I decided to FedEx.

Then I called up Defender Industries in New Jersey and said, "I have too much money and want to have some fun!"

The tele-jockey at the other end wasn't stupid. "Fun?" he asked. "Fun... hmmm... fun... furn... FURUNO!"

Thus I end up buying a Furuno 1623 radar for *Wild Card*.

Of course, there were some technical issues I hadn't considered. For instance, radars require electric power. This was a problem. Between my wife's vibrator and me (adoringly) staring into my high-wattage light bulb ringed make-up mirror—well, we don't have a lot of 12-volts left over.

"What should I do?" I asked my wife. Alas, she was in no mood to help. She obviously wasn't terribly pleased with my recent purchase and wasn't too subtle hiding her disgust. "Kiss off!" she snarled.

Well, it was an idea. I mean, I'd been to Trinidad many times and had drunkenly stumbled passed the little store-front window where they assembled the units. And, wasn't it the only Caribbean company with enough balls to brazenly put the word 'stupid' right in their name? Yes, I'd order a KISS (Keep It Simple, Stupid) wind generator from Doug Billings at Kiss Energy Systems in Chaguaramas, Trinidad—and solve my electrical needs forever!

Needless to say, the installation of both of these units wasn't easy.

I'm sort of clumsy.

The only tool I regularly play with is my own. The radar was the worst. The axe I used to chop a hole in my aluminum mast kept getting dull. The electric cable was too short—so I had to run it efficiently—directly through the main cabin to the nav station. Yes, I put a 'duck!' sign on it so that really dumb people wouldn't think it was a sort of electro-handrail.

Now this is a modern radar. I grew up aboard in the 1950's with an old-fashioned one with a long black hood to block out light. Yes, they were huge and cumbersome, but, hey, they were way-cool too! I mean, put a certain type of cigarette in one of 'em and, hey, you could see actual vivid colors on a B&W screen!

And, it was a convenient place to throw-up into, if you didn't like the guy on the following watch!

But this new unit is as small as my talent—or, very small as my wife likes to point out.

The main reason I wanted it was because of its 'watch' and 'guard' features. Basically, the unit mostly sleeps (like me) but occasionally wakes up and peeks (unlike me). This gives me a lot of confidence—so much so, in fact, that when recently, a passing freighter hailed me on Channel 16 and said frantically, "We're about to collide!" I just glanced at my blank radar screen and said smugly, "No, we're not. In fact, you're not even there!" (Newbie hint: never set the gain to zero!)

I was amazed at how sensitive the Furuno 1623 was—once you find the proper settings and adjustments. I can watch my wife row ashore (alas, we can't afford dinghy gas) to weed her taro patch. (Yes, she has desperate hopes of eating in the distant future.)

The wind generator was a lot more fun to install. Obviously the installation manual was written by a Trini: "Put in wind," it read. "Connect. Drink cold Caribe beer!"

Well, it wasn't quite that simple.

I think the main mistake I made was installing it on such a windy day. I mean, bolting those blades on while the hub spun faster and faster...wasn't easy, I'll tell ya!

But soon we had more volts and amps than we knew what to do with. And so, I had to buy one of those 'e-meters' as well—just to tell how wonderfully the wind generator pumped out the mega-juice.

"What's it say?" I asked my wife as I connected the meter. "You're right," she said in techno-amazement. "It does say watts!"

So there you have it: *Wild Card*, pathetic little world-weary yacht that she is—has a new radar and a new Kiss wind generator to power it. And we're dead broke.

In essence, things are back to normal. Of course, we're still basically the same. All this 'electro-convenience' doesn't make us better people. We still bicker.

"Stop interrupting and distracting me," I recently yelled at my wife when she asked me, as I peered into our shiny new radar, if I saw any "famine relief" ships on the screen.

An Irreverent Look at the America's Cup

The America's Cup is truly an American institution. By that I mean that it is based on trickery, deceit, unfairness, rule-bending, spying, cheating, greed—and many other qualities that most Americans greatly admire.

Of course, cheating isn't a new concept. But few countries other than the United States of America could muster the unmitigated gall to cheat the rest of the world *for over a hundred years*. That's audacious. That's American.

Let's back up. The desire to cheat started even before the *America* was launched. Her owner, John Cox Stevens, signed a contract with her builder/designer, George Steers, that said Stevens didn't have to pay the $30,000 asking price unless the vessel could "beat every yacht of her size in the U.S. and England." She *was* able to do so, and, thus, Stevens was forced to pay Steers.

In the fateful "All Nations" race of August 22nd, 1851 in England, *America* won the 100 Guineas Cup, but her win was not a clean one. There was some question of whether she sailed the proper course. The leader of the 15 boat race, *Volante,* sprung her bowsprit off No Man's Land, and was forced to retire. *Arrow* went aground; *Alarm* stood by to assist. *America* crossed the finish line 19 minutes ahead of *Aurora,* true. However, if she'd have been racing the *Aurora* under the New York Yacht Club's own rating rule of the day, *America* would have *lost* the race by almost an hour. Luckily for the Americans, it was strictly a boat-for-boat race.

Once they got the Cup to America, they conspired to make sure that no one would ever be able to carry it off. How? By making a million rules: the challenger had to sail across the Atlantic on its own bottom, all of its gear had to be from the country of origin, that the race be held in an area in which local knowledge was important, that only American officials be allowed to officiate, etc.

To stack the deck (sic) even further, they allowed themselves to "defend" with an entire fleet of boats, while the challenger was limited to a single vessel. In the first America's Cup defense, the *majority* of the American vessels in the fleet beat *Cambria.*

The next challenge seemed far fairer. A single challenger and the defender faced each other on the race course. However, it was still completely lopsided. The challenger was a single vessel named months in advance, while the defender was any one of a number of diverse racing vessels in a large fleet—picked on the very morning of the race. Thus, on a heavy air day the NYYC would pick a strong, heavy boat, while on a day with light winds they would pick a light-weight centerboarder.

By this point, cheating (or perhaps "unsportsman-like conduct" would be a better choice of words) was so ingrained in the character of the NYYC that they probably didn't even know they were doing it. It was as if the club's official motto was: "You lose: we win!"

Let's face it, there is something decidedly peculiar about the entire America's Cup mystique. The more America cheated by creating an unlevel playing field, the more the rest of the world wanted to wrestle away the Cup.

Consider Italian businessman Paul Gardini of Italy. He is probably the only man in the world to spend 100 million dollars to come in dead last in a yacht race! (Later Gardini committed suicide. The accepted version is that he was about to be arrested for corruption…but I can't help but wonder if, perhaps, he wasn't going through his old sailmaker's bills when he pulled the trigger.)

Another strange fact: this is considered a sport. This makes Dennis Connor, in some weird and twisted way, a Great American Athlete—even though he's misplaced his chin, can't see his toes, and gets winded after signing a couple of autographs.

Of course, Conner's multihull defense against Michael Faye's 120 foot mono-maran challenge was a classic. Both men seemed to be saying "It's not about competing, it's about winning."

But despite all logic and common sense, another America's Cup will soon be upon us. Men with egos greater than their countries national debt will once again spend many millions of dollars to make their plastic toy go faster than the other guy's plastic toy.

The French will continue to smash their boats into other vessels amid much shouting. (How can they expect to win when they have to shake each other's hand during every tack?)

The Aussies will pout, the New Zealanders will grimace, and the Japanese will attempt to sell everyone tiller extensions with tiny little waterproof transistor radios within.

And the Americans will attempt to cheat.

Ah, yes! The America's Cup. International competition at its very worst. I can barely wait!

The Financing of Used and Abused Boat Gear

I seldom replace anything on *Wild Card*, our 38-foot S&S-designed Hughes sloop. Instead, I kick it overboard if it falls from the rig, toss it in the water if it is a stray piece from the cockpit, or carry it on deck to 'deep-six' if it's a piece from the interior.

Occasionally, alas, this doesn't work. I mean, there actually *are* some things on a modern vessel that are needed for it to function safely offshore.

Take my bow rail, as example. When I hauled *Wild Card* off the bottom after Hurricane Hugo in 1989, I knew I'd have to replace the bow rail immediately.

It was bent like a pretzel.

But, after pricing a new bow rail, I figured that I'd just 'unpretzel' it with a pipe-bender.

This worked—sort of. I managed to vaguely get it back into the original shape. By that I mean, if I showed some sailors a picture of it and asked them, "Is this a bow rail?" 56% would answer affirmatively. (However, if I asked them *what* it was, they'd reply, "I dunno—a pretzel made out of stainless steel tubing?")

The bow rail was a cheapie to begin with. It had 'iron-rot' from the inside and soon developed dozens of cracks in the tubing.

"Don't worry about that," I told my long suffering wife, Carolyn. "Just don't touch it!"

I, of course, never go on the foredeck nor mess with the (dirty, dirty) anchors. I stay in the cockpit.

"But..." sputtered Carolyn, "isn't the whole idea of a bow rail to keep us from falling overboard?"

"Who told you that," I scoffed. "*El contraire*! I mean, if you start to fall into the bow rail—*leap* over the side immediately. Whatever you do, don't jar it!"

"But..." she sputtered again, and I could tell she was attempting to sucker me into an argument. But I cleverly headed her off with, "Hey, Carolyn, why does it always have to be about *you*, eh? We're talking bow rail here, not bodacious-babe! Honey, I love you... yeah... cherish you, even... but everything on the boat isn't... er, Carolyn-centric, if you know what I mean. So don't... you know, stupidly damage the boat's bow rail if you foolishly fall over. That's all I'm saying!"

This 'don't touch, don't tell' policy went on for about a decade or so.

Alas, even untouched, the bow rail continued to deteriorate. The cracks on its surface became larger. A couple of its welds rusted through and the bottom tube started sagging away from the top one. The screw-holes in the deck were gradually enlarging and whole rattling-basket was getting loose-as-a-goose. It would flop from side to side when we tacked. If a large wave hit it, it would lift up a couple of inches. It seemed to be made less-and-less out of stainless steel and more-and-more out of jello.

Occasionally Carolyn would screw up and flick it with our anchor snubber or touch it with her hair while bending over our anchor chain... while I bellowed from the cockpit, "Damn it, Carolyn! How many times have I *told* you?"

Then one day a horrible thing happened: a seagull landed on it. It wasn't a big seagull nor a particularly hard landing—but it broke the bow rail forever.

There was a horrible 'clang' as the tubing fell to the deck. Both of us were belowdecks, and I couldn't see Carolyn—so, natch, I blamed her.

"Was that you," I screamed. "Did you do that?"

"What are you talking about," Carolyn said, "I'm in the head!"

"Maybe you reached out the porthole or rigged a line through the hatch?"

"Don't be silly, Fatty," she said while furiously pumping, "And why automatically blame the woman whenever something bad happens?"

"Why," I said, and relished the looming argument. "Remember the Garden? You and the snake? The Apple? Do you think guys like me forget little things like that?"

Alas, this 'martial riff' didn't help the bow rail at all.

We were in Coral Bay in the Virgin Islands at the time, and Carolyn gently suggested we save up our pennies for a new bow-rail. "A 'nuther round," I slurred to Mean Jean, the bartender at Skinny Legs. "And you got any of those bow-rail-thingies back there?"

"Bow rails?" Mean Jean asked with a grimace. "No, Fatty, we just have booze & burgers back here."

I raised my hands pathetically to Carolyn in a gesture of perplexed helplessness. "Hey, I tried," I hiccupped at her. And I shouted back at Mean Jean, "Then gimme a Slim Jim, babe, and a brewski!"

Of course, we had an ocean to cross. A wide one. The Pacific. So it was important that I fix my bow rail.

I did. With duct tape. A *lot* of duct tape. Many wraps. I used chopsticks for splints, and plastic wire-ties to bind it all together.

"There, that should do it," I said when finished, "unless a fly or a mosquito lands on it!"

That was over a year ago and, in the interim, numerous parts fell off (Galapagos/Tahiti/Tonga) as we went along. Finally, last week in Whangarei, New Zealand, the entire device turned into a jagged pipe splinter and collapsed with a puff of salt-stained rust.

Buying a new one was out of the question. I priced a 'custom made' one which was more than the price of the boat! Stealing one was, of course, a traditional option—but a tad risky in a small harbor. ("What makes you think, kind sir, that the bow rail I installed on my boat this morning is the bow rail which was stolen from your vessel last evening?")

Luckily, I discovered a used one for sale at Stanley's Used Marine Gear. Yahoo!

It was even reasonably priced at $100 dollars—although this would put a serious dent in our meager cruising kitty.

"Excuse me," I said to Stanley, "how much is this? I mean, I see a stock number but no price."

"No," said Stanley, "that's the price—a hundred bucks."

"What?" I screamed and clutched my chest as if having a coronary. "Are you serious, Stan…for *this piece of crap*?"

Unfortunately, Stanley knows me. He simply ignored all the people I sent into the store to criticize the quality of the bow rail, its price, condition, construction, designer, finish, etc. Why, he even ignored the guy who tripped over it and threatened to sue!

I didn't give up, though. I persevered. Finally, Stanley saw the light and reduced the price—ten cents. This worked out to about a penny-a-day for my hard-nosed, *mano-a-mano* negotiations.

"I knew I'd wear you down in the end," I bragged to Stanley as I carted away the bow rail and he counted his 99 dollars and 90 cents.

The installation went fairly well—once Carolyn managed to serendipitously pry the proper-sized galvy nails from the planks of the dock we were tied to. (Here's the trick to nailing into fiberglass: *BIG HAMMER!*)

In fact, we were just admiring how 'yachty-snotty' *Wild Card* looked with her new bow rail—when a dock-strolling Kiwi family fell screaming into the harbor, because of some, er, loose dock planking.

There were four of them frantically dog-paddling around in the water: father, mother, daughter, and son.

"Quick!" I shouted to Carolyn. "Toss me the boat hook!"

She did, and within an instant I'd snatched the mother's purse out of the water. "Reward!" I screamed happily.

The Limitlessness of My Stupidity

I was pulling up to the Red Hook fuel dock recently when some old friends spotted *Wild Card*.

"Congratulations on your circumnavigation," they shouted.

I turned, puffed with pride and started to think of something clever to say—as I rammed the dock at about four knots and raked its length with my port-side-projecting boom.

The impact must have been considerable. They were knocked to their knees and began writhing around on the sliver-filled planks while frantically covering their head in anticipation of my rig falling down upon them.

In any event, as they scurried for the relative safety of shore I meekly called after them, "We got a *lot* of practice sailing—but *very little* practice docking!"

Making a vast number of very stupid mistakes seems to be the one constant in my life. If I'm not actually *doing* something stupid, I'm *saying* something stupid.

I don't know what prompts me. Example: I was recently talking to the guy who signed me up on Radio One WVWI (my Saturday morning show is now its sixteenth year) and said, "I *love* doing a talk show! I mean, radio is a medium-without-content—*perfect* for guys like us!"

Somehow he managed to take it the wrong way.

Ditto, the DPNR (Department of Planning and Natural Resources). I breezed into their offices to renew my boat registration and said, "Ahoy... how's zit wid de Oppressors?" and failed to get a single laugh.

I did the same sort of suicidal thing with the Feds. While at Customs clearing back into the United States, I blurted out, "I warned 'em, I warned 'em!"

"Who did you warn?" asked the uniformed beefy guy inspecting my Malaysia and Indonesia-stamped passport.

"Muslims," I said, hoping to get on his good side. "I told 'em to start shopping at Wal-Mart or, with sincere regret, we'd kill 'em all!"

This statement bombed too.

The whole reason I was refueling at Red Hook was because I'd failed to 'save money' by jugging diesel fuel out to my vessel.

Yeah, it's true: I'm so cheap I squeak. That's right; I squeeze my pennies so hard Abe Lincoln cries. We cruise the world on the pocket change that frugal Scotsmen throw away.

I admit it: I'm way-cheap. So I decided to save a few pennies by jugging my diesel fuel out to my boat.

My first mistake was to use ten gallon jugs instead of five. My second mistake was to attempt the transfer during heavy weather—in order to use the large seas to 'lift' the jugs from my dinghy to yacht rail.

Amazingly enough, I did manage to get the first jug on my side deck without problem. I timed it perfectly and it almost 'levitated' itself aboard. Pleased, I tried again. This time I knocked over *all* the remaining jugs in the dinghy *and* the jug I'd already lifted aboard! (It wasn't a big deal: only about half their contents leaked out before I managed to re-straighten them!)

Of course, if you really want to plumb the depths of my idiocy—my recent depth meter fiasco is a good example.

In 1974, exactly 30 years ago, I purchased a Datamarine depth meter. It finally stopped working and the manufacturer adamantly refused to send me a brand new one free-of-charge—just because its fine-print guarantee was "way out-of-date, man, like—expired by decades" according to some heartless, legal-eagle bean-counter in its PR department.

Anyway, I needed a new depth meter.

Being a careful, prudent shopper, I turned to Practical Sailor for advice. They recommended a unit which was just as good as the competition—and $50 cheaper!

"Excellent!" I said to Carolyn. "We'll save some money!"

Now, I had just recently hauled *Wild Card,* so I planned on installing the new transducer while in the water.

I do risky 'macho-marine' stuff like this all the time: regularly replacing through-hulls, bolts, and speedo sending units, with me in the water relaxing and Carolyn inside screaming, "Where's the wrench, where's the frig'n wrench!" while being fire hosed with a two-inch stream of salt water.

There was only one slight problem. The new transducer's stem wasn't three-quarters of an inch as expected but one and an eighth inch!

"I am *not* drilling a large hole through our boat with a powerful 110-volt drill while it is in the water," balked Carolyn. "I mean, I have no desire to be the first female VI sailor to make the Darwin List!"

I know when I'm licked. So I went to my favorite shipyard and asked to be hauled out briefly to replace my transducer.

"An hour at the most," I said, "I'll be all ready to go."

A crowd gathered as I slid *Wild Card* into the slings. And I was only-too-happy to be able to pontificate on the finer points of yacht maintenance, ship's husbandry, and other topics I know knowing about.

As I hopped off the boat, I moved the aft lifting strap a foot forward. The guy driving the lift climbed down, moved it aft. I angrily dashed back to grumpily replace it where I put it the first time.

"That's fine—exactly right!" I told him, and turned back to chatting with the crowd as the travel lift revved.

Suddenly I noticed all their once-admiring faces getting a haggard look. Jaws dropped. One or two glanced away. I turned around and looked at *Wild Card*.

The strap, entirely through my fault, was not on the counter or keel—but wrapped around my folding Max prop instead.

Everything held for an impossible moment—and then my prop shaft sickeningly bent 45 degrees.

The boat jolted.

And I heard a very expensive 'snap, crackle, pop' sound.

"Well," I said brightly, "at least we can now accurately mark where *not* to put that strap!"

Not only was the shaft pretzeled, the cutlass bearing was oval/ruined and the shaft tube end shattered as well.

"Gee, Fatty," Carolyn smirked, "aren't you glad you saved the fifty bucks on this particular depth meter?"

"Well," I parried, "you know how I love to discuss liver damage with my buddies at Bottom's Up!"

It took sixteen days of hard work and our entire cruising fund to splash *Wild Card* once again.

Yes, the cruising lifestyle isn't an easy one—especially for a brain-dead, empty-pocketed, know-it-all sailor such as myself.

But me—I always look on the bright side.

Such experiences are good for our sea-borne marriage. They strengthen it. Our mutual suffering unites us—and is one of the few things we can regularly afford.

Carolyn, of course, puts it slightly differently.

"The only reason I stay with you, Fatty," she says ruefully, "is because every day you manage to do something stupider than the day before. And after 35 years of living aboard and sailing together, I just can't believe you still are able to top yourself!"

"Hey," I blushed, suddenly all shy and girlish, "stop with the flattery, okay?"

The #1 Boat Maintenance Task

Fatty and Roma maintaining their sense of humor

If you only maintain one thing on your boat—let it be your sense of humor. Let's face it: life continuously offers us opportunities to either laugh or cry. Laughing is more fun. Yes, the key to successful cruising isn't so much what happens, but how you respond to it. Is the approaching rain squall an ordeal or an adventure? It's your choice.

"Of course, we've got a *huge* advantage over most cruisers," I often say. "Because we're broke, our $3,000 boat is mess, and we're both complete idiots."

It's true. Our pathetic attempts to survive—even *thrive* within the global sea gypsy lifestyle—provide us with endless opportunities to laugh both *at* ourselves and *with* our friends. Plus, we have to earn our living as we sail…which is even crazier!

When I first started writing, my wife, Carolyn, called my manuscripts "homing pigeons" because no matter where I'd send them in the world—they'd fly right back.

Yes, it *was* a tad ego-bruising. I mean, even the sloppiest Caribbean "fish-wrapper" would not have me. I applied to one such local publication and the guy said, "We don't pay!" Since I needed to get a Topsider in the door, I said, "Luckily, I'm a rich, trust-funded brat and I'll write for free."

I did so for a couple of months. Finally, the guy came back and said, "You're fired, Fatty. Your stuff isn't worth what we're paying for it."

I was flabbergasted. "But you pay me *nothing*," I reminded him.

"Exactly," he replied.

But I have never let abject, total, complete, and/or utter failure stop me.

Finally, I applied to Jim Long at *Caribbean Boating*. I was hopeful because he'd hired Andy Turpin (now senior editor of *Latitude 38* and a dear friend.) So I knew Jim Long lacked good judgment—hell, *any* judgment!

Jim hired me. But when I went to collect my pay check, he gave me an address in Red Hook instead. "I owe you money and this guy owes me money," Jim said smoothly. "So all you have to do it collect it and keep it and everyone is happy-happy-happy!"

The guy in Red Hook owned a "going out of business" fish wholesale operation and didn't have any money. But he did begrudgingly give me a couple of frozen fish heads instead.

At this point, Carolyn wasn't used to being a writer's wife, and thus asked in wonderment, "You get paid in dead fish?"

The next week was the same thing only different. Jim Long gave me the address of a "going out of business" grocery store in Brenner Bay. They weren't nearly as cooperative, but I did manage to swipe a couple of jars of Planters as I ran out the door shouting, "Even-steven, okay?"

That evening, Carolyn, realizing I was now being paid literally "peanuts," said, "I'd prefer dead fish."

Thus, I started working for Radio One, WVWI. Nicky Russell, Rick Ricardo, and Tex Murphy told me the key to success in radio was having pre-recorded "actualities," not just yak-yaking into a microphone. This was around the time when the St. Thomas US Coast Guard safety office was just beginning to institute "random drug testing" for all USCG captains.

Thus in the middle of my Saturday morning "Marine Report" radio show, there came a loud pounding on the radio studio door and (at least this is how my pre-recorded spoof sounded to the Radio One listener) a group of shrill US Coast Guard drug testers burst in—violently thrusting a paper cup at me.

"But I'm 'live' on the radio," I explained, "I can't do a drug test right now!"

But they insisted, pointing out that "random, unannounced" drug tests were just that.

So I…peed into a paper cup "live"…while on-the-air.

I thought this was *very* funny. Many people did not. The phone lines lit up like a Christmas tree—oops!

The following Monday morning, station owner Bob Noble called me into his Franklin Building office to dismiss me for "intentional audio urination."

I couldn't believe it. "Nobody told me I couldn't take a leak on the air. It ain't fair!"

"What do I have to do, Fatty," he sputtered in anger, "give you a list: no peeing, no crapping, no farting, no vomiting?"

In the end, I managed to sweet-talk my way back into my radio journalist job. Bob Noble really was a great guy who treated everyone with dignity and respect—while paying 'em about ten cents an hour.

Ah, yes! The immense joys of being a much-loved, seldom-paid Caribbean journalist!

It was incidents like the above that forced me back into the more serious print journalism.

I remember the first time I sent off a sailing yarn to a national sailing magazine. "Do you realize trees have to die so you can write this dribble?" was the response.

I figured I was aiming too low and too narrow. So I sent off a story to one of the top literary magazines in New York—whose editor must have been in a particularly foul mood to scrawl, "In twenty-five years of editing, this is the worst manuscript I've ever received."

Just to show him I wasn't discouraged, I sent him another one. Just to show me he was of the same opinion, he replied, "I stand corrected. Your previous submission was the *second* worst of my career."

"How's the writing going," Carolyn would ask me at the end of each literary day.

"Well," I'd respond doggedly, "A lot of editors say I'm writing memorable stuff!"

Of course, it is wonderful to be married to an understanding woman like Carolyn. Our marriage vows should have included a warning about "...being forever the brunt of his jokes until death do you part."

"We've ocean-sailed together now for over thirty-seven blissful years," I often tell new acquaintances, "And if she is good for just another three years, I'm gonna allow her ashore."

Once she mentioned the word divorce, and I responded angrily, "What? *Wild Card* needs to be hauled, could use a new mainsail, and to have her chain re-galvied—and you bring up something frivolous? I mean, don't be so *selfish*, okay?"

I can't believe she puts up with my shenanigans. "She's only said two wrong things in her life," I say, "'I' and 'do' were both of them!"

Or, "How could someone that smart be so dumb when it comes to men?"

Of course, she can dish it out too. "We're poverty-stricken because they pay my husband what he's worth," I heard her tell a friend. On another occasion, "My husband's a realist with low self-esteem." Or, "What he lacks in intelligence, he more than make up for in stupidity!"

One morning I awoke and said to her brightly over the galley table, "I'm feeling optimistic today," A couple minutes later I heard her telling my mother-in-law, "Now he's *delusional!*"

Yacht racing, of course, provides another fertile field for laughter. I've learned, for instance, never to say, "What reaching mark?" while in the protest room. Ditto, "But how could you know that we hit the starting pin on the side *away* from the committee boat," is another.

You have to be careful how you brag to a yacht racer. For example, BVI International Judge Robin Tattersall wasn't too impressed when I told him, "Why, I've never seen a sailboat I couldn't make go slower!"

I mean, a line like that will have cruising sailors rolling in the lee scuppers—yet leaves yacht racers cold.

"I've been passed by jellyfish! Sandbars silt in faster! Why buy a knot meter when calendars are free? Sure, I factor in continental drift. Did I ever tell you about the time I cruised Alaska and was overtaken by a glacier?"

Navigation is another area filled with laughter-potential. I mean, the reason they called it "dead" reckoning before GPS, was because that's how many navi-guessers ended up. My sailing father used to repeatedly quiz me as a young lad on the finer points of coastal piloting: "What's the difference between deviation and variation?" he'd demand. And I'd answer, "The latter is a small, easily held magazine, and the former is non-missionary fun?"

Yes, I remember when even Jimmy Cornell spelled noonsite differently. And when peering each evening through a telescope at celestial bodies didn't mean you were named Tom. It was a simpler time when "shoot the moon" meant something truly innocent.

Sailing around the world can be a tad ego-deflating. In fact, at first I was even confused by the basic terminology: I grimaced, grabbed my crotch, and twisted away in mock pain before a more knowledgeable, globe-trotting sailor set me right with, "Not circum*cision*!"

Nor was geography my strong point. Carolyn had to set me down in mid-Pacific for some serious global tutoring: "Let's see if I can put this in terms a male sailor can easily understand—the South Pacific, think laughing women with flowers in their hair and easily removed pareos," she instructed me. "Let's see, heading west—I feel sheepish even mentioning New Zealand but that probably explains why the 'roos are so quick in Oz, eh? Bali *High* says it all, doesn't it? Thailand—massage parlors. Burma—foot-fetish—you'll love the curly-toed shoes, Fatty! India—Kama Sutra. Africa is the dark continent."

Even the most basic of marine maintenance tasks can sparkle with the right perspective. Recently a wooden boat owner was complaining about keeping up his extensive bright work, and I told him, "The only thing varnished on *Wild Card* is our toilet seat. And I polish it twice a day!"

He seemed a tad confused. "With what?" he asked.

"Soft pads," I replied.

Yes, sailing, especially racing, with some of those "traditionalists" is a bit strange. Once, during the old St. Barths Regatta, we raced on a giant sexually-confused brig. Carolyn was helping to man the foredeck, and its sailing master was intent on catching the large gaffer just ahead. He wanted every possible scrap of sail up. Carolyn had all the flying jibs aflutter and even the topsails topping—and he still wasn't satisfied. "Spanker!" he cried.

"Over my dead body," she spit back.

Ah, the perils of nautical lingo!

I personally feel that this trend can be carried too far. I don't want to end up steering my vessel from a "male-member-pit." These linguistic subtleties are especially important to a writer. Sure, it is easy to say people hanging around waterfront bars love seamen—*if* you spell it correctly!

A lot of cruisers have kids. It's a short jump from rug rat to bilge rat. I grew up on a boat and enjoyed every second of it. Well, I did until I was a teenager and started working on George's Bank aboard the old (1924) riveted iron offshore lobster vessel *Winthrop*. The only reason I signed up was because its skipper, Cap'n Georgie Morten, had been a *Master Mariner* aboard square-riggers in his youth. Anyway, my job was to pitch-fork fish heads into the large wire-mesh pots, to manually bait the lobster traps as they were being swung overboard. It wasn't easy work, but I did my best. One day Cap'n Georgie came down from the pilot house to joke with me. "You're getting pretty good at baiting. Soon you'll be a Master...."

I tossed the pitchfork onto the deck, raised both my fists and hissed, "Don't say it!"

Yeah, teenage boys are sensitive about that.

Generally speaking, sailors are easy-going. But there are limits even among seafarers. For example, soon after *Carlotta* was christened, I had family members aboard for a sail. We had a great day tacking around Boston harbor. It had been years since I'd sailed with my sisters Carole and Gale. Since my ten-foot Lawley tender wasn't very beamy, I'd had to ferry family members out two at time. When it was time for the return trip ashore, it was afternoon and even rougher. Plus, we'd all had a few drinks. Thus I was happy to have just purchased a new two horse outboard for my dinghy. My friend on the boat next to me wasn't so well equipped: he rowed his small pram with a single paddle. And he wasn't making much headway as I putt-putted passed with Carole and Gale.

I slowed when he waved his paddle. "Can I borrow your oars," he asked. I'd patiently waited for just his set of circumstances for almost a decade. "No," I shouted back, " they're my *sisters!*"

Alas, it is traditional-yet-contemporarily-bent jokes like the above which makes my wife's life so crazy. Recently she was signing our 38-foot sloop *Wild Card* up for little "fun" regatta in Vava'u, Tonga and was asked by one of the form-shuffling race officials, "What's your handicap?" Carolyn replied without missing a beat, "I'm married to Fatty Goodlander." The race official must read this publication because he blanched, reached out compassionately, and said with almost a sob, "You poor dear!"

Picking Up the Mooring, Fatty-Style

Basic seamanship and small boat handling seems to have eluded me. This is strange. I mean, I teethed on "Chapman's." I've spent most of my life with a tiller in my hand. I took the Coast Guard safe boating course when I was in diapers. I learned celestial navigation before I learned to drive. Hell, I once even dated a nattily-uniformed girl from the USCG Auxiliary.

Yet I still make the stupidest mistakes.

Example: I recently single-handed into Coral Bay for the Blues Festival. Instead of anchoring, I decided to pick up an empty mooring that a friend of mine told me I could use.

I wasn't exactly sure which one it was, and went to the wrong mooring first. There was a strong, gusty wind blowing. The brisk breeze was kicking up quite a sea on the rocks just to leeward. "Oh, well," I thought, "I'll just have to 'execute' the maneuver perfectly."

I did. I brought *Wild Card* straight into the wind which allowed her to stop dead in the water with the buoy directly under the bows—absolutely perfect *except* for the fact that it was the wrong buoy.

Damn!

I spotted the correct buoy just downwind. *Wild Card's* bow paid off and she trotted off directly at it, as if a faithful dog. This was fine with me. I wouldn't have to return to the tiller, rev the engine and circle. I'd just be able to grab it on the fly.

Wild Card did her part perfectly. She actually bumped the large white mooring buoy with her stem. I had no problem reaching the small float with my trusty boat hook. However, the mooring hawser was extremely heavy because it was a large coil of wet, slippery, tangled line. I wasn't expecting this. Thus I was unable to quickly secure it to my bitts. In fact, I couldn't lift it aboard as I trotted down the port side of the moving boat.

Since the boat was moving with almost 20,000 pounds of inertia, I knew better than to attempt to stop it without taking a bend around something strong.

But by now, I was running out of boat. I decided that I'd lunge forward, gain some slack and secure the seaweedy mooring pennant to my genoa sheet winches.

This would have worked perfectly, if I hadn't had to go around my Bimini supports to gain a fair lead. I fumbled this simple maneuver for one nano-second too long, and thus was one millionth of an inch shy of being able to secure it to winch or cleat.

I grimly decided that I would just have to stop her by brute force. Unfortunately, I was not braced well and the massive pull toppled me off my feet. Thus I began being dragged aft.

Damn!

Quick as a wink, I passed the pennant around my stern rail and horseshoe buoy, braced both my feet, gulped, and took the full load of the moving boat with my flabby arms—with my suddenly considerably longer, flabby arms. Here was a job for Popeye, and I hadn't had any spinach with my rum in a long, long time.

No, maintaining my grip (both on the rope and reality) was not easy. I could feel my muscles tearing, hear my tendons popping, sense my lower back protesting—but I held firm, damn it. I was resolute. Utterly. Thus, I stopped her. Hurray!

The only problem was I could not let go to do anything else. My arms were fully extended beyond the transom. Sweat was beaded on my forehead. Every muscle in my body ached. My brain screamed, "Let go, you damn fool, let go!"

I desperately looked around the cockpit for a piece of line. Normally, my cockpit is littered with spare coils of line. However, we'd just straightened up the boat for guests and I was out of luck.

Double damn!

I glanced up and was puzzled to see a bunch of people in dinghies sort of rafted-up-and-drifting nearby. I hadn't notice them when I'd pulled in. Strange. But before I could fully consider this new development, the wind gusted strongly. I was again being pulled aft—sort of "strained" through the maze of stern rail uprights, antennas, GPS sensors, SSB co-ax, self-steering control lines—a complicated spider-web of expensive & fragile items of great importance.

"Arggghh," I croaked as my turned-away face was mashed into the stainless steel tubes of my Monitor windvane.

"Tsk, tsk, tsk," clucked the vaguely sympathetic folks in the rafted dinghies.

There was no denying it now. I had an audience.

I smiled sickly, as if this on-going nautical situation was a mere trifle, a normal-if-silly event of no real consequence for an experienced sea dog of my caliber.

I knew I had to do something quick. I was hyperventilating. My pulse was off the Richter scale. I was cramping up. And, worse, my audience was growing.

With a desperate lunge, I let go with one hand, snatched the bitter end of a nearby jib sheet, bowlined it to the mooring pennant, then belayed said line to a cleat—and fell backwards onto my cockpit cushions.

I was now officially attached to the mooring. There was one small problem. My boat was backwards.

"No worries, mate!" as my Aussie friends would say.

I reached into my cockpit locker and grabbed a hundred-foot piece of line. Excellent!

Now the trick to appearing "way-cool" while doing complicated boat-handling maneuvers is to not rush. Just move slowly, and everyone will think you're super-together, right?

So I tied the 100-foot line onto the mooring pennant, cast off the pennant, passed everything outside of everything nonchalantly, and leisurely—oh-so-coolly—began to stroll up to the bow.

I knew that the long line would allow me plenty of time to get there. Unfortunately, I'd forgotten about my dinghy. I'd been towing it and it had been hiding "out of sight, out of mind" on the other side of my boat. And, evidently, it had become entangled with the mooring ball.

Suddenly the dinghy appeared, shot forward, and snagged its brand new outboard motor on my extension line.

Now *Wild Card* was being held at a 45-degree angle off the wind in a complicated triangle of dinghy painter, mooring pennant, and extension line.

Triple damn!

I attempted to flip the extension line off. Again. No luck. I took a deep breath and calmed myself. One more time—yes, I finally got it flipped off, and realized I was out of time.

I dashed for the bitts like a meth-crazed madman! I almost made it—just a couple of inches shy. "Oh, God, no!" I heard escape from my lips as I started being dragged backwards towards the shrouds.

It was agonizing. Demoralizing. Horrible!

I was stumbling backwards like a drunken Ed Munster. Humiliation was imminent. My boat was now almost completely sideways to the gusting wind.

"Oh, boy!" I was chanting, "Oh, boy!"

I managed to hold on and clamber over my life lines at the same time—and just snag the lower shroud with my left hand as the pennant line took up in my right.

"TwaNG!!!!!"

I was now acting like a human rubber-band between boat and mooring, my feet kicking crazily in mid-air. Even worse, because a sideways boat has more windage, there was far more strain on the line than before.

I could feel my arms elongating even further. I was getting wider, wider, and wider instead of my usual fatter, fatter, fatter.

And I could now hear an increased buzz from the dinghies. "Is that *really* Fatty," someone asked, "or did an incompetent landlubber steal his boat?"

"Maybe he's making a what-not-to-do video," suggested another, craning his neck to spot the camera boat.

"I told him he should stop the drugs long ago," lamented a third.

Needless to say, I couldn't join in with the laugh track. The pain in my arms was so immense I was having difficulty estimating how many tons of force were required to blow out two 53-year old shoulder sockets.

And the rocks weren't all that far away to leeward.

Quadruple damn!

Cap'n Eliot, from the three-masted schooner *Silver Cloud*, majestically putt-putted by in his dinghy. A true gentleman, he gave me the professional courtesy of pretending not to be staring as he passed. I silently vowed to buy him a drink upon our next meeting.

Now, of course, all I would have needed to do was nod and a dozen Good Samaritans would have rushed to my assistance. But, hey, aren't being stupid and pig-headed two of the things I'm most famous for?

I mean, I've got a Caribbean-wide reputation for Depth-of-Dumbness and now didn't seem like a good time to attempt to change it.

So I grunted. Strained. My face turned red. My entire body started to quiver. Yellow liquid ran down my leg. My tongue protruded from between blue lips.

But, I finally began to pull the line in, inch by inch. Once or twice the wind gusted and I had to stop, hold fast, and pray to a Higher Power. But then there was a lull long enough for me to clamber back inside the lifelines, fall backwards with a crash (clipping the back of my balding head on a ventilator,) and brace my feet on the toe rail.

There was a smattering of half-hearted applause from the dinghies. But the general sentiment was voiced by one big guy off a half-sunk powerboat, "What? Cap'n Fatty's Fabulous Mooring Show is over after only half an hour?"

I didn't reply, being too busy trying to remember my cardiologist's telephone number, how many aspirins I should start chewing, and if my Last Will & Testament (which leaves my entire dog-earred collection of *Mad* magazines to the KATS kids program) was up-to-date.

During all this time, my long-suffering wife, Carolyn, was impatiently waiting on the dinghy dock. Suddenly she was surrounded by a laughing, leering group of excited sailors: my highly entertained, bursting-to-tell audience.

"You wouldn't *believe* what Fatty just did," giggled one of the sailor-girls.

"Was it utterly stupid?" Carolyn shot back brightly. "Unbelievably ignorant? Completely dumb? Totally unnecessary? Infinitely infantile?"

"Yes, yes, yes," the crowd sang out with glee.

"Well then," Carolyn said from hard experience, "then I *would* believe it!"

Of course I didn't know any of this when I picked her up at the dock after carefully Mercurochroming a dozen of my larger wounds.

"How did it go?" she asked.

Luckily I answered with the whole-truth-and-nothing-but-the-truth. "Just another Fat day in Paradise!" I said.

Where's a good line when you need it?

The Agony of Dried Snot

I hate owning a fiberglass boat. I mean, at least wooden craft rot out from under you. Sure, a wooden boat will send you to the poor house, divorce court and insane asylum—but eventually it has the decency to quietly slip beneath the waves and allow its seafaring victims some small, final respite.

Not so a fiberglass boat. No, it is almost eternal in its damnation!

Take our 38-foot Hughes as example: it is always bedeviling us in new and unusual ways—after 18 solid years of repair.

I once showed my family a slide show of our first circumnavigation. One of the innocent children asked me aloud, "Why are you always working on the boat in the pictures. Don't you ever go ashore for fun?"

Fun? What is fun? I mean, I don't have *time* for *fun*—I'm a boat owner! And, yes, circumnavigating is, if the truth be told, really just doing boat maintenance in exotic ports. I wish there was more to it, I really *really* do!

The fact of the matter is that, there are a lot of boats afloat today that look just like boats—but aren't. See, boats are really supposed to be "marine structures" that have structural integrity. Picture an egg. An egg has structure. You can't break it by squeezing it in your hand because it distributes the load. Now picture a hard-boiled egg that has been cracked in a million places. It *looks* just like an egg, weighs the same amount, has all the same stuff, but it is weaker than—well, my morals!

That's how *Wild Card* was. Is. Always will be.

The first time I sailed it, the deck got pregnant on the windward side by the chainplates. That's right, there was a big, big hump there—like a swollen watermelon. I tacked and the deformed hump changed sides.

"Damn," my wife, Carolyn, said. "It must be the chainplates moving. Look, the whole rig is looser than—your sense of reality."

I dashed below. Sure enough, the chainplates were dangling & tinkling in the breeze like—stainless steel wind-chimes!

I had to stop sailing, return to port, and slobber them with many layers of mat, roving, and biaxial.

This added about a ton of weight, but stopped the "swollen watermelon" problem. However, the rig was still as loose as Paris Hilton, because the entire boat was crushing. That's right; it was *narrower* going to windward and *fatter* off the wind.

So I returned to port and snuck up on an outdoor billboard sign in the middle of the night—when I just happened to have a chainsaw in my hand. (Free exterior plywood!)

Soon I had a complete athwart ship bulkhead fiberglassed (dried snot!) into my boat around the mast. It was as uncrushable as a cinder block—and about as heavy.

This kept the beam of my vessel constant. But the rig was still bobbing up and down like a transvestite's Adam's apple! Damn, back to port *again*!

It turns out the "ship-wrongs," (They darn sure weren't ship*wrights*, eh?) working for Howard Hughes at the Hughes boat yard in Canada were experimental, innovative fellows with a wicked sense of humor. They had mounted my mast on a sort of plywood "diving board" platform instead of a compression post. I guess, the idea was to remove the "stress" of it standing up to the wind. Thus, if we'd get a five knot gust, our sails would fill, rigging tighten, mast lower, mast deform, sail-shape change, & depower—cool, eh?

Well, no actually. I mean, we like the wind to push our boat forward, not our mast down. Thus I chain-sawed off the top of a local dock piling (don't tell the marina managers, okay?) and jammed it under the mast.

This did the trick. Sort of. I mean, my "erection" was now completely rigid for weeks. No lumps, no crushing, no pumping. The only problem was—my mast pushed away my keel!

The engineers at Hughes, knowing that the keel of these boats were as weak as a Bill Clinton promise, attached it to the hull by—Velcro! They didn't set the mast on the keel because they knew it was just bolted through "jello-glass." (This looks like fiberglass but has all the structural integrity of...the dessert food.

Thus I had to haul out and fiberglass the front half of my keel on; the mast, now being stepped on its front, sagging lip.

Whew! I had it dicked now, eh? Finally! Mast up, keel down—classic yachty stuff!

Unfortunately, I stupidly tightened my forestay to remove the "foot or two" of headsail lag I had—and tightened and tightened.

My boat now looked like a banana. My jibs were suddenly too long, by two feet. So I slacked the forestay and twisted up the backstay—until I heard a crack and everything got loose again. That was the *aft* edge of keel breaking away from the boat—and it was right back to the shipyard again.

Damn!

Now, some owners of "flexible flyers" like *Wild Card* say that their adjustable backstay is useless. But I don't agree. I use mine to align my engine. Works like a charm!

Now that I finally had the mast and keel glued together, *Wild Card* sailed like demon. It was so fast, in fact, that she cracked the leading edge of her rudder, because there was actually some force on it.

Oh, dear.

This was, evidently, carefully made in two halves and glued together with top-quality, marine-grade—Bazooka chewing gum.

I never knew what sadism *was* until I owned a Hughes 38. I mean, where were the Hughes marine engineers—in jail, angry, and reading DeSade's *Justine* or *Juliette*?

Now, my particular model Hughes doesn't have much water tank capacity—because the topsides are balsa-cored, which is really just a hi-tech name for "sponge."

Yes, we carry plenty of water. Alas, it is uselessly trapped in our "sandwich construction." (This is labeled "sandwich construction" because it is about as strong and non-porous as Wonderbread.)

Even better, our boat has a "full pan" to hide its unsightly electrical wires. This, of course, makes finding and repairing deck leaks nearly impossible. (The original electrical wires only lasted a few months, because they were laying in the puddles of water trapped between the underside of the deck and the pan, ha-ha!)

The "built-in Dorade boxes" were nothing of the sort. The "pan" just shed the buckets of water pouring in long enough for the gullible new owner to sign the bill-of-sale in the dry boat show shed. (Actually, at one point Canadian Mounties were assigned to the Hughes booth at boat shows because so many of the irate owners were having—well, "issues" with Howard!)

Other than the above, I think my boat is pretty well constructed.

So Carolyn and I sail around the world, while regularly tossing "blankets" of wet, resin-impregnated fiberglass cloth at weak pieces of our vessel, as they break off with astounding regularity. We're getting pretty good at it—like brave bullfighters, wielding our life-protecting capes.

"Are you sure this is how it is supposed to be," Carolyn recently asked me, as she frantically attempted to galvy-nail down a hatch that was beginning to lift off when our too-flexible deck was being swept by giant, breaking seas.

"Yep," I said. "If you wanna sail around the world on the pennies that Scotsmen throw away!"

St. Valentine's Day, Sea Gypsy Style!

A lot of potential cruisers—men, mostly—are interested in enticing their spouses offshore. Here's how.

#1) Bribes. Yes, diamonds work well. But bribing your spouse need not be expensive. For instance, I save all my popsicle and ice cream sticks for my wife to use when she does my epoxy work. She seems genuinely impressed with my thoughtfulness and husbandly consideration.

It isn't the amount on the price tag; it's the thought that counts. Example: instead of buying her expensive deck mops or yacht scrubbers, I just cut old manila hawsers into chick-sized chunks and scribble her name in magic marker on a strand. Oh, man-o-man, she practically wears the foredeck's gel coat away when I give her a new one!

Incidentally, it *is* nice to personalize some of these gifts, but it is best not to get too specific. For instance, a "First Mate" coffee mug or a "Bodacious Babe" embroidered bikini will look just as nice with the next wife as it does with this one. (Bottom line: think ahead, sailor!)

#2) Gifts are a bit more subtle than bribes. I mean, "Ten bucks for a half-and-half," isn't considered exactly romantic by the fairer sex. Thus I make sure to "ruffle it up" with bright wrappings and "sensitive man" candlelight—whenever I "gift" my wife on her birthday with a pair of welding gloves, knees pads, or some new grinding disks.

#3) Dinner Out Ashore! This *always* turns on my wife. So I make a *point* of inviting her ashore for dinner at least once a year! The Big Night Out is always fun—if you avoid a few simple mistakes. For instant, your wife will smear herself with make-up and douse herself in perfume. Why, my wife broke three combs just attempting to untangle her hair! Regardless of how ridiculous she looks tottering down the gangplank in her duct-taped high heels, tell her she is beautiful, stunning, captivating, etc. Don't worry; it is *impossible* to lay it on too thick. No matter how lavish the praise, she'll find your compliments stingy.

One more thing: beware the posterior! That's right, woman are ass-adverse! Butts can only be described as "itty-bitty" or "slender" or "tight." Why, you can descriptively go all the way to pedophile and not worry!

If she's an experienced cruising wife, she'll bring a large open-at-the-top duffle bag purse, to catch any left-over or "extra" food that might "fall off the table" (if you catch my meaning.) She might not remember what the menu is for, or might begin to eat by shoving her face into the plate. Or she might yell graphic "Barnacle-Bill-the-Sailor" obscenities throughout the meal. If you're surrounded by other yachties at the restaurant, this won't be a problem. They'll have the good sense to ignore her "offshore" table manners. However, if you're seated amid landlubbers, watch out, a few of them may vomit.

It is best not to take too big of a risk on the actual restaurant itself. I prefer Mickey D's whaleburger with extra ketchup, if you desire a specific recommendation.

#4) Out for Drinks! This is similar to eating ashore except you might do it far, far more often—say, every month or so if your spouse is an alkie.

The important thing during these candy-is-dandy, but liquor-is-quicker "booze foreplay" shore excursions, is to demonstrate the depth of your love—real, genuine, caring love for her, for her mind, her body, and, yes, even her liver!

Don't let her drink too much. When she glances away, take a large gulp from her glass. When she goes to the "little girl's room" polish off her drink. Accuse her of being forgetful when she returns suspicious.

If she tries to order a third drink, cut her off. Yes, apply tough-love, and she'll adore you for it. However, don't be *too* mean. Example: I allow her, for the next four or five hours, to idly play with the melting ice in my discarded drinks, and to lick my swizzle stick or chew my lime rinds. Who says I ain't nice?

#5) Movies Out! This isn't so bad, if you tell her straight off "no popcorn!" My three favorites: "Titanic"," Jaws"*,* and "The Perfect Storm*."*

#6) Rental DVD's aboard. Since Harry Reems, retired, I prefer Seymour Butts or Ben Dover.

#7) Girl Time! Yes, it important that females have a chance to bond, too. Group activities are best: filleting fish and learning the complete song lyrics to "Frig'n in the Riggin'" are good female-friendly tasks to start with.

#8) Praise & Flattery: the two cornerstones of every watery relationship. Like my father once told me, "Son, always praise people. Ninety-nine percent won't realize you're doing it and the other one percent will appreciate it!" Wise counsel, eh?

This is dead-easy, once you get the hang of it. Just blurt it out, don't worry about how it sounds. "I like the way your breasts swayed while you were cutting up that octopus for bait," is fine. So is, "I liked the way your hair looked during the dismasting." Don't worry if it sounds odd to a male ear, it will sound smooth as honey to a female one. "The way the mud squishes between your toes in the shipyard—pure sex!" or "Your braided nose hairs, and those damp dreds under your arms—Richter Scale wow!" or even, "I love your cedar bucket sounds!"

See how simple it is?

#9) Sex. Yes, sex itself is a powerful motivator. For instance, my spouse knows that if we pitch-pole, we'll have sex immediately afterwards if we're alive. This gives her something to focus on other than fear. Ditto, severe gales. I mean, I think of our hard-used Para-Tech sea anchor and our new Jordan series drogue as—well, "time-out adult toys" if you get my drift—or, hopefully, lack thereof.

And I won't even mention what I've promised to do to my wife if she crews with me around Cape Horny!

#10) Flowers. I don't know why, but even hardened sailor-girls are crazy for flowers. This is why sex is so casual in the tropics: flowers are easy to steal. But that's not true in more northern climes. And modern florists are expensive! However, here's a money-saving tip: their trash bins are seldom locked and "dumpster diving" is a required skill for a frugal circumnavigator on a budget. True, some women are a bit put off by wilted and/or almost-dead flowers. But, hey, if it is in the latter part of a romantic relationship, what could be more appropriate?

Of course, we've been primarily focusing on the fairer sex. This is not only sexist, it is unfair. Many men don't go to sea because of—er, "performance" problems.

"This is ironic," one sad cruising wife told me, "especially since he's surrounded by all those *other* erections: like his main mast, his mizzen mast, his stout spinnaker pole, his rigid inflatable, the hard dodger, his autopilot ram, his bow-thruster—grim reminders never end, eh?"

Hints for woman:

#1) Don't be too spatially accurate. Even the smallest cucumber is six inches and can get you into a pickle!

#2) Praise his Macho-ness. If your wheel-chair bound husband uses his cane to press the button of your electric Barients, just say, "Oh, baby, you sheet *hard*, honey!"

#3) Never forget the exterior play area of your vessel was not named after a rooster—no matter what your mother told you.

#4) When going ashore for dinner or drinks, Hooters is always a safe choice.

#5) If you want to be a successful gold-digger, find a man with a large goldplater. This isn't terribly difficult. Just go into a sailor's bar and find the old silver-haired duffer in the yachting cap whose waist size and age match. Tell him stuff like, "I find fiberglass dust erotic," or "I don't want a *thing* until your yacht's sail inventory is complete!" or, just bluntly blurt out,

"I'm—*wet* around boats!"

If the old duffers wife is there, just signal your intentions by asking stuff like, "Did the same surgeon who did your eyes do your tummy tuck? Thigh lippo? Nose job?"

This should endear her to you.

#6) In Mixed Company. Obviously, you'll be spending a lot of time with other sailing couples should you marry a rich-yachtie-about-to-croak. So always put a positive spin on things. Or, to put it another way, the more active your Romeo is, the sooner he won't be. Thus, if the subject of, say, multiple orgasms come up—just gush air-headedly, "Well, I don't know how to count that high, sugar!" or "He don't need no Viagra. Hell, once I had to shoot him with an elephant tranquilizer gun!" Or, if your husband is from the same country Rocky Balboa is, "That Italian Stallion stuff ain't no lie!" Or, "Our boat don't just rock, she Tsunamis!" Or, "Thank God for the extra carbon fiber that Swan put into the master stateroom's bunk support brace!"

#7) Continuing Education. Yes, it can be fun for sailormen and sailorwomen to stay active during their sunshine years. And nothing is better for an active lifestyle than learning. Thus, entice your skipper with a "How to Drink Beer" instructional video. If he isn't interested in learning, but you'd still like to continue your education alone, why not a night course in "Preparing Snacks for your Football Watching & TV-adled Husband!"

The bottom line: cruising together is a team. It only takes a few seconds for a cruising wife to e-mail-forward her husband some porn hyper-links—or for him to give her a large, floating, waterproof credit card holder.

Yes, cruising together towards the Pearly Gates can be fun—especially for fun-crazed, sun-dazed, geriatric sea-gypsies!

The Writes and Wrongs of Slinging Ink

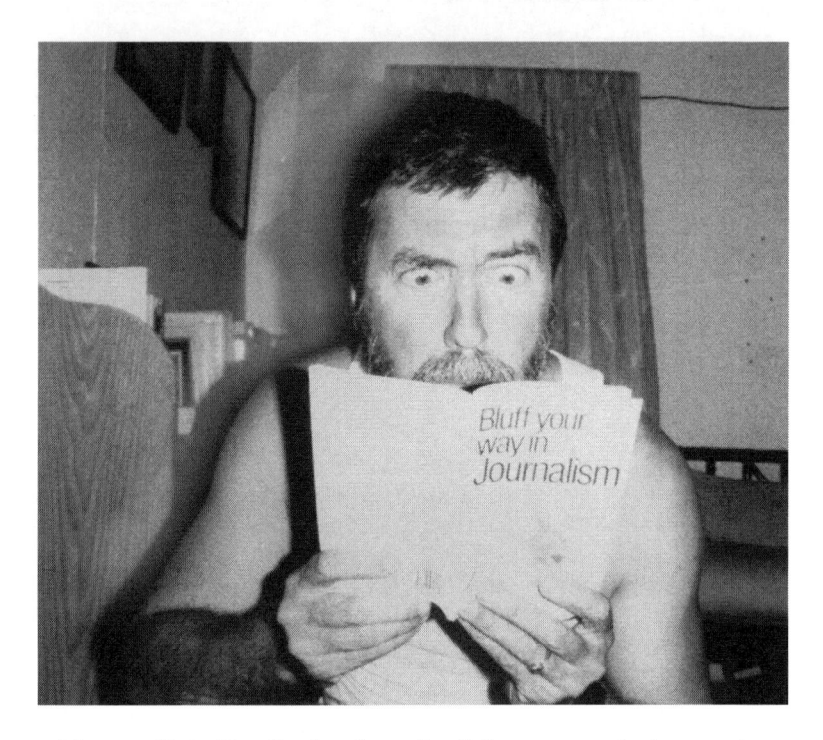

"Are you Fatty Goodlander, the writer," the woman asked me as she approached tentatively at the St. Thomas Yacht Club. I was a bit wary because she didn't look like a typical fan of mine. In fact, she didn't look like she had any mental problems at all. She was nicely dressed, relatively clean, and even wore a gold Rolex watch on her wrist.

I peered at her intently. She didn't flinch, look guilty, or throw up. The more I stared at her, the more nervous her stylish appearance made me. She didn't look like anyone had ever broken her nose, there were no track marks on her arms, and all of her teeth appeared to be her own.

What the hell could she want with me?

Needless to say, I was on my guard. "Yes, Madame," I said. "I'm Cap'n Fatty. Guilty as charged."

She hesitated for a moment, indecisive, and then blurted it out in a rush. "I've read all of your books," she said breathlessly. "And just wanted to tell you that when I read them I laugh so hard I *pee!*"

Not all the comments I've had on my writing are so deliciously complimentary. "You don't need an editor," angrily slashed another slush pile surfer at the bottom of my rejection slip. "You need a *therapist.*"

The first review of my book "Seadogs, Clowns, and Gypsies" was hardly a rave. "In his preface, Cap'n Fatty infers he is not a skillful writer—and then conclusively proves his point throughout the remainder of the text."

When I released "Chasing the Horizon," one literary critic thanked Cap'n Fatty for "...making the paper of his second book *softer* than his first." I've had people hint that my writing was crappy, but never so literally.

I bore that in mind when I read a totally scalding review of one of my books. The reviewer totally savaged it. I was at my sister's house at the time, and went into her bathroom to cry in privacy. While there, I scribbled an angry note to the heartless reviewer. "I'm in the smallest room of the house, and I have your recent review in front of me. I'll soon put it behind me..."

Part of being a successful writer, of course, is dealing with the public. "What kind of stuff do you write," I'm often asked. "Oh, it varies," I usually reply. "According to most editors, it varies between poor and worthless!"

Even after I laboriously learned how to write a simple declarative sentence, I *still* had to endure some harsh criticism.

By the late 1980's, I was a decent enough wordsmith to work for *Boat International* of England. Sir Kenneth Wilson was its highly respected, awarding winning artistic director—and a publishing hero of mine.

"I say, Fatty old boy," he told me, "the next time you're passing through London, stop by my office to show me some of your marine photography."

Again and again, I told him that I wasn't a skilled photographer. But he insisted—and even hinted that they might stop buying my stories if I refused.

So a few months later I was in his office, showing him twenty color transparencies "...which I just happened to have in my pocket." which were, in reality, the very best photographs I'd taken in the last three decades of being a marine shutterbug.

As he carefully placed my color slides on the light table, and quickly (yet thoroughly) inspected each one, he lightly chatted about the London metro and the day's weather. And I realized that the rest of the distinguished *Boat International* staff were gradually getting quieter and quieter—while awaiting Sir Kenneth Wilson's pronouncement on the quality of my photos and my talent as a marine photographer. "I say, Fatty," he almost shouted as he casually handed my slides back to me. "I say, Fatty—so you're a *writer*!"

Needless to say, a writer needs a massive ego just to survive. Early in my career, Carolyn used to refer to my manuscripts as boomerangs because "No matter where he sends them, they immediately come back!"

There was a time when I briefly considered getting into scribbling some porno under a pen name. I had a friend who was highly successful at it. "What's the best part," I asked him. He replied, "Why, the *research*, of course!"

Successful freelance requires a good head for business—something I've never had.

My first attempt at commercial ghostwriting was disastrously comic. A tongue-tied neurotic on his way to visit Doctor Kevorkian—hired me to ghost write his suicide note. But I foolishly failed to get the money up-front.

Damn.

There seems to be no limit to my ignorance. Once, on my St. Thomas radio show, I described my fiberglass boat as being "...totally impervious to marine orgasms."

My wife of thirty years could only sadly nod her head in rueful agreement.

Even my 16-year-old daughter is now aware of how—er, unusual—her father really is. Once, when a fan of mine commented on how I made my living by playing the fool—my daughter relied sorrowfully, "Yep, Mom and I used to think it was an act too!

Fatty taking a photo of Glenn and Erja on their boat, Aku Ankka

Write On, Peter!

Peter signing his book "Adrift on a Sea of Blue Light"

I was in Borneo. It was night. Pitch-black. We were anchored off an illegal logging camp in the middle of a disappearing rain-forest—far up an uncharted, croc-guarded river.

Dyak Indians slid silently passed in dug-out canoes—as if ghosts from another era.

Fireflies lit the gnarled trees.

Snakes swam.

Decay.

Rot.

Death.

I was scared and worried and thrilled—which is just how I like to be. I felt alive. Lit up. High! I was getting exactly what I came for—a writer needs to kiss life full-on-the-lips if he is to write well. There is, alas, no substitute for hard-earned, knuckle-busting, ego-bruising experience.

I mean, if you haven't squatted in some ditch in South America, Africa, or Asia, and disparagingly crapped on your ankles—how are you gonna accurately convey the reality of the Turd World?

But the writing life isn't all fun and games—there are boring parts too. Later that evening, just before I fell off to sleep in my mosquito-netted, (hopefully) malaria-free bunk, I rummaged though a pile of old American magazines to do a little market research.

I usually enjoy this—especially if the articles are poorly written. It gives me hope. Anyway, I just happened to flip open one of the glossier mags to a story about some guy sailing in the Med...

...and the words immediately rang true. He'd been there. Done it. Tasted it. Tongued it. Kissed it. Licked it—wow! *Good stuff!*
And so I flipped back to his byline—P. Muilenburg...and smiled a big fat smile.

How do you measure a man? By many yardsticks Peter Muilenburg falls woefully short. He is poor in the empty-pockets, kite-string-for-a-belt, duct-tape-on-his-eyeglasses sense. He seems to have no idea how to use the levers of power. After forty years in the same small place, zoning boards, bank presidents, and real estate developers haven't the foggiest of notion who (or what) he is. (If they do, they certainly don't care.)
...even his yacht is... well, not very!
...and his tie-dyed 60's politics—please!
And yet Peter Muilenburg is the man I most admire on St. John... the man that I'd most like to become.
How can this be?

It was a typical St. John party—during which I drank so much that I drank myself sober. (Or even worse, believed I had.)
It has since gone down in Coral Bay legend as the Party of Three Fiddlers—a musical extravaganza which 'just sort of happened' when the Sun Mountain Fiddler (Dick Solberg), Dave Dostal, and Peter Muilenburg all uncased their fiddles... while Joe Colpitt, Sexy Thea, and I beat on our guitars. (Even Lou Lou Magras from St. Barths wobbled a tune or two!)
Rafael, Peter's older son, was there—tilting his head in that quizzical, analyzing, deep-thought way of his. He was perfectly at ease with his parents and his younger brother. The Muilenburgs are first-and-foremost family, true... but they are also best friends and mutual supporters as well.
At one point Rafael was playing the bongo drums off in a corner... eyes rolled back in his head, his mouth agape, shoulders undulating... not looking at all like the Ivy-league, West Coast lawyer he'd become.
Diego, the younger son, is handsome as a movie star. He's such a straight-ahead good kid, he is almost surreal. Once I hired him to a job for me for a few weeks. When I paid him what I promised, he said, "That's too much!" as he attempted to hand back the money.
Across the noisy, smoke-filled room was Dorothy. Dorothy is Earth Mother. She is quiet, reserved, private, easy-going, and soft-spoken—the perfect school marm. But it would be a mistake to think that, because Dorothy is so caring and kind and considerate, that she is weak. She is not. She is strong—in some ways stronger than the rest of them combined. There is stainless-steel in the soul of this woman... and only a fool would cross her.
Peter was playing fiddle—blinking, halting, jabbing.
Now Peter's fiddle playing... is enough to make an alley cat in heat consider giving up sex. But that doesn't stop Peter. He's a hootenanny-type player who knows the joy is in the music, not the technique. And so he just sails right into the tune... scratching and jabbing away until he finds a note... any dang note... jiggles it... and bends it... and bows it... for all that note is

worth. Every once in awhile his fiddle spits out a brief melodic run... and afterwards Peter sort of stops, allows the fiddle to fall from his chin... as if, he too, is thinking, "I wonder where that came from?"

I glance over at Dorothy—the love for Peter so fierce and plain in her eyes.

Peter had just gotten, I knew, some bad news about his Parkinson's disease. But he didn't let it show.

I was nodding off—misplacing my drink, losing my ashtray, stupidly allowing my guitar to slide down a wall.

And I was looking at Peter while hearing my own father say, "It is not what happens to you, son, that people judge you by... but how you deal with it."

I decided right then and there that Peter was 'dealing with it'... and *had* dealt with life... pretty well. So the following day when I woke up in the late afternoon, before I lost the good-vibe feeling, I penned Peter a brief note.

Why? Because we so often don't say the things we should to those we love. If we're in some bar and an asshole annoys us... sure, we might loudly tell him off... but almost never do we tell the people who delight and nurture us... that they have.

"Ahoy Peter," my letter said. "Just a quick note to tell you that I think you've got it... got it pretty much right."

Yeah, I suppose it is unusual for one man to write another a love letter like that—but if you act out of kindness, what you do is seldom wrong. And as a person that's enough. I like and admire Peter, told him so, and that's that.

But as a writer, of course, it falls short. I owe the reader more—to illuminate Peter... to allow my heart to speak in ways my head cannot.

Here goes: there is a certain endearing boyishness—an eager Eagle-scout-ness—which is at the very core of Peter. He is earnest in the best sense of the word. Oh, Lord, yes, he's a preacher's son—even if he's rejected the specifics of the Christian message. Peter cares. There are rules in life. A higher being. Sin exists. We, as human beings, have choices. We can go this way or that.

And sometimes it is important which.

Peter is one of those rare individuals who isn't full of shit. By that I mean morality isn't a theoretical equation to him—but a daily struggle. He doesn't just *believe* in racial equality—he put his life on the line as a freedom rider in the American South in the early 1960's of desegregation. He doesn't just mouth words of peace—he refused to go ("Hell no, we won't go!" was the chant.) and *still* refuses to go along with the war-mongers of today.

And he's modest about it. When I questioned his work in the Cause... his time in the Movement... how it felt to be locked up that one night... in a jail cell... hiding behind a post... waiting to be shot at by those good-ole-boys creeping around out back...

...he dismisses it.

"Aw," he says, "I don't want to make it a big deal. It was fun. I was young... as much interested in getting laid as anything else."

Not too many people have put their life on the line for any cause—let alone the civil rights of others. Those few who have... seldom let us forget that they did—which is their earned right. Peter is the only man I've ever met who has done one without the other.

He doesn't suck up. The only person who has ever visited St. John who Peter was rude to was Richard Milhouse Nixon.

He doesn't net-work—he'll keep a senator from St. Thomas waiting as he chats with a homeless drunk in Coral Bay... because the later needed the kindness more than the former. Example: I bumped into Peter at the 2004 St. John Carnival. I was in full party mode: dancing, singing, drinking

Peter was there with St. John school teacher Doris Jadan. Doris is a wonderful woman with a huge heart—but she's getting old now. She is frail. Unsteady. But Doris has been really swell to me over the years and I wanted to say hello to her. But it was never quite convenient: too many old friends to greet, too much food, another cold beer. When I finally decided to make time for Doris—it was too late. She'd tired. Peter had brought her home.

That's Peter—always doing what the rest of us would be doing... if we were better people.

The last time I saw Peter, he was walking alone down the road in Coral Bay. It was hot, and his bald spot sweated in the scorching sun. His left arm was held stiffly at his waist and his right hand gripped the backside of its open palm. He shuffled.

"That's courage," I thought to myself. "That's class."

On Ports and Passages

Fatty walking on St. Barth's

My wife, Carolyn, and I were recently asked, "What's the best part of cruising?" We immediately responded in unison with different sides of the same coin. "The passages," I said, while she replied, "The ports!"

I think this is common. Many cruising couples have a male sailor who loves to travel combined with a female traveler who loves to sail. (Not all, of course.)

Most of my personal cruising pay-off is within the ocean journey itself. I feel at peace, in harmony, and filled with joy while at sea. Carolyn, on the other hand, enjoys the passages, true, but looks more forward to the destination.

When we share our adventures with others, Carolyn talks of the wonderful things that happened to us on terra firma, while I fondly recall the magical moments within Mother Ocean's bosom. Of course, I have the same stock answer for both the "what's your favorite ocean" question and the "what's your favorite port" question as well.

"My last one!"

It's true. After forty-five years of living aboard and ocean sailing, I can honestly say that it just gets better. Why? Wasn't it better before bareboats, GPS, DVD's, ATM's, cyberspace, and jet-travel? Well, yes, in a way it was. But, I personally, wasn't better. I was more judgmental then, I carried too many societal yardsticks. Now, I realize I have none of the answers—so I can enjoy the questions more fully.

Everywhere I sail in the world somebody rows out to me as I'm dropping my hook and says, "You should have been here ten years ago!" What this person is really saying is: "I was, you weren't—so, I'm cool!"

That's fine. That's a part of human nature. But the important thing to remember is: these are the "good ole days" right now. We'll never have another moment as perfect as this one to live life fully—especially if it is upon the deck of a small vessel on a large ocean.

The word "travel" comes from the French *travail* or, "to work." Sailing offshore is a *lot* of work in many ways. That why the ports are so sweet. You've earned them. Yes, airplanes go to windward well. So what? At the very core of the cruising lifestyle, is the slowness of the passage; its languidness, its serendipity, its unknowable, unfathomable, hidden delights.

Anais Nin, one of my favorite word goddesses, once said, "When you travel, you don't see what is, but who you are."

True.

To travel is to peel the onion of oneself; to discard your many unexamined prejudices.

Carolyn and I have had many wonderful times in crappy places; merely because we don't accept the external labels of others to cloud our reality. Sure, India is crowded, dirty, noisy, and a complete bureaucratic nightmare. But, it is also one of the most mystical, enjoyable places in the world, especially glimpsed from the deck of a small boat.

The most magical port I have ever experienced was (natch) during the most magical period of my youth—in the late 1970's, while in my late twenties, with Carolyn, aboard *Carlotta*, in St. Barthelmey, West Indies.

It was, for a freedom-loving hedonistic sailor like myself, the Harbor of Eden. The very air intoxicated me. There were sailors from all around the world, a regular UN of yachting. Music was everywhere. Champagne flowed. Poets spouted. Painters brushed. Potters potted. Writers scribbled. Hey, was that Mikhail Baryshnikov? Raquel Welsh? Jimmy Buffett? Harrison Ford? Bob Dylan? Mick?

Did Philippe Poupon just tack into the harbor on *Fleury Michon*? Was that Mike Birch on *Third Turtle*? Bernard Moitessier, roaring drunk on *Joshua*?

...was that demented woman in the hooker outfit I'd given the hiccup-punctuated music appreciation lecture to last night at Le Select *really* a classical pianist with the Berlin Philharmonic? (I ashamed to report she was!)

Oh, what style St. Barths had! I decided (and still believe) that if I could ever have one-tenth the class of Marius Stackelborough or Lou Lou Magras or Fast Eddie of Gustavia—that I would be *far* cooler than Brando, Bogart, and James Dean combined.

Carolyn and I stayed for almost a year without ever coming up for air. It was as if we'd always known, deep within our hearts, that life could be this good—a sensuous, artful, dance-crazed, intellectually-lit fairy tale... and yet were somehow shell-shocked to discover our core-belief was actually true.

Ah, but is this just the naiveté of youth talking—a Caribbean coming-of-age fable?

I think not.

Thirty years later Carolyn and I felt the same way about a completely different place: the lonely deserted isles of Chagos in the middle of the Indian Ocean.

There were no bars, no rock stars, no beautiful people—but everything I'd ever wanted in a group of 33 deserted islands—and less!

No people. No government. No—hassle!

I'd never experienced life under such Utopian conditions. Wouldn't it be near-perfect?

Yes, is the answer. Yes, indeed! And, like St. Barths, we had to sternly force ourselves back to the unreality of accepted daily existence or go native forever.

I love America, too. I've been down the Mississippi River three times (*Elizabeth, Corina, Panique*) and would love to make the muddy, treacherous trip again. It is true that "people on the river are happy to give" as the Creedence Clearwater Revival song (*Proud Mary*) says.

Traveling down America's sewer pipe to New Orleans is a continuous delight. I don't think anyone can gunkhole with King Al (the Neptune of the Mississippi) for a couple of months without falling in love with the people of rural America: so unpretentious, so hardworking, so down-to-earth.

Georgetown, South Carolina, was another special port for us. We'd just blown up our diesel, we were broke, and we didn't know a soul in the Deep South. But the entire town banded together (thank you, Ken & Robin and Tim & Katie!) to help us get back to sea again.

St. Augustine is our favorite stop in Florida. Somehow I briefly commanded their (St. John's county) library system when the head librarian, Louise Darby's, husband died. And, since I had no degree in library science, I had to bill myself as an info-manic instead! (See, you can *never* anticipate the best, weirdest parts of cruising!)

The finest place I've ever lived under the American flag was St. John, USVI, Caribbean Sea, Earth. It was the first island I ever lived on where the word "brotherhood" was never spoken, but practiced every day in every way.

I was then, and still am, enraptured with the entire Caribbean Sea. Bob Marley still reigns there. I've explored its nooks and crannies for over three decades, and still haven't scratched the surface.

We must go back to the San Blas Islands. The Kuna Indians have much to teach me about living in harmony with nature.

Every port in which we anchored in the Tuamotus (French Polynesia) was a wonderful mystery to be unlocked. Palmerston Island, in the Cooks, has to be the most welcoming rock on the planet. We love Indonesia. Bali is a Hindu dream. Thailand is still the Land of Smiles. We can't wait for the thugs to be tossed out of charming, long-suffering Burma, so we can cruise there. Does time really stand still in the Maldives? It seems to. Madagascar has been slowly moving away from the rest of the world for 100 million years of continental drift—the most unique chunk of dirt on the planet.

Africa is—home. For us. Mankind, I mean. What an odd feeling to come over a hill, see a plain full of wild animals grazing to the horizon, and think, "I'm home. This is where—where my people began."

St Helena is so lonely in the middle of the wind-swept South Atlantic that the family (okay, it is a big family but obviously one-blood) that lives there, makes a special effort to welcome all hearty sailors—and has since Slocum.

Yes, there are hundreds of harbors on this watery planet of which I can say, depending on mood, are the "best place I've ever sailed into."

Which ocean do I like best? Certainly the two great trade wind passages are the Cape Town to Brazil run up the middle of the South Atlantic, and the Panama Canal to Torres Straits "Coconut Milk Run" across the wide Pacific. Given the right time of year, sailing conditions will be near-perfect the whole way.

Yes, the North Atlantic has its own circular charm of Bermuda, Azores, Gibraltar, Canaries, Caribbean, and the good ole US of A.

But my favorite ocean is the southern half of the Indian. I like its big swells, high winds, and majestic seas. It is totally untamed, uncivilized, uncaring and, thus, it is seldom visited. Almost deserted. "Seriously empty," as one storm-tossed sailor joked to me. And there are almost no places to stop. But the tiny specks that exist are beyond compare: Christmas, Cocos Keeling, Rodriquez, and Reunion.

The biggest problem I have as an eternal sea gypsy, is deciding where to sail next. There's an embarrassment of riches. It isn't easy to make a mistake. And, if I do, I just tack away. What could be better?

But my perfect harbor, via my favorite ocean, will not be yours, nor should it be. I am not advising you to follow my route, only my example. The future awaits. The whole world is, if you just allow it to be, your oyster *if* you are a sailor. You've been thinking about it your whole life, haven't you? Why not make today, the someday you've always dreamed of? Why not allow the glorious future to be now?

Kuna sailboat in the San Blas Islands 2005

Zen and the Art of Sailing

I have a confession to make: I've discovered Zen.

Zen is a system of thought by which people like myself can follow a simple, logical, step-by-step approach to conclude they aren't as dumb as they are.

Nice, eh?

The key to Zen is "The Now."

This can be complicated but basically it means no guilt. Example: to your friends you can honestly say, "I've pooped on you in the past and will poop on you in the future; but within this glorious moment of "The Now," is a moment of relative non-pooping. So why are you on such a lower-plane-of-consciousness as to still be mad at me?"

In the 1960's this was called "laying on a guilt trip" but now it neatly comes under the much broader heading of Zen.

Yes, Zen Masters (why be modest?) such as myself know to ignore the "History and Mystery" of life.

Being a Zen Master is kinda fun. You get to order people around in incomprehensible ways, while looking wise. And you can smirk when they get confused. Example: "The Past is History and we all know you can't change history! So why worry about the past? And the future is a mystery! In fact, we don't even know if we have a future. We only have the present. And, aw-shucks, when things happen in the glorious 'here and now,' we don't even know if they are good luck or bad!"

Did you understand the above?

Neither did I.

That's Zen.

And that's why it is so nice to be a Zen Master: you get to watch your students and devotees attempt to fathom such gibberish.

Of course, you have to keep your students/slaves/zombies motivated. I mean, enlightenment is always *just* around the next corner—until you get to that corner and discover it is, alas, One More Path!

"How you say," giggled a Thai monk at the wheel of a silver BMW with a diamond-studded ying/yang symbol hanging from his mirror, "we play 'em like fish, no?"

If your students begin to waver, you just zap 'em with a parable in the fine old mumbo-jumbo tradition. "Once there was old live-aboard sailor who adored his son. One day the son found a Jet-ski drifting through the anchorage. He rode it proudly, throwing up great rooster-tail wakes and making irritating noises like an angry bee. The old foolish man rushed to the wise Harbor Master and said, 'Oh, this is great luck! Now, we will be able to harvest our barnacles better!' The Harbor Master said, 'Maybe so, maybe no.' The next day the spoiled-rotten son rode his Jet-ski into the side of a Tortola ferry and broke his leg. 'Oh, this is horrible luck,' the old man told the wise Harbor Master. 'Now my son won't be able to help me during the barnacle harvest!' And the Harbor Master merely repeated, 'Maybe so, maybe no.' The following day, the DPNR raided the harbor and sent all the young men without broken legs to fight and die in the Global War Against Litter and Literacy. And, because the local barnacle-harvesting labor shortage made the market price of Caribbean barnacles triple—the father and son got rich."

See how easy it is? Remember: the more you avoid any logic or common sense in your Zen parable, the better it will stand the test of time.

Don't worry; your students will accept anything: "Money is evil! Possessions are evil. You don't know the Path. You are lost. I will help you. But first you have to pass a spiritual test: what is your credit card pin number?"

I know, I know—it would seem they'd balk but they don't.

Such is the 'wisdom of Eastern thought.'

Since I've Zenned-up-to-speed I haven't lost a single argument with my wife. True, she's in the right 99% of the time, but I just dismiss her with, "How sad to choose being right over being kind! Don't you know that 'right' is stupid? That True Wisdom only arrives when you are willing to admit being wrong when you are not? Is your ego so out-of-control—so fragile—that it has to grasp at such weak straws as the truth? What the matter with you, honey, is that you must pretend to know what you know, as if you know it."

If she's wrong, the process is more streamlined. "Dummy," I say.

Zen and the Art of Sailing is a natural match—but it really doesn't matter. You can make money off of almost any silly idea—motorcycles or something equally nonsensical. Westerners are that gullible.

The hardest part is keeping a straight face. Only the capitalistic Chinese are honest enough to show Buddha laughing (all the way to the bank).

Example: if someone is missing their wallet and confused about where it is—and I happen to have possession of it, I don't stoop to explain its physical location. I merely say, "Two days from now, tomorrow will be yesterday. What's it really matter?"

Of course, California is the place to cash in. One Tibetan scammer who conquered LA was so happy, he screamed gleefully, "Rich people here are so screwed up they think I can help them!!!!!"

L. Ron Hubbard is, of course, one of my heroes. A writer of such limited skills he was forced to write trash for sci-fi nuts, he had to supplement his meager income at writer's conferences. There he'd tell his audience something like, "If I was really a crook, I'd get involved in religion. That's where the real money is!"

Yes, it is 'clear' to me he was a genius. He even knew the best way to hoodwink the gullible was to include the lofty word 'science' in the title!

But I digress. The real question, Grasshopper, is; will Zen make you a better sailor? Yes, is the answer.

You'll learn there is no such thing as the 'true' wind because truth is relative. Ditto the apparent wind—what has wind direction to do with raising a child anyway?

If you happen to lose your vessel on a reef, call up your insurance company with a light heart. "I once had a water glass. It was a perfect water glass. Every morning I'd drink cool mineral water from it. I liked it. It felt nice in my hand. But I knew someday it would break—that it would someday shatter into a million pieces and not be able to be put back together again. So now it has. Of course, I realize I have three choices and one bad option—and the bad option is denial. I am not in denial. The glass has shattered, the ship is lost. True. I can't change it. Nor can I just 'leave' the reality of the shipwreck. No, I must accept it. And if I was able to also accept an insurance check for $247,000—well, all the better to show me The Way and Wisdom of Zen!"

This doesn't always work. Not all insurance agents are enlightened. In fact, some need a little prodding by an aggressive agnostic with a law degree—but, alas, I hesitate to mention such sad, sordid legal realities.

And if we should happen to meet someday and I punch you in the nose—don't hate me for it. See my innocence, instead. Seek to understand me, not judge me. Look 'beyond behavior.'

I do. I really do. I practice what I preach. For example, the editor of this publication originally rejected this piece on the premise it had nothing to do with boats and/or the Caribbean.

"Expectations are just set-ups for disappointments," I placidly informed him. "Impatience is just a denial of the Now. We all have separate realities. There is no good and evil. You are only a thought away from a happy feeling. Change is the only constant. Let us all learn to love 'love' lovingly. I can see God's fingerprints everywhere. Let us celebrate! Embrace! Rejoice!"

The Perils Of Pearls

My wife, Carolyn, cannot sail past a pearl farm without drooling. This is unfortunate: there are strict laws in French Polynesia regarding the sale of pearls, possession of pearls, and/or export of pearls. Penalties can be extreme: confiscation of the vessel is just one arrow in a quiver of draconian choices. When I mentioned these disconcerting enforcement facts to my wife, she bristled and bluntly suggested that the "French colonial oppressors" should perform an impossible sex act upon themselves.

"Honey," I said, "be reasonable...." But, of course, I was wasting my time. She's a hopeless addict and her lust for pearls knows no bounds. She will never be reasonable when it comes to nacre: she wants more, Bigger, *BETTER* pearls! Yes, she's a classic addict is the sense she needs an ever greater 'dosage' of *Pinctada Margaritifera* just to maintain her oyster-scented, greedy little high.

Currently, we're in Tahiti. It took us a long time to sail here because, well, we made a couple of... unscheduled 'emergency' stops in the Tuamotus. Poor *Wild Card*! She wallows sickeningly; dangerously overloaded with... with... her, er, furtively-gotten gains!

That's right: the bilge is full. So are the starboard water tank ("Shh!") and that secret compartment under the head... that's chock-a-block, too!

We have a pearl, singular. We have lots of pearls, plural. Bags of 'em. Sacks of 'em! Strings of them! Small ones, big ones, nicked ones, scarred ones, and carved ones! Black ones. White ones. Fresh and salt ones! Ones that 'flash' eggplant and wink pink and stammer silver... pearls of every race, creed, and color imaginable.

Of course, some got away. They roll around the cabin sole of our vessel like expensive, pretty, berserk ball-bearings, ever ready to 'banana-peel' the skipper onto his arse—damn those pearls! They bedevil me! Mock me! Taunt me!

Carolyn, of course, is barely visible anymore. She'll sink like a stone if she ever falls in: ironically dragged to the bottom by her heavy pearl earrings, large necklace, fat bracelets, huge rings—all of which would be returning, rightfully, to their natural, watery habitat.

"Perhaps you should make small PFDs for your larger ones," I suggested meekly, but she savagely retorted with, "Don't get smart with me, Obese One!"

She's utterly shameless about it. Recently she was talking to a Tahitian pearl farmer, and flirting like crazy. He finally, reluctantly, showed her some of his '*poe ravas*' (black pearls in Tahitian). So the other islanders would not see his stash, he and Carolyn turned their backs on the rest of us. He brought out a silk handkerchief from his soiled pocket, carefully unfolded it—while Carolyn 'oh-ed and ah-ed' over his collection.

Finally, just to taunt me, she turned back to face me and shouted loudly, "Oh, honey! He's got a *BIG ONE*!"

I don't know how I take it.

This is one tough broad on my ego, I'll tell ya!

"Funny how times change, isn't it?" said the kindly-smiling chief of the little lagoon community in the Society Islands. "I mean, when Captain Bligh first came here, Tahitian women would offer themselves for a ship's nail. Now the shoe is on the other foot, eh?"

I grinned sickeningly, obviously not as good a sport as his gentle ancestors had been. Damn it! I hate the way the primitive savages we continuously seek out to visit always turn out to be smarter than ourselves!

Of course, Carolyn doesn't want to just *own* the largest, most beautiful pearl in the world—she wants the world to know she does. Thus, she is a tad—well, insensitive when it comes to the baubles of other ladies.

"Did you see the mal-formed, misshaped, nicked, dull, poorly-oriented little pearl-abortion that sailbag was wearing?" she'll snicker. "I mean, what does she do—look at it with a magnifying mirror!"

"Please, honey," I scolded her. "Don't chortle! And that yachtswoman probably doesn't consider herself a 'sailbag' as you disparagingly referred to her. And, lastly, not everyone has a pearl necklace the size of golf balls—let alone a pennant which is... well, big as a breadfruit!

"You noticed." she winked shyly, "Wanna see more of my—charms?"

Yes, aphrodisiacs exit. Old Chinese men covet rhino horns. The Japanese favor shark fin. Carolyn prefers pearls.

Of course, pearls are delicate things. They can't take abrasion. Each should be individually packaged and kept separate from the others. Thus I wasn't completely surprised when I came down belowdecks on *Wild Card* and found my camera equipment dumped in a pile on the floor.

"I need the waterproof Pelican case for my pearls," she informed me curtly. "You can put your silly cameras—oh, stow them in a pillow case under the dodger or something, okay?"

"Wait one second," I said foolishly. "Aren't pearls... like, waterproof?"

"Damn it, Fatty!" she spat at me. "Are you a graduate of the GIA? No! Am I? *YES*! So let's both just do what we do best, shall we? You be captain, I'll be queen!"

"And, exactly, what does a captain do?" I asked and fell right into her trap.

"Earn," she hissed, "and the more silently, the better!"

It is true. She is, alas, a graduate of the GIA, the Gemology Institute of America. I am not sure exactly what this group is. I thought she told me she was getting involved with the 'C'-I-A, but, evidently, it is a much shadier, more disreputable organization.

Basically, GIA alumni tour the world stating with scientific certainty (backed up by microscopic analysis and a lot of gobbly-gook mumbo jumbo) that their gems are worth a *lot* of money and that *other gems* aren't.

"Have I got this right, Carolyn," I asked her recently. "Or is my perception skewered?"

"You'll be skewered if you don't get off the boat for awhile and allow me to sort my keshi(*) in peace!" she told me. (*I think of keshi as ugly and deformed but Carolyn spins "each keshi pearl is naturally and uniquely formed, and utterly individual in shape.")

Obviously, this whole pearl-addiction-crisis is affecting our relationship. I was horrified to discover a stash of love letters she'd recently written to Robert Wan (largest pearl farmer in the Pacific) and that she'd begun praying nightly to the Great God of Mikimoto!

Even worse, she is beginning to deify Petero Tupana, the Tahitian fisherman who, in 1968, discovered the secret to seeding oysters from the Japanese—and freely shared it with his fellow Polynesians for the financial good of all. (No, Miki wasn't pleased!)

I mean, once Carolyn and I were having an argument and I said something disparaging about her pearls. "Don't utter another hateful word," she shrilly demanded. "They'll hear!"

"What?" I said.

"They're sensitive," she said dreamily, "after all, they're *cultured* pearls, remember?"

How do you deal with that? The woman is completely (and utterly happily) delusional.

Recently we were getting into the dinghy to head ashore and I noticed she was... "Aren't you forgetting something," I queried. "Mightn't we need something else for a shore trip?"

"Let me see," she mused aloud. "I've got the necklace and the earrings on. Do you think I should wear my pearl tongue-stud too?"

"Clothes," I said sadly. "I want you to put on some clothes!"

"You are *so* middle-class," she lamented as she flounced back aboard.

Of course, it was almost impossible to yank her away from French Polynesia. She refused to leave, and demanded 'just a few more gross' of pearls. She had become utterly childlike, and, so, like the parent of a brat, I was forced to bribe her.

"Ah," I said, "but it would be a shame to miss the opals of Australia, wouldn't it? The diamonds of South Africa? The zircons of Zurich?"

"I've always wanted an opal," she said, and began to warm to the subject. "But a big one, okay?"

"Absolutely," I promised. "The size of—a jet ski, how about?"

"Yes," she said, as if hypnotized by her internal vision, "And a diamond the size of?

"A 55 gallon drum!" I shouted, "*If* we can leave tomorrow."

"Yes, My Hero," she swooned, "Absolutely! We leave at dawn, My Captain!"

Fatty's black pearl carved by Becko on Makemo

Showboating at the Boat Show

Cap'n Fatty at the Strictly Sail Pacific Expo

I should never leave my vessel. Every time I do, things go wrong in a major way. Example: My dear mother asked me if I would attend her 90th birthday party in Santa Cruz, California. Since she asks for so little and deserves so much, I promised I would. However, I was in Southeast Asia at the time. This is far, far from the reality of America. And it is so expensive and time consuming to fly internationally, especially when you are exactly half way around the world. But I'm a faithful son and felt I had no choice. So we immediately started making plans, scheming scams, and dreaming up new dementedness for the coming family debacle.

The first question was; how to afford it. I'm a marine writer who makes his living writing about wild & crazy sailing adventures, not wholesome, family-oriented, shore-side ones. Oh, well. Nothing ventured, nothing gained. So I dashed off many e-mails hither-and-yon, in hopes of shot-gunning a solution.

While waiting, my wife and I made love. We enjoy this. We're still thrilled with our good fortune; we both having married avid heterosexuals. (Isn't it swell how life works out sometimes?)

Where was I?

So, I got a response from a national Stateside publication I work for: Would we be interested in giving a seminar at the "Strictly Sail" boat show in Oakland? And if so, on what subject?

I was naked and sweaty as I read the e-mail at the nav station of *Wild Card*, the modest 38-foot, $3,000, globe-trotting, sloop-rigged garbage scow we call home. We both laughed at the silliness of any sane person being interested in our dumb "dessert-first" advice. I was just about to say we'd speak on "Love and Lust" when Carolyn leaned her lovely... er... body over my shoulder and suggested "Sailing with Love and Laughter" as a more PC title.

See why I married her?

Let's be brutally honest for a second: I'm not often in the United States and thus am seldom able to help take care of my 90-year-old mother. She lives alone and is fiercely independent. But, of course, she occasionally needs a bit of assistance—and then calls my brother or one of my sisters. They usually are able to drop everything and help—but, not always. This occasionally irritates my mother, who then complains to the only siblings who are available to complain to.

Thus, the people who help her most are always listening to her say, "Too bad Fatty isn't here. He is a real loving son and would be able to solve this situation instantly."

This is so unfair.

Thus, while I was in America, my family decided that not only would I sort-of "host" her 90th birthday party. But I'd also have the good fortune to deal with her and her "tiny" problems the entire time.

I'm not complaining about this. This was fair, more than fair. And, normally, this would not have been a problem because my mother is almost totally self-sufficient.

Alas, this is where cruel fate stepped in.

My mother loves to dance. At her 87th birthday party, we could not get her off-stage. For almost an hour, she gyrated sensuously across the dance floor, making the TV hoofers of "Dancing with The Stars" seem like young, flat-footed clods. Twice, I tried to hustle her off towards her rocking chair—but she was far too elusive.

Alas, as I was just touching down on US continental soil for the first time in many years, she was in the middle of her daily dance rehearsal—and got pains in her stomach. Within hours, she was in surgery, with various medical types tying bowlines, carricks, and reef knots with her ancient intestines.

She was not happy about this, to put it mildly. "Stop your foolishness and sew me back up," she ordered them. "I have a party to go to!"

Yes, we Goodlanders are genetically focused on fun.

My mother and I both hate hospitals. Thus we launched a plan. I'd continue to order the party hats and she'd "get well quick" in rehab. This she did extremely well—so well that the medical establishment was dumbfounded. Soon she was back in her Santa Cruz apartment with days to spare before the Big Bash. All Goodlanders not in mental institutions or jail would attend, flying in from all over the world.

Alas, a couple of days before her 90th birthday, she fell and fractured her starboard femur.

"I don't feel any pain and I'm alright," she'd say each time I touched her leg and she'd inadvertently shriek in agony. Then she'd follow up with, "How's the party-plan coming, Fatty. Are we still on track for mega-fun?"

It was a pirate costume party, of course, because, even at 90 years of age, my mother openly lusts after Jack Sparrow. It went extremely well. Over fifty guests attended—many under their own names. We rented a huge house right on the beach.

Of course, I had to give her a present. Since I had little money, I wrote a 125 page book called "Celebrating Marie" and had it published with a private print run of 100 copies.

The book and the party were a giant success. Andy Turpin, senior editor of *Latitude 38*, played banjo in the sea-gypsy band that kept our toes a'tapping.

My mother glowed with happiness.

The following day I wheeled her into surgery once again. They screwed and bolted various titanium bits onto her upper femur in hopes she would eventually walk again.

Obviously, there will have to be a transition period from hospital to home-recovery. And eventually, she'll probably have to fly up to live with or close-by one of my sisters.

Thus, many complicated things had to be swiftly put in place—like a home nurse, for example. And all of them cost vast sums of money.

America is, in case you've forgotten, rather expensive. At first, I was mentally dividing the price of everything by 35 baht, as I do in Thailand—*WRONG!*

Thus, I unexpectedly discovered myself homeless and penniless in America—and 15,000 miles away from my vessel.

At this point, I knew I'd have to "shake the money tree" hard at the "Strictly Sail Sailboat Expo" in Oakland, California.

Frankly, I had hoped things would go smoothly and make sense. HA!

It turns out "Strictly Sail" was half powerboats—go figure. The boat show and the people who ran it had One Overriding Objective—to convey to the world that the "sky wasn't falling" within the marine industry. Alas, everyone I spoke to within the industry that was specifically charged with this Herculean task, would soon burst into tears and sob, "I've just been fired!" and demand my weary shoulder to cry on. (I was happy to oblige, but the next boat show I attend—well, I'm gonna wear a terry-cloth shirt.)

The astounding part was that all but one of my seven seminars was standing-room-only. And there were plenty of strange/sick people there, because my books sold like hot-cakes, earning me just enough money to fly back to Southeast Asia—with empty pockets and a rueful smile. (And with my brother Morgoo-the-Magnificent resuming his care-giving role, thank gosh.)

A final note: It will be awhile before I mingle with the dirt-dwellers of America again. But it was fun!

Hot Oil Massage, Fatty-Style!

I'm a confirmed sail-boater, an avid stick-boater, and an ardent blow-boater who, naturally, spends most of my life upside down in the bilge—working on my diesel engine. This is ironic. I'm not good at it. In fact, I'm terrible at it. On a scale of one to 10, I'm a minus-three. I'd claim I was completely incompetent—but that would be boasting, as I'm far worse. Engine mechanics reveal me for what I am: an idiot.

Of course, I'm a married man. I don't have to suffer alone. During these "engine traumas," we co-suffer. I swear up a blue streak, my wife, Carolyn, rolls her eyes. I throw a tool, she winces. I burst into tears; she daintily offers me a grease-smeared hankie. I ying, she yangs.

Here's what happened: we arrived back in Malaysia (dead-broke) from two expensive months in the Good Ole USA and we were horrified to discover no oil in *Wild Card*'s diesel engine. Not a drop.

"Bastards," I shrieked. "Those evil Somalia pirates must have broken into our boat and stole our lube oil! Wow, that's brazen—I mean, right outta the freak'n crank case!"

"Perhaps," Carolyn said gently, "it wasn't pirates, Fatty.... perhaps... your perfect macho-mano engine has a hole in it—and the oil leaked out ignobly?"

"Impossible!" I shouted. How dare she say such a nasty thing? But, eventually, reality began to rear its ugly head and, well, my eyes misted up. I felt betrayed. After all, my engine is almost brand new. Wait, maybe that's not quite accurate. Let's see, I installed it in 1995... okay, my engine has run almost flawlessly for over 13 years. And I basically have ignored it all that time. Still, I felt deeply betrayed.

I realize this isn't fair. Nor logical. Nor just. But that's how I felt. I felt... less of a man. As if, by losing command of my engine I'd somehow lost command of my... of my... well, castration images jumped into my addled, horsepower-deprived brain.

Now, the first thing that I do when I have a diesel engine problem anywhere in the world is to Skype (via the internet) Diesel Dan Durban at Parts & Power of Tortola, patiently wait until he comes onto my computer screen, and then burst into tears. I know, I know... admitting such sissy stuff in print does not speak well of my moral character (or lack thereof.) But that's the truth, that's what I do. I grovel. I beg. I plead. I promise crazy things like, in this case, my first-born son.

Now Diesel Dan knows me well enough to know that he doesn't want to know me better—and thus is motivated to get rid of me as quickly as possible. "Wipe 'er down, fill 'er up and see where it drips out," he growled.

Now that advice sounds pretty basic and simple *after* you've heard it, doesn't it? But it was like a breath of fresh air into my clueless head: suddenly I had a sense of purpose and a specific direction. Yippee!

So, instead of getting to work on the engine, I strutted around the expensive marina where we were now trapped, and said sagely, "Once I detect the dribble, dab the drop, and latch onto the leak; it should be no problem to... well... to do what needs to be done!'

Carolyn and I quickly determined that there was a hole in the oil pan. "Great," Diesel Dan warbled over Skype, "I'll send you a new one. Just yank the engine, slap it on—and you're all set!"

The problem with 'yanking' the engine is all the goofy stuff that's attached to it: secret hoses, unidentified wires, strange cables, unlabeled pipes... lordy, lordy!

But, with the help of wire cutters, bolt cutters, hacksaws, axes, and a small jack hammer; the engine was soon ready to be lifted off its beds.

"Are we gonna hire a crane to lift it," asked Carolyn with a worried tone in her I'm-getting-too-old-for-this-crap voice.

"Don't be silly," I scolded. "We're sailboaters, ain't we? We'll use the traditional methods that Joshua Slocum pioneered—the main halyard! It will be easy. I'll be down here watching and you'll be up there on the halyard winch cranking."

"But since you're strong and you go to the gym every day we're in port," she parried, "why don't *you* crank while I watch?"

This is the type of marital situation you run into when you attempt to train a novice spouse into the fine art of marine diesel mechanics. Luckily, I was prepared for such nonsense.

"My dear," I said gently, reassuringly, "first off, there's a legal problem because—for liability reasons—I had to sign an insurance waiver at the gym. It's a legal waiver which forced me to promise to only use these muscles for recreational purposes—so, there's that. And then there's my heart problem... what if... while getting my own cup of coffee or something... I had a heart attack and died... wouldn't you feel guilty? And we all know that, well... too many captains spoil the soup, eh? So why don't we just relax and do it the logical way... my way?"

Engines are heavy things. Our half inch halyard was about three-eighths in diameter when the engine finally began to lift off its beds. "You're getting it," I shouted up to a grunting Carolyn on the deck above me. (I could have glanced up at her, but did not—fearing I'd get eye-strain if I did.)

Soon the engine was swaying around our main cabin, at a height of four feet above the cabin sole, spewing oil, salt water, coolant, tranny fluid, etc., everywhere.

"Shouldn't we—at least remove the settee cushions or something?" Carolyn asked as she came below and saw the dripping beast in all of its ugly glory.

"Oh, there's no need to 'gild the lily,'" I laughed gaily. "We can clean the boat's finery later—right now it's work time, my dear. Why don't you massage the engine with hundred dollar bills while I hit it hard with my rusty wrenches?"

Getting the old oil pan off was easy—though how much used oil splashed out of it was a Tsunami-like surprise. Soon we were both covered in grease and oil and sweat... soon all our knuckles were bleeding... soon we wore only snarls... soon nothing but obscenities were being ripped from our frothing, foaming lips... *YES*!

Removing the old gasket presented the only real problem. Diesel Dan had warned me about not touching/nicking the pristine parts and thus I was very careful with the sledge hammer I used to beat it off.

Occasionally, of course, a boat would go by. Its wake would jostle our 38-foot sloop and suddenly the engine would become a violent, demented pendulum swinging around the belowdecks, crashing into bulkheads, shattering picture frames, and knocking us over. "Hold it, hold it," I'd scream frantically at Carolyn during these stressful moments, "If the rope breaks, just set it on your lap. I'll have it re-attached in a jiffy!"

The oil pan had 36 bolts holding it on. These needed to be 'torqued' to a specific number which was stated in kilo-centimeters or grams per second or some such Euro-techno-bull. Besides, I didn't have a torque wrench.

"Pickle jar," I told Carolyn. "You know those big pickle jars that are difficult to open and you have to hit 'em hard with the palm of your hand and then use a couple of grunts too? That's exactly the amount of force I'll apply to these bolts—simple, eh?"

"How amazingly scientific," she mused.

"Oh, it must be marvelous working with me," I agreed, "and you're so obviously learning a lot!"

I pretended not to notice her burying her weary head in her greasy, blood-flecked hands.

Once the engine was finally lowered back down onto its beds, we had to begin the job of hooking it back up. "Gimme some hose clamps, tie-wire, duct-tape, wire ties, paper clips, silly putty, STP stickers, flame-decals, chewing gum—that should do it," I said.

We worked together for a while in silence, and then I blurted out. "Next is bleeding."

"But I'm already bleeding," she said, holding up her hands and pointing at a sliced thigh and a smashed toe.

"Now's not the time to discuss the pink issues, dear, let's stick strictly with the blue ones until this sucker runs. I was talking 'bout the *fuel* system, babe. We have to bleed the fuel system."

Carolyn and I have done this a lot in the last 39 years we've cruised together as a loving couple. Here's how, step-by-step, we do it. 1.) We both watch the engine closely. 2.) Carolyn pumps the hand-operated priming pump. 3.) I open a petcock. 4.) We get squirted in the face by diesel oil. 5.) When there are no more bubbles in the fuel squirting us in the face, 6.) I close the petcock while Carolyn 7.) stops pumping.

If we do this well, only about a gallon of fuel gets in our hair and/or ears.

"What about shaft alignment," Carolyn asked.

I squinted wisely over a yard stick, said "kick it to port 'bout 'alf a foot," and then, "Fine, that should be within five thousandths!"

Finally, it was time for the big test. We lined our drip pan with newspaper, cranked up the engine, and ran it hard for half an hour. Then we waited for a couple of more hours and removed the newspaper. Not a drop!

"My hero," Carolyn cried out in jubilation, and gave me a big messy 10-40 multi-weight kiss on the lips. We were just getting into it when Diesel Dan chirped up from the computer on the nav station. "Ahoy Fat and Ms. Fatette," he said, wearing his stylish blue Perkins shirt aboard his powerboat in Tortola, "How's it going in Southeast Asia?"

"Fine," I told him, trying to be civil while Carolyn greedily attempted to tug me away, "but no time to chat now, Diesel Dan... er, maybe later, during our next major diesel emergency... right now, gotta run!"

Weather Wimp!

I hate to admit it but I'm a weather wimp. Every time the wind gusts to 30 knots, the temperature falls below 80 degrees, and/or the seas build to a foot or so—well, I burst into tears. That's right: I'm a coward. Completely. Don't tell anybody, but I spend a lot of time screaming at my wife, "I want my mommy!"

It has gotten so bad that most international 'weather routers' won't work with me. They just refuse. Can I help it if my standards are high—and, well, me too?

"Help!" I e-mailed the last one frantically. "The wind just gusted scarily to over 14 knots! And, worse, I see a cloud on the horizon. I have a horrible feeling it *could* contain moisture!"

This rattles them. They don't seem to know their place. I mean, *I am the one paying*, right? I mean, I could get bad weather reports for free, right? Let's face it, on some passages I'm just too tired to put up with the 'wind thisa way, wind data way,' crap! So, I hire an expensive weather router *and expect them to deliver*!

One guy tried to wiggle out of his forecasting responsibilities with, "Hey, pal, I don't make the weather." But I snapped backed with, "*You* took the money so *you're* responsible!"

Of course, I'm happy that marine electro-technology has advanced. Example: Josh Slocum didn't have his anemometer wired directly to his EPIRB like I do—so that my Emergency Position Indicating Radio Beacon gets automatically switched on if winds builds to the 'Perfect Storm' level or 20 knots—whichever comes first.

Modern technology isn't fool-proof, however. Sometimes it frustrates me. I guess I have a short fuse. In any event, my weather fax often spits out pieces of paper which are blacker than a politician's heart—unreadable, to say the least. Usually I can handle this, but not always. Sometimes I snap.

Recently, I head-butted my weather fax in frustration. Unfortunately, my wife, Carolyn, happened to be passing by—a woman with almost *no* understanding of how to be a 'macho-manly-man!'

"Whatchadoing?" she asked.

"Interfacing our electronics," I replied calmly as I dabbed my bleeding nose with a paper towel.

Needless to say, I pour over my GRIB files. These are generated by 'computer models,' those sexy, scantily-clad young girls who do 'laptop dancing' in nightclubs. (Why they don't use weathermen, I dunno—too radical and 1960's, perhaps?)

Anyway, GRIB stands for Goofy and Ridiculous Information for Boaters. Of course, the jokers at NOAA (Not Often Accurate ***holes) attach a disclaimer to each forecast that reads something like, "This should not be used for anything by anyone. Wind predictions can-and-will vary... but can generally be relied upon to be within 50 knots, plus or minus. Remember, wave heights are 'average' and can also vary 50 feet or so."

I mean, is this really the best America can do?

Don't even get me started on weather charts. Damn, are they *trying* to confuse us? What's a front? Trough? Low? Ridge? Who is Hector and/or Pascal? Why are some fronts—occult ones? (Could these wx charts be made by... like, Goth forecasters?)

I don't know nor care.

Nor am I enamored with infrared images.

I almost died in a purple splotch and never want to go through another magenta area again!

Yesterday I was advised to visit a weather web page with 'animated' products. What, Donald Duck reads the forecast? Daffy? Popeye?

It used to be, back in the early days, it was hard to get any marine weather forecast, let alone a bad one. Now NOAA broadcasts bad ones continuously on VHF!

That's progress.

I guess.

Nothing seems to make sense anymore. Why is it that, along the coast of Puerto Rico, NOAA keeps warning boaters about the flash floods every few seconds when it is the poor saps who can't afford yachts who keep drowning in them?

Sick, eh?

If there is one thing I hate it is 'pretenders' who try to impress their fellow boaters by saying stuff on their SSB radios like, "...three levels of Q" or "...upper atmosphere shear" or "...scattered stratocumulus!"

I can't even tell if they're putting me on. One forecaster mentioned that while 'raising humility' might cause a super-saturation of the dewpoint... it is best not to worry about it too much. Huh?

I mean, I bolted my barometer to the bulkhead with four large stainless steel machine screws just so it *wouldn't* drop!

They're even messing with the tides now: suddenly there is a diurnal one. (I thought this was a prostrate condition!)

And it is all getting more personal and touchy-feelie as well. I mean, I know hurricanes are depressing. Why mention it so often on the Weather Channel? And who buys all those tornado videos they're always hawking—some pervert who likes to munch popcorn while watching trailer parks explode?

There are times I think I might be losing my mind. If hail stones are usually the size of golf balls, what size are the vegetables in squash zones? Am I right? I've never even *seen* an isobar—let alone a compressed one. What sort of climo-deviant labels a weather chart used for prognosis and analysis *ANAL PROG*? Why do stupid sailors always seem to get caught in the doldrums? Can anyone tell me why sea level is so mean? If it is 'raining cats and dogs' will you step in a poodle?

Nor do I put much stock in that stupid 'Rhyming Simon' weather folklore. I learned most of my 'weather-wisdom' sayings in the 1960's and, alas, they haven't held me in good stead. While "red sky at night, druggies delight" might be accurate, "red sky in morning, heads take warning" is too ambiguous to be useful.

Of course, the whole world is shocked by El Nino and El Nina years. Whose bright idea was it to put a Spaniard in charge of global climate control anyway?

And, yeah, scientists *do* seem to be divided on whether global warming is caused by political hot air or not.

Even the Japanese are getting into the act: when two hurricanes hit you while bumping into each other this is known as the Fujiwhara Effect—because it has decimated more tropical islands than WWII, I guess.

I believe, however I should begin to temper my criticism. Even Nicholas Cage in the movie *The Weatherman* didn't like to be humidity-ated. And, I hate to admit it, but my wife, Carolyn, wasn't exactly impressed with this column when she proofed it.

"Surely this piece has the worst puns ever," she grimaced as she read.

"Don't rain on my parade," I snapped back.

Appalling Apia Marina!

I'm often accused of 'only telling the good parts' of cruising. Maybe this missive will change that perception.

Frankly, I'm not too fond of marinas or, to put it another way, I don't like trailer parks even if the trailers float. Nor am I fond of being ordered around. Especially by idiots. So I was a bit shocked, while in (formerly Western) Samoa, to be summarily ordered into their new Apia Marine.

"Why?" I asked.

"Because you boaters have been asking us for a marina for years," said the happy-but-don't-mess-with-me harbor host guy—who just happened to be the head of the bribe-happy Port Authority as well. "And to give us more room in our crowded harbor!"

The harbor was almost empty. You could easily anchor another fifty yachts and six inter-island freighters within it. And, while I'm not against marinas existing as an option, making them mandatory is certainly not a regular practice in the South Pacific.

Plus, I'm not rich. I can't afford to pay $30 a day for dirt-dweller abuse. The simple truth is, I came to Samoa to chase the ghost of Robert Louis Stevenson and Margaret Mead, not to be a profit center for its power-mad Port Authority.

To say the marina was new is a bit of an understatement. The evening before *Wild Card* pulled into it (and ran hard aground twice), it was being furiously-if-incompetently dredged—by a rusty back-hoe on a dangerously tilted barge.

The first vessel that tied to a piling—pulled it over... like a candle-in-a-cake. On the day of the grand opening (yes, the Prime Minister made a stirring speech) one of the big-boat finger piers broke loose in two knots of breeze—without anything tied to it.

A couple of minutes later the gleaming shore-power/water box across from our slip, keeled over like a felled tree—again, with no one around.

Not only was this the marina-from-hell, it was haunted!

The very first evening, the blissfully-happy security guards went around to all the yachts and shook their crews down for beer, rhum, or worse. The second evening the security guards brought their own kava bowl, which evidently gave them the munchies. "Do you have any food aboard your yachts, please," they begged. "Perhaps some potato chips or beer nuts?"

No, of course, there were no toilets. Ditto, no showers. "But we are going to build them for you soon, and when completed—no extra charge!" said the Port Dictator with a sleazy, what-more-could-you-ask-for smile.

There were some shaded benches and a picnic table in the marina. But a crudely printed sign said that these were off-limits to yachtsmen—for the use of Port Authority officials only.

For almost a week all ten boats in the harbor were told we'd be ordered into the marina the following day. But nothing happened for five days. The marina opening was, happily, postponed. (Two of the ten vessels actually wanted to go into the marina, the other eight did not). But we were in a foreign country, and, hey, you gotta-do-what-you-gotta do, right? So we hung around our boats to move them instead of day-tripping ashore.

Suddenly, on Saturday morning, the Harbor Master was zooming around in his dinghy yelling at us. "I've been calling you on Channel 12 since dawn. Why aren't you monitoring the Port Authority frequency? It is time to go into the marina... go, go, go... right now!"

Needless to say, this created bedlam in the anchorage. We all hastily yanked up our anchors and rushed into the marina. An American vessel named *Marcy*, with Captain Peter of Washington State, was in the lead. Wham, he came to a sudden halt. "I'm aground!" he said.

We'd been promised there was a minimum of 15 feet in the marina when, in reality, there were numerous spots with only four feet. Some slips for sixty foot sailing vessels had less than three feet of depth!

"I'm aground," Peter repeated to the Harbor Master who was waiting to catch his lines 50 yards away.

"No, you are not," said the Harbor Master.

"What..?!?" said Peter. He was in total disbelief. Not only was he obviously hard aground—not 100 feet from the Harbor Master who told him he wouldn't be. But the guy was *now* telling him he wasn't.

Peter didn't lose his cool. Instead, he grabbed his six foot long boat hook and speared it into the water—where it stuck in the mud with plenty protruding.

Now all the remaining nine of us were not aware of this, as we were underweigh, heading in. The Harbor Master could have informed us or warned us or instructed us to avoid that particular clump of dredging—but he did not. Almost every boat which drew over 5.5 feet ran hard aground.

It was chaos. A small squall was passing at the time. Many of the vessels, once aground on the trailing edge of their keels, had their bows pivot with the wind. They were in danger of damaging themselves, the docks, and other boats. Some of the yachtsmen, realizing that the Harbor Master was now *knowingly* attempting to force boats drawing seven feet down four foot channels, attempted to warn their fellow boaters. They shouted from docks and from their boats. One fellow even ran out on the seawall. "Turn back," he shouted. "Slow down! Reverse!"

There were numerous boats aground at the same time—with the Harbor Master yelling, "More throttle. Give it some power, Skipper!"

I have, in my 47 years of living aboard, never seen anything quite like it.

I mean, it was an incredibly funny scene if it wasn't happening to you!

Needless to say, many of the skippers weren't too happy—and expressed their displeasure forth-rightly to the Harbor Master... who was amazed how ungrateful these foreign sailing wretches were. They were hollering at *him*!

That was *his* job!

His face turned to stone.

He started to openly yell back. On his HH VHF, which all vessels were required to monitor, he contemptuously referred to his (now five-minute old) customers as "bloody asses."

And the new instructional signs were a laugh riot. As you came into the marina, the first important sign you saw said, "Upon entering the marina, shut off your engine."

Perhaps they wanted total chaos, eh?

Now various people, even ones who didn't want to be there, had various expectations and agendas. For instance, Floridian Duncan, the sailor on *Good Karma* speaks fluent Samoan which he learned during his years as a Peace Corp worker. He figured this would be a good time to give his Samoan family a tour of his boat.

But the Harbor Master said no. "No Samoans allowed aboard or anywhere in the marina," he said.

My wife, Carolyn, figured she had misunderstood. Surely, a Samoan wouldn't be making a racist rule which eliminated people such as himself. Why he and his workers would be in violation—at the very moment he uttered the rule!

"No Samoans," he said. "None. Never! No exceptions."

(There is a serious theft problem in Samoa, so this could be behind his strange logic, although it was completely silly because, of course, *all* the visitors {and mechanics, boat-workers, etc} to the marina were Samoan— hell, we were in Samoa!)

"You have to wear your marina badge at all times," said the Harbor Master. "No exceptions!"

Now Carolyn is slow to anger, but she is of Italian heritage... and when she starts waving her hands around—well, I know she's about to go off.

"What badge?" she asked.

"The badge I am going to give you," said the Harbor Master.

"Okay," Carolyn said. "Then give it to me."

"Two dollars," said the Harbor Master.

"Then you aren't giving it to me, are you," Carolyn vented. "You're selling it to me. You're already asking us for more money. You're hitting us up with hidden charges, within minutes of arrival!"

"You have to sign-in and sign-out every time," said the Harbor Master to change the subject. "And you need to have your pass to leave the premises or get back in."

This was easily solved. We all just kept our dinghies in the water to avoid the lengthy delay while the not-too-speedy security guard demonstrated, again and again, that he could not spell "wild" nor "card". (I'm sympathetic to the fact English isn't his first language and spelling isn't a high priority in Samoa. But if the *only* way I can go ashore—to find a toilet, for instance—is to have my name, pass number, and vessel's name accurately recorded in his ledger—well, I can only spend five or ten minutes saying "W-I-L-D" and "C-A-R-D" before I blow my top while wetting my pants).

Yes, I could go on. The marina is airless and, thus, stifling hot. Port truck traffic is very loud. Just across the street is a nightclub that doesn't know the disco-craze is over—even at 2 A.M.

When I complained about running aground, the Port guy just grinned evilly and spudded a giant dredge within a couple of feet of my vessel—and dredged underneath me for three days straight—just upwind of me, literally splattering my entire port side with mud.

"Deep enough now, skipper?" asked the Port guy.

"Yes," I wept in frustration, "I guess so—thanks!"

The strangest part is that every other Samoan we'd met during our stay—with the sole exception of the head of the Port Authority—had been absolutely wonderful to us.

Sadly, many vessels that planned to stay for two weeks for the XIII South Pacific Games are now moving on to Tonga. The brand new marina will soon be as empty and as profitless as the empty anchorage.

The Worry Nets

SSB radios are wonderful things. Example: should you be far offshore and surrounded by utter bliss—you can still turn-on and tune-in your radio to find something to worry about. Worrying seems a basic human need. If you are currently happy, you can fix that by worrying about the future. If you tire of that, fret about the past. See how easy it is to drive away happiness?

It is especially important for the 'newbie' sailors to tune into the local worry nets. After all, we don't want them to fall into the habit of enjoying themselves!

Seasoned sailors *know* you can be run down by a freighter, catch fire, explode, or—worst case—lose your DVD movie player at any moment while on passage. Greenhorns, however, need to be reminded.

WHETHER NETS: These are the SSB nets you tune into when deciding 'whether' or not to leave on passage. "I'd like a 12 to 14 knot quartering breeze, sunny skies, low humidity, and flat sea—for the first 70 miles. Then, once beyond Sint Maarten, I'd like the wind to clock 12 degrees to the north."

Yes, it isn't like the old days when we just wanted to survive—when any passage that didn't drown us was considered a good one. I recently heard one grumpy guy complain, "Yeah, the Trades were fine and we beam-reached the whole way. But with the sun that high, it really isn't that good for photography, is it?" Gee, cry-me-a-river pal!

The coolest new development is the professional weather routers who guide you daily through your passage. They really earn their money. "There's a 140 knot hurricane to your south, a savage winter gale to your north, three tsunamis to your east and a couple of 'bergs to the west, but I'm routing you right through the middle of 'em all. Tricky, but—hey, we've got the technology if you're got the money."

I was on the same passage at the same time and would have said, "Trades." I mean, I know people who consult a weather router to go from their slip to the fuel dock! "Leave at 1252 Zulu. You'll have a downwind slide to the fuel dock with a slight positive current. No problems foreseen. Assuming it takes about half an hour to refuel, the tide will have then reversed and the current should again be a positive factor in the 12 minute motor-sail back to your slip. That will be $100, please."

Oh, yes, money is a factor. Nobody listens to me. What does an amateur know? But a guy in the middle of an Arizona desert who has never even *seen* the sea—why, he's a *professional expert*, as long as his credit card machine and customer's gullibility still function.

Some of the SSB exchanges you hear are a tad crazy. "Lookit, pal," one sailor hissed to another via his SSB radio, "I paid $150 bucks for this 14 day forecast. It *better* be right!"

Last month I made the passage from windy New Zealand to squally Fiji. If, as I hoisted up my anchor, Jesus, Mary and Joseph had rowed out to tell me what the weather would be five days hence, I'd have blurted, "Are you kidding? Do I look like an idiot?"

Of course, the weather isn't the only thing to worry about. Lord, no! There are tons of other things.

Safety and Security, for example. Let's face it, a hell of a lot of people cruise to the Caribbean so they can worry about their dinghies. I listened in for a month while cruising the Grenadines in 2004. Finally, I couldn't take it anymore. I shut off the SSB radio, unclamped my outboard, deep-sixed it, and slit my inflatable dinghies tubes. When the whole mess was finally resting/waving on the sandy seabed below me, I laughed gleefully and cried, "Now *that* will fix those little bastards!"

Of course, it is true that an SSB can save you money. We were once anchored in Gustavia, St. Barths, when we heard that limes were 2 cents apiece cheaper in Papua, New Guinea. "Hoist up the anchor," I immediately told my wife, Carolyn. "We're going!"

My all-time favorite is "Treasures of the Bilge." If you ever want to be depressed about human nature in general and capitalism in specific, just tune in. You'll hear stuff like, "I've got a used impeller with two fairly good blades remaining... for a pre-Soviet Russian shower stall pump... manufactured in the 1920's... which I'll let go for 3% off list current price... say $100US... as is, where is."

"I've got some galley scraps," chimed in another hopeful sailor, "suitable for bait or chumming... or, perhaps, starting a small compost pile on your foredeck, say, $3 a bucket... if you get here before it *really* starts to stink!"

I succumbed in Chaguaramas, Trinidad, by announcing on the morning VHF net, "Ahoy all you pitifully cheap sailors, frugal sea gypsies, and tight-fisted Antilles cruisers! I've recently placed various valuable boat bits—used sails, burst fenders, disassembled bilge pumps, opened-up electronic devices, slightly soiled boat cushions, and barely chafed yacht cordage—in the dumpsters and garbage bins of Peakes, Powerboats, Crews Inn, and Coral Cove shipyards... each is for sale for $25—strictly honor system. You can drop off payment marked "Cap'n Fatty, *Wild Card*" at MMS (Marauders Maildrop Service)...

Most Caribbean cruisers get sucked into the SSB nightmare via the 'position report' nets. I've acted as net control for a few—writing down the incoming positions on a small chalkboard so they could be easily erased immediately after.

Yes, some net controllers *do* keep the position reports for the few days: a comfort to surviving family members who love to sagely/sadly point to a chart and say, "They drowned right around here!"

I mean, who cares? I once called-in twice-a-day positions reports for a week and then stopped in mid-ocean. Nothing. Then, about a week later, two people inquired. I owed both money.

Occasionally, of course, I do hear something over the SSB which makes me smile. My all-time favorite is, in a fuzzy, frequency-starting-to-modulate voice, "...low on batteries!"

Getting Older

Growing old isn't easy. Losing your mind, and then forgetting that you lost it, is no fun. "I've got Al-what's-his-name's disease!" my wife recently informed me. "What did you say?" I queried. "I can't remember," she said in confirmation.

Of course, living on a boat just compounds the problem. It isn't easy hiding your adult diapers under a pair of tropical swim trunks. It's also difficult to remember to put in your dentures when a bareboat drags down on you in the middle of the night. And there is no question that keeping your wheelchair properly lubed is time-consuming around a marine environment.

The first aging symptom I noticed was my vision getting as fuzzy as my thinking. "I think I need eyeglasses," I told my wife who was sitting across the cockpit from me. "Would you have married me if you had known my eyes were gonna go so soon?"

"I quite agree you need glasses," said the female form sitting across from me (which, alas, turned out to be my 15 year old daughter).

Things have, indeed, changed. Why, I can even remember when drugs were recreational! Now I've got a massive multitude of multi-colored pills that keep me immune from almost everything—except doctor bills.

In fact, it wasn't all that long ago when "getting juiced" didn't necessarily involve prunes.

As you get older, you get considerably less nimble. This is as equally true for an offshore sailor as a landlubber. Deciding to replace your MOB (man overboard sling) module with a man overboard escalator which cleverly folds into the topsides of your boat is a sure sign you're getting old. So is a "lifting" 12-volt toilet seat to boost you up from your ship's head.

There are other subtle signs: using a boat hook to pull up your trousers, leading the flag halyard aft to a genoa winch to hoist the "Q" flag, using the anchor windlass to haul up a bucket of mop water are all indications that you're no longer in tip-top physical shape.

Referring to the half dozen cans of chilled Geritol in the cockpit cooler as a "six pack" is another dead (almost) giveaway.

Worry and stress play a major factor in aging. In fact, I worried so much that I was going to lose my teeth—that my hair fell out.

I couldn't afford to see a scalp specialist about the above medical situation because I'm so poverty-stricken. Or, as my wife likes to say, "He's so broke, he can't even pay attention!"

Losing my hair didn't even save me any money either. The pennies I saved on hair cream, alas, was more than eaten up by the added expense of slobbering sun block on my bald spot.

Life raft supplies get complicated in your "golden years." Positively buoyant, solar-powered dialysis machines aren't exactly cheap. Neither are EPIRBs (Emergency Position Indicating Radio Beacons) that ring at the geriatric ward of the Mayo Clinic.

Soon after your eyes fail, your hearing starts to go. This isn't all bad. Since I got my hearing aid, I haven't heard my wife complain even once about my (lack of) income! And I've decided that adding sound insulation to my vessel's engine compartment is suddenly far down on my priority list.

There are some money-saving aspects of growing old—birth control devices, for instance. And the eager-if-aged skipper's excited cry of "pole tip up!" isn't just limited to the race course during the final stages of romantic life.

Nudity is no longer as much fun—not after gravity has had its way with your body for a half century. Body parts such as wizened buttocks and sagging breasts can become quite painful after being dragged along all day on nonskid decks.

Being on the move constantly has some benefits for the cruising sailor. I've forwarded (heh heh!) my subscription to Modern Maturity, (with those advertising flyers for burial insurance, and my free sample kit of Polydent Dental Adhesive) to my next mail drop at, er, the Tierra Del Fuego Yacht Club.

As you get older, you also get more set in your ways. In essence, your opinions and prejudices harden along with your arteries. Recently my wife was a perfect example of this. As a young bride she was extremely tolerant of different lifestyles, but such is not the case today.

"I can't stand those unkempt WASP-afarians," she said nastily as an unwashed white kid with dreadlocks strolled down the dock.

There is no question that I'm slowing down physically. I don't see much foredeck action these days—not even during the Heineken Cup Regatta. I guess my aluminum creeper, red cane, and back brace are clear indicators I'm just not as spry as I once was.

There are some positive aspects to growing old as a Caribbean Sea Gypsy. For instance: reading the obituaries in *All At Sea* to see which of my friends took the "Last Cruise." I'm also less fearful of being arrested for a felony now, because being sentenced to 25 years in the slammer ain't so bad if you only have three or four years left!

Of course, I'm a realist. So I'm looking forward to my second childhood as much as my first. Maybe this time I'll get it right. In any event, there's no doubt in my mind that growing older is better than the alternative!

Bon Voyage!

Another Sunrise in Paradise

I awake at first light. Next to me is another human being. She breathes in and she breathes out. I watch. And watch some more. Her head is a tangled storm of dark Italian hair. There is a curve of ass, a swoop of narrow waist, a mound of gentle breast. I look at her 56 year old face, and smile. I know every line, each scar, and every blemish. It is funny. We both grow old. But we also grow more—intertwined. Every wrinkle makes her more beautiful.

We lean on each other—now more than ever. We have aged at different rates. And, thus, as our physical real estate deteriorates, we both—literally and mentally—lean on each other to ever greater degrees. Our flesh is weak but our commitment is strong. Whenever one falters, the other is there.

Thought of one way, this inevitable aging process could make a person sad—or even drive one into the arms of a greedy plastic surgeon. But I prefer to think of it the other way: that as my steps falter and my physical abilities diminish, my appreciation of my life-partner grows.

I love life. Dying is a part of it. Aging is a prelude. I embrace it all.

Sure, we occasionally snarl. I am often a jerk. She is no more perfect. But we're happy with our velvet chains of family. She gave me her youth. She only had one youth and will never have another other—and yet she shared hers with me.

She still laughs at my jokes. Yesterday I told her, "As my memory dims, my conscience clears," and was rewarded with one of her sexy growl-laughs.

Our daughter Roma Orion now lives in Amsterdam—and *not* because of the drugs! What could be nicer?

Thus, I kiss my wife, Carolyn, as light as a butterfly's wing on her sleeping forehead.

I am careful to not make a sound as I roll out of our tiny, toe-kissing V-berth.

Wild Card's interior is neither large nor plush. It is dim inside our cabin. The weak light favors our aging varnish, our tarnished bronze, our faded photographs.

I have found it is much faster to dust without my reading glasses.

If I woke her up right now and we both ran to opposite ends of the boat—we'd still be within 38 feet of each other. Most of the time—the vast majority of my life—I've spent within ten feet of her. There is nowhere in our little watery world where she can't hear or smell me—and I her. Still, she is my Mystery Woman. She has secrets. Hidden places. Private scents. Sweet secretions.

I love the smell of her hair. The way she grunts. How her toes curl.

I really can't tell where my wife and my life begin or end—nor where the world and my vessel intersect. I live within a wonderful fairy-tale movie. It is an adventure movie. It is a movie of a love story. It is a travelogue. It is a porno flick, a family flick, a chick flick.

As I move aft in the cabin, I stop at the nav station. It is silent. Most of my instruments are as asleep as my wife. But a GPS winks in anchor-alarm mode. My depth meter reads 15 feet, over a soft mud bottom. My wind speed reports 12 knots. And my Danforth compass indicates the breeze is from the nor'east.

I check the Link 10. My batteries are down 37 amps, not bad. The solar cells will soon recharge them. If, for any reason, the sun hides—then I'll turn on the wind gen.

I feel in balance.

I take but I give.

I gently lift the companionway screen and move aft into the cockpit. I can tell it is going to be another beautiful day.

Once I had a friend who knew he was going to die soon. I asked him what he wanted. He told me he wanted another perfect day. I asked him what a perfect day was. He told me a perfect day is—any day you're alive.

We're currently anchored off the lovely island of Langkawi in Malaysia. The harbor is huge. Giant fish hawks wheel overhead. Puffy white clouds. The sun sparkles on the water like liquid diamonds dancing.

I force myself to take small, quick breaths—I don't want to hyperventilate with the beauty of it all.

I recently was asked by a questing friend how to find the "Now." I told him, "Find the beauty."

"Where is the beauty?" he asked.

I thought about telling him to look for God's footprints or to find Mother Nature or to look at any tree or ocean wave...

...but instead I said, "It is all around you. If there is ever a time you can't see beauty—it is because you are not looking hard enough. Because awe-inspiring beauty is always there, if you but look."

Even in the midst of atrocity is beauty.

A muezzin starts up singing from one of the nearby shore-side Mosques. I listen. At first he sings all alone. But our harbor is crescent-shaped. We're within hearing distance of five different Muslim houses of worship. Soon the other muezzins join in for what I call their 'calliope of constipation.'

I find all religion ugly, but God beautiful. However, I try to cut 'em some slack. It took me awhile, but now I find the singing muezzins inspiring.

I've cancelled the shipload of Ex Lax I ordered.

And I pat Buddha on the back (No, not on his sacred head for gosh sakes!) for saying, "Don't believe in any of them, dude—me included!"

I find the world both enchanting and *enchanted*. There are more miracles per second than I can count: snowflakes, clouds, waves, and rainbows abound. I recently heard a lecture on string theory—and it made me giggle.

...could it be that art and science—and Las Vegas, even—is God playing peek-a-boo with Himself?

Carolyn and I recently spent a couple of weeks making a beautiful cockpit table. It gleams at me. It is still new enough that I marvel at it. We made in out of local hardwood. We used mostly hand tools: planes, rasps, chisels, and saws. We took turns on the long cuts. I'd saw for awhile, and then she would. We're close to the equator. Sweat dripped off her nose. Sawdust rivuleted between her breasts. One strand of hair kept falling down—and she'd blow it back away with exasperation.

I find it all erotic.

She came aboard to sew up some curtains at 15 years of age, and has been sewing happiness into my life ever since. People are amazed and distressed at America's divorce rate. I am not. Why should couples stay together? She is her own person. People are individual units. She can stand alone. She has everything she needs. Yet still she wants me and I want her.

We've lived together aboard now for 39 years—and been lovers for longer than that. We've traveled the world together. We've mopped up each other's vomit, feces, and blood. And yet she still sparkles to me.

Recently we had a little argument and she said in exasperation, "I just want to grow old with you, Fatty!"

It is the nicest thing anyone has ever said to me.

When I was a young child and growing up aboard the schooner *Elizabeth* we had a conch shell. It was *the* conch shell, our family's conch shell.

Whenever lunch was ready, my mother would blow it—and I would come running from wherever I was in the harbor. Ditto, dinner. If there was an emergency, the person aboard would blow it—and the rest of our crew/family would immediately drop what they doing and come a'running.

I still have that conch shell. It is now aboard *Wild Card*, via *Corina* and *Carlotta*.

Some sons inherit the family farm, I, a true son-of-a-sailor, inherited a conch shell.

And I am honored to be so honored. It is precious to me. It is my history. It is a lifeline to my distant past. It links me to my dead.

Once, many years ago, I thought I'd lost Carolyn. I didn't know what to do. I was in a panic. So I hoisted myself to the very top of my mast and then laboriously hauled up the deck bucket with the conch shell. And I blew that conch shell for as long and as loud as I could. Again. And again.

…as my fellow boaters anchored nearby stared up at me with a combination of sorrow and pity.

She heard it.

She came back.

My reverie fades. I hear her moving below—the sound of the head door, the clank of her tea kettle, the smell of our coffee.

"How is it," she asks me. I don't know if she'd talking about the weather or the boat or the harbor or life in general… or us. But it doesn't matter. My answer is the same.

"Fine," I say.

Writing to Stay Afloat

I didn't hardly go to school—just four or five years total. I spent most of my childhood at sea aboard a 1924 Alden designed 52-foot schooner named *Elizabeth*. My father was a pareo-wearing beatnik who shunned the shore. "Don't ever get involved with the dirt dwellers, son," he'd advise me. "Remember: men and ships rot in port!"

I listened. At 15 years of age, I met a soft-spoken Italian girl, lured her aboard the 1932 Atkin 22-foot sloop-rigged double-ender I'd just purchased, and sailed away into the sunset.

Few people in the world were less suited to be a writer. I didn't know how to spell, the parts of a sentence, or what an essay was. Even talking to people made me uptight: I had a severe speech impediment. I didn't even know how to write cursive—and my alphabet printing was sloppy as well.

But dreams are funny things. My heart was filled-to-bursting with laughter and tears. I knew people would love me if they could just see inside. And I was an avid reader—thrilling to the words of Twain, Steinbeck, and Hemingway.

But if you can't even spell worth a fock, it's hopeless, isn't it?

At the age of 27, I briefly returned to the United States, and sailed up the East Coast, dropping in on old friends along the way. Again and again, the same scene was repeated. My friends would bring out an old shoe box, or large envelope, or a pillow case filled with my salt-stained letters. They'd invite over friends with whom they'd shared those same letters—and those friends, whom I had never met, loved me too.

It was a revelation. Maybe my quest wasn't hopeless.

The following year, just over 25 years ago, I decided to become a full-time professional writer. I had two big advantages: My living expenses were low and my wife, Carolyn, (yeah, same one) believed in me.

We were anchored off St. Augustine, Florida, at the time, in the lee of the Bridge of Lions. I didn't own a typewriter, so I purchased a used portable Olivetti from Goodwill.

"Mrs. Darby will see you now," said the blue-haired woman at the circulation desk of the local library on Aviles Street.

Mrs. Darby was a grey-haired, bifocaled, no-nonsense type of Librarian, so I didn't pull any punches. She cocked her head in amazement as she listened to my spiel, and occasionally jabbed a fat pencil in and out of her hair in exasperation.

"Let me get this straight," she said. "You've never written anything—but you want to write. You need a quiet office five days a week where you can work without interruption. Do you have any money?"

"Well, no," I admitted. "But I've got a strong back. I could pull the weeds or wash your car, or lug some books."

"Do you really expect me to say yes?"

"Well," I said. "I thought that, maybe, if you were into promoting book-reading, that, you know, you'd be into promoting book-writing too."

We stared at each other for a long time. "Follow me," she said, and led me up a narrow stairway to the attic. There were three odd-shaped rooms up there—two of them filled with spilling piles of spine-damaged library books. Our shoes left tracks in the dust. The floorboards creaked. It was stifling hot. Airless. Stuffy. Confining.

"Did you ever read 'The Yearling'?" she asked as she led me into the final room, which was strangely empty, save for an ancient desk and rickety chair facing the lead-glassed garret window.

"Yes, madam," I said. "Marjorie Kinning Rawlings'. Pulitzer-Prize winner."

"Marjorie used to write up here often—when she wasn't at Cross Creek," Mrs. Darby said quietly.

I felt the hair on the back up my neck stand up. My hands were shaking and my throat was dry. I couldn't believe my good fortune. It was an omen—I was on the right path.

"I'm taking a big risk here, young man," she said as she turned and left. "Please don't disappoint me."

The following day, I set up my typewriter and began to stare at it. Day after day I stared at it—hoping it would spring to life. My goal was to get something anything published somewhere within the next 12 months. But my typewriter was mute. And I felt like crying.

I couldn't do it. I couldn't write anything, and if I did—no one would publish it. I was going to fail—for the first time in my adult life, I was going to fail.

Then it dawned on me that unobtainable goals were counter-productive. So, I immediately changed my goals to 'typing' each day for six hours while collecting one hundred honest rejection slips over the course of the next 12 months.

Yippee! Each morning I'd dash up the stairs and start pounding out gibberish on the keyboard—about what I'd just eaten for breakfast, the weather outside, or the color of my socks. It didn't matter. I wasn't 'writing,' I was typing. The pages piled up. I measured my success with a ruler.

It wasn't long before I could easily type 20 pages of gibberish a day. The late afternoons and evening were spent reading about the writing life as well.

One book advised, "Hang out with other writers," so I walked into the editorial offices of the *St. Augustine Beacon* and asked the first person I met if they were a writer. "I'm Katherine Hawk," the woman said. "I write the 'About Town' column."

"Good," I said. "I'm supposed to hang out with you."

"Excuse me?" she said. (Years later, her husband Bob laughed, "I thought you were trying to screw her—I had no idea you were serious about all that writing crap!")

Every day I wrote—oops—*typed* gibberish for six hours.

"The job of a writer is to write," Katherine Hawk had told me at our first meeting—and I took her advice to heart.

Another book on writing advised to 'write what you know.' I decided to become a 'marine journalist' on the way to being a world famous novelist.

I studied other struggling writers, and noticed how many of them seemed to be lecturing, pontificating, and preaching down to their readers. I began to think of this as the 'broom-stick-up-the-butt' school of journalism—and promised myself I'd never fall into it. Instead, I concentrated on entertaining and amazing my readers—and emotionally touching them. (Tears and/or laughter are still the highest compliments I can earn).

One day I happened to stroll by a shoe store that had an advertisement for 'cross-training' sport shoes. Every single thing that happened to me, every single second of every day, during this stage of learning my craft—I thought of in terms of writing. Cross-training? I took out books on acting and I started to practice how each of my characters would walk, talk, and hold their bodies. A text book on costumes helped me to literally dress the part, as I wrote the part. A book on the 'artist's eye' had me concentrating on the intricate-yet-unseen details of everyday life all around me (telephone poles, man-hole covers, parking meters, etc.) A book on the five senses really wowed me: I'd walk around town asking myself what the color blue would taste like; how an orange would sound if it was a symphony.

I started looking deeply at the texture of everything: its grain, heft, nicks, nap, and weave.

I saw a picture of the Mona Lisa and thought about her smile. I immediately dashed to my typewriter and pounded out a story: she'd thought she was pregnant by the Vicar's son—but had just now felt the first trickle—and realized (with immense-yet-oh-so-secret relief) she'd only been late.

My wife asked me if I was going insane. I looked at her, really looked at her. I could see the pores on her nose, musical notes were leaking out her armpits, her breasts seemed to be filled with helium.

"I don't know," I said.

Big news! Another ink-slinging Margaret was coming to town. This time it was British novelist Margaret Walters of Harrogate, Yorkshire, author of the delicately-written, rose-scented thriller "Time Most Precious."

I went down to the hotel where she was staying—but it was bad timing. She was upset. Somebody had vandalized her car. Nothing like that had ever happened to her in England. "Why? Why?" she kept asking. "What kind of person would do such a thing?"

The following morning, right smack dab in the middle of my gibberish, popped a story of *exactly* why I'd vandalized that rich bitch's car—and I slipped the story into her message box at the hotel before my courage deserted me.

We were both uptight at our initial meeting. "Look," I blurted out. "I'm not a vandal. I'm a writer—well, actually, I'm a typer who *wants* to be a writer...."

"What are you talking about?"

I didn't know what to say—so I just babbled. "I can feel everything that has ever been felt. All the anger in the entire world—all the love and hatred and jealousy and envy—all the goodness and evil in the universe is locked within my breast. I know what it is to die—or to be reborn—how spilt ice-cream feels on the hot pavement of a sunny summer's day...."

Margaret Walters looked at me horror—she hadn't been expecting to be tricked into visiting with a dangerous lunatic. But she asked the one question I wanted to hear, "Do you have any more of your writing with you?"

Margaret was in town to give a series of lectures for the Florida Freelance Writers' Association (FFWA). She needed a chauffeur, baggage handler, and go-fer—or, as she so politely put it, 'a young editorial assistant.'

I was soon traveling around the state with her—meeting Dana Cassell, the magazine marketing expert; Janet Groene, the Caribbean travel writer; and Elaine Rocco Chase, the romance novelist.

"Ah, Fatty!" said novelist Jack Hunter, best-selling author of "The Blue Max," which had recently been turned into a highly successful movie. "Margaret was telling me what a fine young writer you are!"

It was a couple of weeks later—I think at the Annual FFWA conference in Orlando—when Margaret read a few of my 'best gibberish' paragraphs and called me up to the stage amid warm applause. I stupidly said something like, "Adjectives suck, verbs are cool," but it was my very first 'public' speech on the art of writing—and I'll never forget how I savored it.

It was time to get down to brass tacks. Each day I'd arrive at my garret, and shout aloud my three main rules of good writing: "Show don't tell, illuminate don't describe, and advance the action!"

Then I'd start pounding the keys. If I began to grind to a halt, I'd shout aloud to the empty room, "Type, you idiot, type!"

I divided my day into two parts: six hours of 'creative' (writing and editing) and two hours of 'business' (manuscript mechanics and mailing, traffic lists, professional correspondence, etc.)

Every Monday at noon, I'd mail off five query letters to major magazines. Each Friday afternoon I'd mail off at least one finished manuscript—and often two.

Every time I'd get a rejection letter, I'd post it on the wall of my office in plain view—one step closer to my goal of a hundred.

"These aren't rejections," I'd tell myself. "These are visible reminders that I'm continuously searching for the markets that will eventually buy my work on a regular basis!"

Before I'd mail off each story, I'd research the five best markets for that story and 'pre-write' the cover letters at the very outset. I did this so the 'sting' of rejection was somewhat less, and so that I could quickly resubmit the article to the next market without hesitation or self-doubt.

At the same time, I met with other writers, editors, and publishers as often as possible: not merely to 'network' with them and promote my own work—but to listen and learn from them as well.

The seventeenth story I sent off sold—to a local paper for ten bucks. I was thrilled beyond—well, words! Fifty-some stories later, I sold another marine-related story—this time to a 'glossy' regional magazine. I'd probably sold around fifty or sixty stories and articles, when a small marine 'fish-wrapper' newspaper called *Caribbean Boating* offered me a regular column.

I couldn't believe it. Within a year of first being published, I was a by-lined columnist!

I started sending 'clips' with my queries—and positive responses shot up accordingly. Some marine-related publications started contacting *me* for articles, and I was thus in a position to command a far higher price. I quickly realized that 'marine- related writing' was a huge growing field which encompassed environmental, travel, industry, how-to, sports, and personal experience writing—as well as general interest stories about boats and boaters.

But, thus far, I'd not sold to a national 'prestige' magazine. So I set my sights on *SAIL* magazine in Boston—and one of its most revered editors, Marty Luray, in particular.

Marty was a sailor's sailor—and a highly skilled wordsmith as well. (Former editor of *Rudder,* etc). In fact, Marty was highly regarded as the most 'literary' of the marine editors currently at work. He was a man who really cared about words and how they lay on the page.

About two years into my writing career, I wrote a story I thought was worthy of sending directly to my hero, Marty Luray. I polished and polished and polished it—until it shone like a 1200 word jewel. Marty purchased it immediately. I send him another story the following month, and got another positive result in the return mail.

Then a horrible thing happened. Marty requested I call him. When I did—he requested I write him an essay.

Well, of course, I couldn't. I couldn't write an essay. I didn't even know what an essay was—something scholarly, I assumed. I didn't know anything about grammar or composition or dangling participles. Hell, I'd only been to school for a couple of boring years. I was just a crude story teller, for gosh stakes, and now I was being 'caught' pretending to be something that I was not.

"And, as you know, I loved the last two essays I purchased from you," said Marty Luray—and I almost burst into tears of relief.

About six months later *SAIL* published a short piece of mine —an essay, actually—entitled "The Last Cruise." According to Marty it received more positive mail than any story he'd purchased for the magazine.

"You're on your way," he told me.

I'll never forget reading the 'Letters to the Editor' in a following month's edition, and staring at the headline "GOOD WORDS FOR GOODLANDER".

I'd finally learned my craft well-enough so that I could show the world my heart—and they'd loved it.

I soon went to Europe to cover professional multihull racing for *SAIL*. While there, *Boat International* and *Yachting World* started buying stories from me, as did *Yacht Vacations, Latitude 38, Sailing*, and (eventually, and best of all) *Cruising World.*

My stories were translated into Dutch, Danish, French, Spanish, and German.

Fodor's Travel Guides asked me to update some of their sailing, chartering, and diving chapters—the beginning of a ten year relationship.

Regional marine publications such as *Caribbean Boating*, the *VI Marine Scene*, and *All At Sea* were delighted to put my name on their masthead—and pay me for the privilege.

The BBC invited me to London to appear on TV, and the Tokyo Broadcasting System sent a film crew down to the Virgin Islands for a week to do a documentary on the life of a writing sea gypsy. WVWI Radio One gave me a weekly radio show—that lasted for 18 years.

I wrote three books, edited a fourth, and founded American Paradise Publishing. (My "Chasing the Horizon" still sells a little better every year.)

I never lost sight of why all these good things were happening, and continued to write six hours a day, five days a week without let up. "The job of a writer is to write," is the best advice I've ever received.

Carolyn and I are currently in Brisbane, Australia, aboard our current yacht *Wild Card* (a sloop-rigged Hughes 38, designed by S&S). For the last twenty years, enough money has dribbled out of my pen to leisurely cruise the Atlantic Ocean, Gulf of Mexico, and Caribbean Sea. We've just spent a couple of years sailing in the South Pacific, and will soon be heading for Bali, Indonesia, India and beyond—merrily writing as we go.

But I can still remember how scared I was when I first sat down at that mute typewriter—how it seemed insane to aspire to become what I now am. I had no skills. None. Zero. Yet I knew I was born to write—so write I did.

Afterword
or
Haven't You Got it Out of Your System Yet?

Langkawi, Malaysia   November 1, 2009

  I recently returned to the United States for my mother's 90th birthday party and a number of people asked, "Haven't you got it out of your system yet?" …as if our cruising lifestyle was a particularly stubborn bowel movement.
  All I could do was laugh—and tell them no, alas, we have not yet come to our senses. We are still "Chasing the Horizon." We are still kissing life full on the lips. We are still madly in love—with our world and each other.
  Everyone makes choices. Some people want a big car or a fancy house—and that is fine, for them.
  Carolyn and I have always focused on less material goals: freedom and learning.
  Freedom is our core-value. It is the single constant which runs through every aspect of our lives.
  Freedom comes in many forms: the freedom to travel, the freedom to earn your living by non-traditional means, the freedom to make love on the foredeck, the freedom to be a citizen of the word, freedom to learn, freedom from racism, freedom to not stand up when everyone else does, freedom from *any* church, freedom to say no, freedom to not wear clothes, freedom from the need of shoes, freedom from cold weather, freedom not to take a number, freedom from land, freedom not to salute, freedom to live exactly how and where we want and still be free to change both at whim, freedom to

evolve together and to change and to grow...

Freedom, freedom, freedom!

I can't think of any life-style that affords more freedom (or more varied fun) than ocean-cruising and circumnavigating. It is an endless delight. We are truly citizens of the world—in all its chaotic, messy, topsy-turvy glory. This planet is, literally, our oyster, our cradle, our home. Most people are restricted to dirt. We're not. Our dreams are bigger. The entire world is our playground, not just the dusty, buggy parts. We aren't merely Americans or Westerners or Chicagoans—we have natural rights that go far beyond these pale borders and quaint, out-dated geographically demarcations.

We stand tall.

We smile.

Best of all, is the amazing diversification of our species: the wonderful people who inhabit this watery planet. They are our brothers. Sure, people-with-agendas keep frantically sticking awkward labels on us (Hindu, nigger, conservative, WASP, nerd, fascist, cracker, zealot, slut, Muslim, Christian, white trash, liberal) but we know these external labels say more about the *labeler* than the labeled.

People are just people. Most of us have the same wants, needs, and desires. We're the same in our hearts—where it counts most.

But if I had to sum up our watery lives in a single word, it wouldn't be sailing or brotherhood—it would be freedom.

Freedom is our drug—and we're drunk with it.

We simply don't want nor need what most people deem a necessity: a house, a car, a mobile phone, a designer wristwatch, or a time-clocked shore job.

We think of these 'land-anchors' as false imperatives—things that *seem* important but are not.

People need feet, not cars. All the best islands in the world share one trait—they are carless. I recently strolled down Western Avenue in Chicago—and went passed so many muffler shops and tire stores and oil-change operations that I began to think that the people within merely existed to service the vehicles—that the vehicles had somehow managed to move up on the food chain while I was dozing.

Mortal beings can't really own anything anyway: we just delude ourselves by selfishly hoarding it for a brief span of time. Nothing lasts forever: not property rights, not countries, not religion—nothing.

The reason we continue to travel, with only brief hesitations, is two-fold: one, is because by traveling we learn about the world and, two, because by traveling we learn about ourselves.

There are many aspects of life—and even of American society—that I couldn't have fully appreciated without touring the world. Ditto, only by squatting in the mud with Karen Indians in Thailand or swinging through the trees with orangutans in Borneo can I properly appreciate the marvels of Google, the advantages of our latest ebook reader, the sophistication of our tack-by-tack GPS onboard navigation system.

In order for mankind to chart a course into the future, it must know where it has been. You cannot do this statically, by staying in one place. You have to be dynamic. You have to move, to 'go with the flow' as we hippies used to say.

Thus we travel.

What's next for *Wild Card* and crew?

...more sailing, of course. But the sailing doesn't have to be long distances or short distances... nor towards any specific geographic goal. We don't want to *get* somewhere, we want to *go* somewhere. The journey itself is our destination. After all, wherever we go, there we are. This is tiny, fragile blue life-boat we all live aboard. We never truly 'leave home' anyway. We're comfortable and at home the entire time we circumnavigate. And we never get lonely for family because we're continuously surrounded by our loving brothers and sisters.

I want to continue to write. I've written a couple of good stories. I'd like to write a good book which will last. I'm still proud of the lustful song within "Chasing the Horizon"—but I can do better.

I will do better.

I'd like to continue writing for *All at Sea* and *Cruising World*—and to alternate between a fiction and non-fiction book each year.

Regardless, I'll continue to put words on paper from 8 to noon every weekday—until God gently takes the pen from my hand.

Most of all, I want to sail into old age with Carolyn. I am blessed to have found the woman of my dreams at 15 years of age—and to have recognized her as such.

I only need her smile to look forward to the morrow.

Cap'n Fatty Goodlander has lived aboard various sailing vessels for 49 of his 57 years. He has written numerous books—including his autobiographical comedy "Chasing the Horizon." At various times, Fatty has been a professional actor, a radio broadcaster, and a newspaper writer. He also had a series of summer travel spots for National Public Radio which are available at NPR.org.

For more info, see: fattygoodlander.com. To purchase one of his books, go to Amazon.com.

He and his wife, Carolyn, are currently heading across the Indian Ocean on their second circumnavigation.

Cap'n Fatty is a featured columnist in *All At Sea* and an editor-at-large of *Cruising World* magazine.

Also available from Cap'n Fatty Goodlander:

Chasing the Horizon is a delightfully demented Celebration of A Way of Life. It is an outrageously funny, often touching, and continuously shocking tale of a modern sea gypsy.

Cap'n Fatty's story is too bizarre to be fiction. Father wears floral skirts; mother is a tad vague. Sister Carole isn't interested in her millionaire suitor; she's too busy smooching with the kid in the cesspool truck.

All seem hell-bent on avoiding the cops, the creeps, and especially the Dreaded Dream Crushers. Dive in!

The Collected Fat represents the very best writing from one of the most outrageous writers in the Caribbean. Cap'n Fatty will enthrall you with his rollicking tales of Lush Tropical Vegetables, Wonderful Waterfront Wackos, and Colorful Caribbean Characters.

A number of these stories will make you laugh. A few will touch your heart. One might change you, ever-so-slightly, forever. All will entertain, enlighten, and amuse.

Seadogs, Clowns, & Gypsies is more than just a book about the remarkable lifestyle of various Caribbean sailors. It is a Celebration of a Way of Life. The people who inhabit these salt-stained pages ("We're all here, because we're not all there!") have a true Lust for Living. They kiss life full on the lips, embrace each new day, welcome every fresh sensation. Yeah, they are louts and cads and drunkards and misfits and fools—and yet, somehow, they emerge from these yarns as a noble, vital people.

Cruising World Yarns is a collection of the best of Cap'n Fatty from more than a decade at *Cruising World* magazine.

Sea adventures don't get any funnier than this!

Order through our website at: **Fattygoodlander.com**
Books and Kindle editions are available through **Amazon.com**
Smashwords.com offers other E-book formats

CHASING THE HORIZON
The Life and Times of a Modern Sea Gypsy
By Cap'n Fatty Goodlander

Cap'n Fatty's Cruising World Yarns
By Cap'n Fatty Goodlander
Editor-at-Large

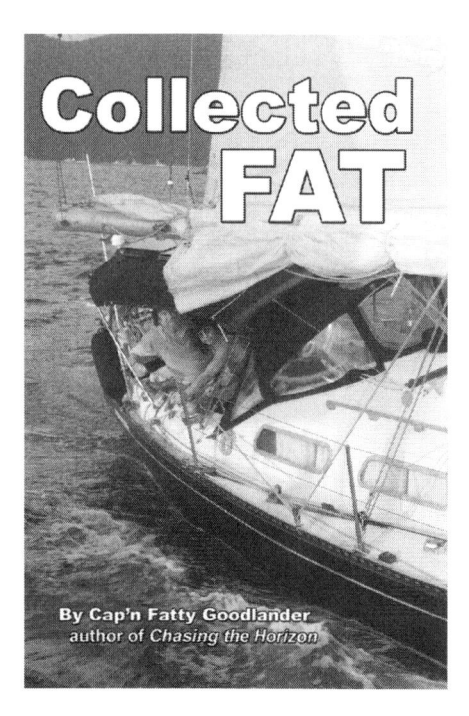

Collected FAT
By Cap'n Fatty Goodlander, author of *Chasing the Horizon*

SEADOGS, CLOWNS, & GYPSIES
By Cap'n Fatty Goodlander

Twenty Modern Sea Stories about Colorful Caribbean Characters, Wonderful Waterfront Wackos, and Lush Tropical Vegetables . . .

Made in the USA
San Bernardino, CA
08 December 2012